Wellbeing, Nature, and Moral Values in Economics

Drawing on more modern expressions of economic analysis, this book explores the interplay between wellbeing, nature, and moral values in economics.

In standard accounts of economics, these three themes are typically treated in isolation from each other, or else overlooked entirely. This book argues that due to this blinkered approach, standard economic analysis is poorly equipped to deal with global contemporary challenges, including climate change, biodiversity loss, sustainability, and the risk of pandemic diseases. The book reviews the economic literature to show that the last few decades has seen the re-insertion into economic analysis of human wellbeing, natural resources, and moral values: three themes present in early economic thought that are highly relevant to the challenges ahead. The book argues for the greater integration of these three themes as the natural environment is crucial to human wellbeing, and moral values are essential for environmentally benign behaviors. The book also focuses on how specific moral values, identified by contemporary moral psychology, *actually* shape economic behavior rather than how abstract ethical principles *should* shape economic behavior.

The book will be of significant interest to readers in economics and social sciences, particularly behavioral economics and social psychology.

Heinz Welsch is Professor Emeritus of economics at the University of Oldenburg, Germany. He formerly held positions at the universities of Cologne and Bonn. His fields of research include environmental, resource, and energy economics; economics of subjective wellbeing; and the role of norms and values for economic behavior. He has published extensively on these topics. His publications on "environment and happiness" were among the first contributions to this field.

Routledge Frontiers of Political Economy

Marx and *Le Capital*
Evaluation, History, Reception
Edited by Marcello Musto

Permanent Economic Disorder
Shahzavar Karimzadi

Temporary Economic Crises
Shahzavar Karimzadi

Money and Capital
A Critique of Monetary Thought, the Dollar and Post-Capitalism
Laurent Baronian

Modern Money and the Rise and Fall of Capitalist Finance
The Institutionalization of Trusts, Personae, and Indebtedness
Jongchul Kim

Innovation, Complexity and Economic Evolution
From Theory to Policy
Pier Paolo Saviotti

Economic Growth and Inequality
The Economist's Dilemma
Laurent Dobuzinskis

Wellbeing, Nature and Moral Values in Economics
How Modern Economic Analysis Faces the Challenges Ahead
Heinz Welsch

For more information about this series, please visit: www.routledge.com/Routledge-Frontiers-of-Political-Economy/book-series/SE0345

Wellbeing, Nature, and Moral Values in Economics

How Modern Economic Analysis Faces the Challenges Ahead

Heinz Welsch

Routledge
Taylor & Francis Group
LONDON AND NEW YORK

First published 2023
by Routledge
4 Park Square, Milton Park, Abingdon, Oxon OX14 4RN

and by Routledge
605 Third Avenue, New York, NY 10158

Routledge is an imprint of the Taylor & Francis Group, an informa business

British Library Cataloguing-in-Publication Data
A catalogue record for this book is available from the British Library

Library of Congress Cataloging-in-Publication Data
Names: Welsch, Heinz, 1955- author.
Title: Wellbeing, nature and moral values in economics : how modern economic analysis faces the challenges ahead / Heinz Welsch.
Description: Abingdon, Oxon ; New York, NY : Routledge, 2023. | Series: Routledge frontiers of political economy | Includes bibliographical references and index. |
Identifiers: LCCN 2022042660 (print) | LCCN 2022042661 (ebook) | ISBN 9781032072562 (hardback) | ISBN 9781032072586 (paperback) | ISBN 9781003206163 (ebook)
Subjects: LCSH: Well-being. | Economics--Moral and ethical aspects.
Classification: LCC HN25 .W466 2023 (print) | LCC HN25 (ebook) | DDC 301--dc23/eng/20220923
LC record available at https://lccn.loc.gov/2022042660
LC ebook record available at https://lccn.loc.gov/2022042661

ISBN: 978-1-032-07256-2 (hbk)
ISBN: 978-1-032-07258-6 (pbk)
ISBN: 978-1-003-20616-3 (ebk)

DOI: 10.4324/9781003206163

Typeset in Bembo
by KnowledgeWorks Global Ltd.

Contents

Tables

1 Introduction

Economics and the Challenges Ahead

Some Challenges Ahead

The first decades of the 21st century have seen several challenges of a global scale, notably the global financial crisis of 2008–2009 and the Covid-19 pandemic starting in late 2019. While the financial crisis was tamed by the collective efforts of central banks and governments worldwide, the pandemic has not only killed millions of people but also spurred a recession from which the global economy recovers only sluggishly.

The financial crisis and the pandemic are challenges that have been, or promise to be, accommodated within relatively short periods of time. In this sense, they were *events* – single occurrences of limited duration. Nevertheless, they were manifestations of underlying *structural challenges*: systemic risks to the world's financial and public health systems, both of which are closely related to and amplified by globalization.

Beyond global financial and public health risks, other pressing problems are facing the world and challenging economics as a discipline. One set of challenges led the United Nations to formulate their Sustainable Development Goals. These include the elimination of hunger and poverty, good health and wellbeing, reduction of inequalities, combatting climate change, and the sustainable use of marine and terrestrial ecosystems, particularly to halt biodiversity loss (United Nations 2021).

The new problems have not gone unnoticed by students of economics, and an interest in understanding and tackling them is a major motivation for students to choose this field of study. Over the years 2016–2018, more than 4,400 students from 25 universities in 12 countries were asked the following question on the first day of their introductory classes: "What is the most pressing problem economists should be addressing?" While "unemployment" was still on the minds of students, "inflation" played a much lesser role. The overwhelmingly dominant concern was "inequality", followed by "environment" and "sustainability". Among the students at Humboldt University in Berlin, Germany (2016, 2018), "inequality" and "sustainability" ranked equally as by far the most important issues. This emphasis on environmental issues is not an outlier: In a more recent edition of the overall survey

DOI: 10.4324/9781003206163-1

(from 2019), "climate change" rivals "inequality" in importance (Bowles and Carlin 2020). This accords well with the title of the Nobel Prize lecture that William Nordhaus delivered in 2019: "Climate Change: The Ultimate Challenge for Economics" (Nordhaus 2019).

Students' concerns about inequality and environmental sustainability seem well justified in terms of real-world data. The distribution of income is highly unequal both across and within countries. In Singapore, the richest country by 2014, the average incomes of the richest and poorest 10 percent were US$67,436 and US$3,652, respectively. In Liberia, the poorest country, the corresponding incomes were US$994 and US$17. Evidently, thus, the poorest 10 percent in the richest country were more than three and a half times richer than the richest 10 percent in the poorest country. More than that, the poorest 10 percent in the richest 10 percent of countries are richer than the richest 10 percent in the poorest 10 percent of countries (Rodrik 2011). Overall, inequality between countries thus seems to be more serious than inequality within countries. Nevertheless, within-country inequality is large. By 2014, the income ratio of the richest to the poorest 10 percent (rich/poor ratio) amounted to 18.5 in Singapore and 58.5 in Liberia. Even in a relatively equal income country such as Norway, the rich/poor ratio was 5.4; in the United States it was 16 (CORE Team 2017, Unit 1). Over time, income inequality as measured by the income of the richest 1 percent tended to drop in the middle of the 20th century in Europe and the United States but has increased in the past several decades. In the United States, for instance, the income of the richest 1 percent of the population rose from about 9 percent of national income in the early 1970s to about 23 percent shortly before the financial crisis, after which it temporarily dropped slightly below 20 percent. Similar patterns existed in many other developed and emerging economies (Piketty 2014).

With respect to environmental sustainability, the most pressing issues are climate change and the loss of biodiversity. As is well-known, the problem of man-made climate change is that carbon dioxide (CO_2) and other gases released by human activities accumulate in the earth's atmosphere and thereby change the earth's radiation budget (so-called greenhouse effect), leading to an increase in temperatures, which is associated with far-reaching ecological, economic, and wellbeing damage (Archer and Rahmstorf 2009). Importantly, it is the global sum of emissions, irrespective of their place of origin, that causes climate change. Between 1950 and 2020, this global sum rose sixfold. A reduction in greenhouse gas emissions is associated with benefits in the form of avoided climate damage, and these benefits accrue to everybody in the world. At the same time, it is associated with costs in the form of a loss of prosperity that results from limiting the activities that cause the emissions, in particular the use of fossil fuels (coal, oil, and gas).

Several estimates of the benefits and costs of the transition to an economy without CO_2 emissions (decarbonization) exist. An in-depth assessment estimated the global benefits of decarbonization to be around 5 percent of the world's income and the costs at 1 percent (Stern 2007), whereas another study came to a much more moderate assessment of climate damage and thus of the benefits of emission reductions (Nordhaus 2019). Both of these estimates, however, do not take into account the possibility of exceeding so-called tipping points of the climate system (Steffen et al. 2018) – with catastrophic and irreversible consequences – so that the damage can be significantly higher and may not even be quantified at all. In view of this, Stern's estimate does not seem to be exaggerated and may be considered as a central benchmark.

Biological diversity (biodiversity for short) is a complex phenomenon that involves both the number and distribution of biological species, where a smaller number and a greater evenness of species indicate less biodiversity (Brock and Xepapadeas 2003). Biodiversity, in economic terms, is an asset, or commodity, as it contributes to human societies by enhancing agricultural productivity, by providing insurance of agricultural systems against new diseases as well as genetic knowledge relevant to biotechnological processes, and by giving ecosystems the stability required to yield a variety of services (Heal 2000), ranging from the capture and storage of CO_2 by forests to providing humans with recreation sites. In the pharmaceutical industry, a large proportion of the drugs in use are derived from biological sources, and the potential for developing new ones critically depends on the diversity of those sources. Given these contributions to prosperity and wellbeing, biodiversity constitutes what has been referred to as natural capital, similar to produced capital and human capital. While stocks of the latter have been strongly increasing over the past decades, estimates show that the stock of natural capital per person declined by nearly 40 percent between 1992 and 2014, mainly driven by land-use changes and a variety of economic activities, notably unsustainable food production practices (Dasgupta 2021).

The Challenges Ahead as Public Good Problems and the Role of Moral Values

The challenges just discussed are so demanding because they involve the provision of public goods. A public good is one that has two properties: consumption by one person does not interfere with consumption by another person, and the provider cannot prevent non-payers from benefiting from the good. Such goods are said to be non-rival and non-excludable, in contrast with private goods, which are both rival and excludable. A seat in a football stadium is a private good: if I sit in it you cannot, and the management can certainly exclude non-payers from seeing the football match. Law and order, in contrast, is a public good: it benefits everyone in the region in which it is enforced, and the benefits cannot be restricted to those who have contributed to its costs.

Non-rivalry and non-excludability have important implications. Non-rivalry implies that once the good has been produced, there is no scarcity of it: everybody can enjoy the benefits it yields. Non-excludability suggests that a producer or provider of the good will not be able to make people pay for it, and will thus not be able to recover the costs of provision. This, then, means that no markets will evolve for public goods: markets are unable to provide public goods; public goods are nonmarket goods.

Rather than the market, the standard institution to provide public goods is the state. Law and order is a paradigmatic example of a public good provided by the state. There is, however, an important way in which the challenges discussed, that is, climate change mitigation and biodiversity conservation, differ from law and order. The latter is a national public good, which is provided by the respective nation-state and benefits mainly their citizens, whereas the former are global public goods that benefit everybody in the world. Thus, when a nation decides to limit its CO_2 emissions, its citizens will bear the costs, but, depending on the nation's size, the benefits will mainly accrue to noncitizens – due to non-excludability. For instance, if the United States (with 330 million citizens) cuts down its greenhouse gas emissions, almost 96 percent of the beneficiaries will be noncitizens. Even in the case of China (with 1.4 billion citizens), the beneficiaries outside the country amount to 82 percent of the total. In general, the smaller a nation, the larger are the external benefits relative to the internal ones. In contrast to the benefits, the costs of reducing CO_2 emissions accrue to the citizens of the respective nations.

Thus, in the case of national public goods, such as law and order, the group of beneficiaries coincides with those who can be made to pay for their provision (the taxpayers), whereas in the case of global public goods – due to non-excludability – the group of beneficiaries is much larger than the group of those who bear the costs of provision. Therefore, while nation-states are able to provide national public goods in amounts that are adequate in benefit-cost terms, they tend to under-provide global public goods, as their benefit-cost calculus typically fails to adequately account for the benefits to noncitizens.

In the language of economics, under-provision of public goods is an instance of social inefficiency (so-called Pareto inefficiency), that is, a state of affairs where at least one of the parties involved could be made better-off without any other party being made worse-off. In the case of public goods, under-provision even means that *every* party could be made better-off, if adequate action were being taken.

Nation-states thus have insufficient incentives to provide adequate (that is, efficient) levels of global public goods. The inadequacy (inefficiency) is larger, the more nations are involved and the smaller they are. At the extreme, nations have strong incentives to try and free ride on others' efforts altogether, rather than contributing to the public good themselves. Evidently, however, this calculus is self-defeating, as the "others" follow the same logic. This failure to voluntarily contribute to public goods in the face of non-excludability is the essence of the "tragedy of the commons" (Hardin 1968). The tragedy, obviously, is even more pronounced when we consider as decision makers the close to eight billion individuals in the world, rather than roughly 200 nations.

While curbing climate change and preserving biodiversity are paramount examples of global public goods whose provision poses major challenges to the world community, most of the other challenges discussed also involve the voluntary provision of public goods. Measures to control the spread of infectious diseases, such as Covid-19, and regulations to ensure financial stability satisfy the criteria of non-rivalry and non-excludability. Different from climate change mitigation and biodiversity preservation, however, the overall level of the respective public goods is not necessarily the sum (across nations or individuals) of measures taken. For instance, measures to control the spread of an infectious outbreak may be location-specific in their effectiveness, so that the overall level of control is a weighted rather than a simple sum of the measures. Global financial stability may even involve a weakest-link technology, that is, the smallest contribution of the world's nations determines the overall level of stability (Buchholz and Sandler 2021). Other international challenges, such as the control of transboundary air pollution (acid rain), are regional public goods because the benefit from mitigation measures taken in one country is geographically limited to a relatively small set of other countries.

As to the other "most pressing problems" mentioned by economics students, controlling inflation and unemployment are public goods, even if national ones. Specifically, unemployment is not just detrimental to the individuals and families actually affected. Rather, the overall level of unemployment affects those who are employed, as it signals the level of their risk of being laid off, as well as the risk that unemployment contributions and taxes may rise or social tensions increase (Frey and Stutzer 2002). General unemployment thus constitutes a "public bad" that affects everybody in a non-rival and non-excludable way. Similar reasoning applies to inequality and, specifically, poverty. Even the non-poor may worry about the possibility of becoming poor themselves in the future and feel anxious about economic and social instability (Collier 2018; Piketty 2014).

The discussion so far has revealed that some of the most pressing challenges ahead involve public goods whose provision requires cooperative efforts by nations and individuals worldwide, and that there is a serious threat of under-provision due to inherent free rider incentives. But aren't there mechanisms that promote taking efforts oneself rather than free riding on others' efforts? One such mechanism involves private goods jointly produced with a public good, that is, goods whose benefits accrue solely or mainly to those who provide them (Olson 1965). For instance, a nation that cuts down on the use of coal contributes not only to the global public good of curbing climate change but also reduces domestic air pollution – a private good from the nation's point of view.

The idea that the existence of jointly produced private goods may further the provision of public goods relies on consequentialist calculus: actions are being taken because they yield, or are expected to yield, favorable consequences. The consequentialist paradigm, in this sense, has been the dominant approach in economic analysis for more than two centuries and, in fact, has been the basis of the discussion of public goods provision so far. The opposite of consequentialism is deontology, which maintains that it is not (only) actions' consequences that guide decisions but some intrinsic value of actions themselves. With respect to voluntary public goods provision, an intrinsic value of charitable giving has been suggested under the buzz phrase "warm glow" (Andreoni 1990).

While there are several reasons for why some actions may be chosen independent of consequences (e.g., social conformity), an important source of deontological evaluation of actions is whether they are morally right or wrong. The moral aspects of actions are of paramount importance for the voluntary provision of public goods because, as maintained by a functionalist view of human morality, moral systems have emerged in biological-cultural evolution precisely because they facilitate the cooperative creation of common goods by curbing free rider behavior (e.g., Tomasello 2016). As concisely stated by a leading scholar in the field: "... moral life is really about cooperation and alliance ..." (Haidt 2012, chapter 4, note 10).

Absent from economic analysis for more than two centuries, deontological considerations, in general, and moral values, in particular, have made a remarkable comeback in modern economics over the past three decades, not least with respect to the provision of goods that are of ever greater importance and for which markets are poorly equipped.

Nature, Wellbeing, and Moral Values in Economics: Past and Present

Over much of the 19th and 20th centuries, economic analysis has equated welfare and wellbeing with the abundance of produced goods, thereby neglecting the important role played by nature and other goods that are not the result of economic activity. Since produced goods typically are private goods – characterized by excludability – the focus of economics was on competitive markets as the adequate institutions to supply consumers with what they needed. As famously noted by Adam Smith (1776) in his *An Enquiry into the Nature and Causes of the Wealth of Nations*, markets work like an "invisible hand", which promotes the interests of society without market participants having to pursue anything but their self-interest – provided that the interests of society come down to wealth, understood as the abundance of private goods. Smith's assertion later was shown to be correct in the sense that market outcomes that result from self-interested behavior are socially efficient (Pareto efficient) if all goods are private goods, markets are perfectly competitive, market transactions do not affect third parties, and there are no information asymmetries between market participants (Mas-Colell et al. 1995).

What came to be the standard economic model is thus characterized by a predominant neglect of the welfare significance of nature and other non-private goods, a narrow notion of "welfare as wealth", and a focus on self-interest as the driver of economic behavior. With these characteristics, the standard, or neoclassical, model is narrower than its predecessor, classical economics, in which a recognition of the economic significance of nature, a more holistic notion of "welfare as wellbeing", and an acknowledgment of moral – as opposed to interest-related – aspects of behavior had all been present. All three themes went into the background as the neoclassical model was crafted and made a comeback not before the last quarter of the 20th century.

Nature had been present in classical economics mainly in the form of land. Economists' concerns about land focused on the quantity and quality of land available for agricultural production in the face of growing populations and their demands for food, and land as a deposit of extractive resources. Different from the nature-related challenges that bother us today – climate change and loss of biodiversity – land scarcity is the scarcity of a private material good and thus poses no generic problems to the working of markets. In addition to agricultural and extractive uses of land, its role as a source of amenity values (such as scenic beauty), whose relative importance would rise with improved material conditions, was recognized (Mill 1857), but the issues related to it received only marginal attention.

Land and other natural resources gradually disappeared from the economic agenda with the rise of industry in 19th-century Europe and the relatively smaller role of agriculture. The concern for natural resources diminished as economists' focus shifted to the *value added* to them by using and transforming them through the use of labor and capital. An emphasis on "value added" prevails in economics to the present day, as the standard measure of economic performance, gross domestic product (GDP), by construction is a measure of value added.

The state of affairs by around 1970 was that natural resources hardly played a role in standard economics. However, almost out of the blue, the 1970s saw the start of their re-insertion into economic analysis and policy. Spurred by the "oil crisis" on the one hand and increasing pollution on the other, natural resources and the natural environment became topical issues and started to be the subject of textbooks (Dasgupta and Heal 1979; Mäler 1974, respectively). This tendency was reinforced by increasing awareness of global climate change in the 1980s and 1990s (Nordhaus 1994).

Natural resource and environmental economics is now an established field of study that, according to the subject classification of the *Journal of Economic Literature*, covers agriculture, energy, the use and conservation of renewable and nonrenewable natural resources, pollution and waste, climate change and global warming, and ecosystem services and biodiversity conservation. Issues addressed include the valuation of environmental effects, and environment-related market failures and their correction through government policies. Traditional economic approaches, such as benefit-cost analysis, are increasingly complemented by transdisciplinary perspectives from the other social sciences and from physics and ecology, giving rise to a widening of *environmental economics* toward an *ecological economics*, which strives for a more holistic understanding of the interactions between economic activities and nature.

Closely related to the focus of neoclassical economics on produced goods (value added) is its understanding of welfare as wealth. By contrast, classical economists' notion of welfare was wellbeing, often referred to as utility or happiness. From the point of view of *utilitarianism*, welfare was "the greatest happiness of the greatest number" (Bentham 1780), where happiness was understood as the predominance of "pleasure" over "pain". Economics was conceived of as a science of happiness, and happiness continued to be viewed as the ultimate object of the calculus of economics, even in early neoclassical thought (Jevons 1871).

Understanding utility as happiness soon met with criticism on the grounds that measuring utility, in this sense, was deemed impossible and that the concept of cardinally measurable utility was unnecessary to conducting economic analysis. Utility rather came to be understood as an indicator of preference: if an individual prefers object A over object B, A is said to yield greater utility than B. Utility is thus an ordinal, not a cardinal concept, that is, the "difference" in the utilities generated by the two goods is not a meaningful concept, nor is the difference in utility enjoyed by different individuals.

If the objects considered are market goods, their prices reflect consumers' willingness to pay for them, which, in turn, indicates the utility they derive from the goods. The quantities of goods produced over a period of time, weighted by their prices, then constitute the wealth created (income), and the wealth of an individual or nation is the measure of individual and national welfare.

While national welfare was identified with aggregate income, as measured by GDP, over much of the 20th century, doubts as to GDP's welfare significance arose not only from conceptual flaws (such as the neglect of nonmarket activities) but also from the observation that tremendous increases in the GDP of developed economies after World War II were not accompanied by corresponding increases in individuals' life satisfaction (as reported in surveys) and similar measures of subjective wellbeing (SWB). While initially established with respect to the United States (Easterlin 1974), similar evidence has been found with respect to practically all economies that have passed a threshold of wealth (Easterlin et al. 2010).

While the concept and measurement of SWB – also referred to as happiness – was initially met with skepticism by economists, using SWB data (elicited in surveys) is meanwhile widely accepted in the economics profession. SWB data are now routinely used to identify determinants of wellbeing other than market goods and to estimate the SWB-constant trade-offs individuals are willing to make between market goods (measured by indicators of consumption or income) and those nonmarket determinants. The latter provides a new approach to the difficult problem of economically valuing nonmarket goods.

Also related to the focus of neoclassical economics on privately produced goods is a neglect of moral or ethical considerations as determinants of economic behavior. As discussed earlier, the socially efficient provision of private goods is ensured by the pursuit of self-interest under some well-defined conditions. Public goods, by contrast, are under-provided if the respective activities are guided by self-interest alone. This is where moral behavior comes into play.

Moral behavior, interestingly, was the subject of a book Adam Smith had published 17 years before he praised the "invisible hand" in *The Wealth of Nations.* In his *Theory of Moral Sentiments* (Smith 1759), he argued that human behavior is partly guided by inner feelings of what is right and wrong, not by reason. These feelings give rise to obligations or duties toward others, which come in different intensities. The strongest duties arise from personal familiarity. They apply most strongly and unconditionally to our children and close relatives but also extend to everyone we know. The weakest obligation is to distant people in need. To illustrate the latter, Smith cited the example of people hit by an earthquake in China.

Smith's work on moral behavior is remarkable in several ways. First, Smith's conception of what behaviors are right and wrong makes no reference to the behaviors' outcomes or consequences. This differs from the consequentialist utilitarian doctrine, according to which the measure of what is right and wrong is "the greatest happiness of the greatest number". Second, Smith takes an intuitionist approach to morality, that is, he views moral obligations as arising from inner feelings rather than justifying or "deducing" them by logical reasoning, as is typically done in moral philosophy. This approach is very similar to the intuitionist approach to morality taken by modern cultural anthropology and moral psychology (Haidt 2012). Third, Smith's idea of intensities of moral obligations depending on (mental or geographic) proximity nicely aligns with modern moral psychology's distinction between group-focused (parochial) and individual-focused (universalist) morality: while the former applies to members of one's own group (however defined), the latter applies to all individuals in an impartial way (Haidt 2012).

Moral or ethical considerations did not play a large role in economics until recently. Smith himself turned his focus to a domain where social efficiency does not rely on moral behavior – undistorted markets for private goods – and so did most scholars who embarked on creating what was to become neoclassical economics. Ethical considerations were of concern only in a niche called welfare economics, which deals with issues of inequality and distribution rather than efficiency. As noted by one leading welfare economist, the study of normative (ethical) judgments had almost disappeared from the economics agenda by the end of the 20th century (Atkinson 2001). Reasons for this disappearance may lie not just in economists' "preference" for studying issues of efficiency rather than distribution, but in methodological skepticism about the very concepts of welfare and utility that welfare economics relies upon.

While largely absent from economics until recently, moral behavior and its underlying values made a comeback with the increasing awareness of the large-scale public goods problem whose solution calls for other-regarding or moral behaviors. That such behaviors are a reality and not just wishful thinking has meanwhile been demonstrated in countless studies in behavioral economics, one of the most strongly growing fields in economic research.

In sum, recent years saw the re-insertion of nature, wellbeing, and moral values into economics as the degradation of the natural environment made it increasingly inadequate to identify social welfare with wealth, operational measures of welfare-as-wellbeing became available, and global challenges became visible that cannot appropriately be addressed by self-interested individuals and governments, but require moral behavior. This book describes how these themes have been integrated into modern economic analysis.

Aims and Scope of the Book

The book offers a concise and accessible account of how modern economics addresses three interrelated themes that mattered to the founders of the discipline, got lost along the way, and made a comeback responding to real-world challenges of our time: wellbeing, nature, and moral values. The book differs from accounts of economics that treat these topics in isolation from each other or not at all. While some recent books address intersections between wellbeing and the environment (e.g., Maddison et al. 2020) and between ethics and economics (e.g., Hausman et al. 2016; White 2019), the present work differs from these books in several ways. First, the combination of wellbeing, nature, and ethics/moral values is unique. Second, while the aforementioned volumes are designed to be large reference works and assume considerable specialist knowledge, the present book strives to provide a concise account of its topic and assumes only a very small amount of prior knowledge. Third, in contrast to existing works on ethics and economics, moral values are discussed mainly from the perspective of the voluntary provision of public goods, notably environmental preservation, rather than the usually taken perspective of fairness and justice. Fourth, the discussion of the connection between ethics/moral values and economics focuses on how specific moral principles, identified by contemporary moral psychology, *actually* shape economic behavior (positive perspective), rather than the moral principles, derived from moral philosophy, that *should* be observed (normative perspective).

Overview of the Subsequent Chapters

The subsequent chapters are organized into two parts. Part I (Chapters 2–4) shows that the public goods whose provision was stated to constitute important challenges, in fact, impact people's wellbeing and, importantly, impact wellbeing strongly relative to private goods.

Chapter 2 deals with the measurement of welfare and wellbeing by means of subjective data. It discusses recent efforts taken in the academic and political spheres to overcome the exclusive identification of welfare and economic performance with income and GDP, the introduction into economics of subjective wellbeing (happiness) as a welfare measure, and the methodological and critical issues involved. The chapter describes the elicitation of happiness data through surveys, how such data can and have been used to track the progress of society at the national and regional levels and as a tool for benefit-cost evaluation, and the advantages and limitations of using happiness data as a welfare measure and valuation tool. A focus of the chapter is on different conceptual dimensions of subjective wellbeing (affective and evaluative) and on issues of measurability of happiness traditionally raised by economists.

Chapter 3 is concerned with the state of research concerning the economic determinants of subjective wellbeing. It discusses how income (both personal income and GDP) and income growth, individual and macroeconomic unemployment, and economic inequality affect subjective wellbeing. Major issues addressed are the finding that GDP growth ceases to be associated with greater happiness once a threshold GDP level is passed (Easterlin paradox) and explanations of this finding. The latter include relative income effects, which imply that increases in personal income are psychologically annulled by increases in other individuals' incomes and a – largely unforeseen – psychological adaptation to higher incomes. The chapter proceeds with a discussion of the relevance of findings from wellbeing research for public policy, focusing on the importance of mitigating unemployment and inequality, relative to enhancing economic growth.

Chapter 4 addresses the role of environmental quality for wellbeing, focusing on a variety of issues that are key challenges needing to be faced by economics. It describes how wellbeing relates to air pollution, climate change, land use and green spaces, and species diversity. A focus of the chapter is on the use of wellbeing equations for eliciting the willingness to pay for environmental quality. With respect to air pollution, results reveal a surprising concordance between the calculated willingness-to-pay measures and research assessing the effects of pollution on mortality and productivity, a finding that attests to the validity of the wellbeing approach to nonmarket valuation. While green spaces and species diversity significantly contribute to greater wellbeing, hotter temperatures and extreme weather events spurred by climate change have large and significant negative wellbeing effects. The chapter also discusses evidence of greater subjective wellbeing stemming from individual pro-environmental behavior, which is consistent with the notion of a warm glow.

Having established the stated challenges' relevance to human wellbeing in Part I, Part II (Chapters 5–7) is devoted to how – responding to those challenges – norms and moral values have been integrated into modern economics.

Chapter 5 deals with the relationship between ethics and economics. It starts by discussing the two broad approaches to behavioral analysis and ethical thought: consequentialism and deontology. The chapter states that the traditional behavioral and ethical foundation of economics is consequentialist, focusing on behaviors' outcomes and disregarding behaviors' intrinsic (deontological) value. It then discusses how consequentialist theories prominent in standard economics, in particular utilitarianism, address ethical issues and that the issues addressed in this way mainly refer to distributive justice (e.g., with respect to income inequality or intergenerational justice in the use of natural resources and with respect to climate change). The discussion then departs from normative (prescriptive) ethical theories to positive (descriptive) accounts of ethical behavior in economic analysis. Referring to experimental evidence from behavioral economics, the discussion establishes that people often reveal altruistic (other-regarding) preferences when issues of distribution are concerned.

While the discussion in Chapter 5 focuses on matters of fairness and justice – the traditional domain of ethical thinking in economics – Chapter 6 shifts the focus to a class of socioeconomic issues to which moral considerations have been applied only recently: social dilemmas, that is, situations characterized by a discrepancy between what is individually rational and what is socially rational. A focus of the discussion is on global public goods, in particular the mitigation of climate change. The discussion differentiates altruistic behavior, which is guided by expected outcomes (for others), from deontological behavior, which is guided by a behavior's intrinsic moral quality, and establishes the failure of altruism in large-scale social dilemmas such as climate change. The discussion then highlights the potential of deontological behavior to fix the failure.

Chapter 7 is devoted to how norms and morality have entered recent economic analysis. It starts by providing a general account and classification of various approaches. The chapter then discusses evidence on the importance of social and moral norms with respect to global public goods, with a focus on the mitigation of climate change. With respect to moral norms, a distinction is drawn between philosophical accounts of ethics, which come down to postulating moral norms and duties (a "normative approach to norms"), and anthropological and psychological accounts, which describe the actual moral values and intuitions that evolution has installed in humans to deal with social dilemmas (a "positive approach to norms"). The chapter proceeds by discussing an influential positive moral framework recently proposed – Moral Foundations Theory – and reviews how moral foundations can be and have been incorporated into economics in recent applications to climate change mitigation.

The concluding chapter ties together the three topics of wellbeing, nature, and moral values from the point of view of how they can enable the discipline of economics to better address the major challenges of the 21st century. It provides an account of economists' assessment of how a set of public goods problems will affect subjective wellbeing to the middle of this century, to what extent economic analysis has addressed those issues, and how important it is that they be addressed. It discusses how the probably most important issue – climate change – has been addressed in leading professional journals of economics, and the role that human values and feelings play for social cohesion and the working of our political institutions. Placing more emphasis on both subjective outcomes and drivers of economic activities is identified as being essential for an economics that helps to address the challenges ahead.

Bibliography

Andreoni, J. (1990), Impure Altruism and Donations to Public Goods: A Theory of Warm-Glow Giving, *Economic Journal* 100, 464–477.

Archer, D., Rahmstorf, S. (2009), *The Climate Crisis: An Introductory Guide to Climate Change*, Cambridge: Cambridge University Press.

Atkinson, A.B. (2001), The Strange Disappearance of Welfare Economics, *Kyklos* 54, 193–206.

Bentham, J. (1780), *An Introduction to the Principles of Morals and Legislation*, London: T. Payne and Sons.

Bowles, S., Carlin, W. (2020), What Students Learn in Economics 101: Time for a Change, *Journal of Economic Literature* 58, 176–214.

Brock, W.A., Xepapadeas, A. (2003), Valuing Biodiversity from an Economic Perspective: A Unified Economic, Ecological and Genetic Approach, *American Economic Review* 93, 1597–1614.

Buchholz, W., Sandler, T. (2021), Global Public Goods: A Survey, *Journal of Economic Literature* 59, 488–545.

Collier, P. (2018), *The Future of Capitalism: Facing the New Anxieties*, London: Allen Lane.

CORE Team (2017), *The Economy*, Oxford: Oxford University Press (e-book available at https://Core-Econ.Org/the-Economy/?Lang=En).

Dasgupta, P. (2021), *The Economics of Biodiversity: The Dasgupta Review*, London: HM Treasury.

Dasgupta, P., Heal, G. (1979), *Economic Theory and Natural Resources*, Cambridge: Cambridge University Press.

Easterlin, R.A. (1974), Does Economic Growth Improve the Human Lot? Some Empirical Evidence. In: Paul A. David and Melvin W. Reder (eds.), *Nations and Households in Economic Growth. Essays in Honor of Moses Abramovitz*, Amsterdam: Elsevier, 89–125.

Easterlin, R.A., Angelescu McVey, L., Switek, M., Sawangfa, O., Smith Zweig, J. (2010), The Happiness-Income Paradox Revisited, *Proceedings of the National Academy of Sciences* 107, 22463–22468.

Frey, B.S., Stutzer, A. (2002), What Can Economists Learn from Happiness Research? *Journal of Economic Literature* 40, 402–435.

Haidt, J. (2012), *The Righteous Mind: Why Good People Are Divided by Politics and Religion*, Harmondsworth: Penguin Books.

Hardin, G. (1968), The Tragedy of the Commons, *Science* 162, 1243–1248.

Hausman, D., McPherson, M., Satz, D. (2016), *Economic Analysis, Moral Philosophy, and Public Policy*, 3rd edition, Stanford, CA: Stanford University Press.

Heal, G. (2000), Biodiversity as a Commodity. In: S. Levin, G.C. Daily, J. Lubchenko, and D. Tilman (eds.), *Encyclopedia of Biodiversity*, Cambridge, MA: Academic Press.

Jevons, W.S. (1871), *The Theory of Political Economy*, Harmondsworth: Penguin Books (1970).

Maddison, D.J., Rehdanz, K., Welsch, H. (eds.) (2020), *Handbook on Wellbeing, Happiness and the Environment*, Cheltenham: Edward Elgar.

Mäler, K.-G. (1974), *Environmental Economics: A Theoretical Inquiry*, Baltimore, MD: Johns Hopkins University Press.

Mas-Colell, A., Whinston, M.D., Green, J.R. (1995), *Microeconomic Theory*, Oxford: Oxford University Press.

Mill, J.S. (1857), *Principles of Political Economy*, New York: Augustus M. Kelly (1865).

Nordhaus, W.D. (1994), *Managing the Global Commons. The Economics of Climate Change*, Cambridge, MA: MIT Press.

Nordhaus, W.D. (2019), Climate Change: The Ultimate Challenge for Economics, *American Economic Review* 109, 1991–2014.

Olson, M. (1965), *The Logic of Collective Action: Public Goods and the Theory of Groups*, Cambridge, MA: Harvard University Press.

Piketty, T. (2014), *Capital in the Twenty-First Century*, Cambridge, MA: Harvard University Press.

Rodrik, D. (2011), *The Globalization Paradox: Democracy and the Future of the World Economy*, New York, London: W.W. Norton.

Smith, A. (1759), *The Theory of Moral Sentiments*, London: Andrew Millar (1967).

Smith, A. (1776), *The Wealth of Nations*, London: J.M. Dent & Sons (1910).

Steffen, W. et al. (2018), Trajectories of the Earth System in the Anthropocene, *Proceedings of the National Academy of Sciences* 115 (33) 8252–8259.

Stern, N. (2007), *The Economics of Climate Change: The Stern Review*, Cambridge: Cambridge University Press.

Tomasello, M. (2016), *A Natural History of Human Morality*, Cambridge, MA: Harvard University Press.

United Nations (2021), *The Sustainable Development Goals Report 2021*, New York: United Nations.

White, M.D. (ed.) (2019), *The Oxford Handbook of Ethics and Economics*, Oxford: Oxford University Press.

Part I

Welfare, Wellbeing, and the Environment

2 Measuring Welfare

Introduction

Discussions of national wealth and social welfare typically take gross domestic product (GDP) as a point of departure, as it is the most common measure of a country's economic performance. First developed as a concise statistical concept in the 1930s, GDP is now the key indicator from the System of National Accounts (SNA) for measuring the level of aggregate economic activity (United Nations 1993). GDP measures the value of all goods and services produced by the resident units (private firms and the public sector) of a country during a given period of time less the value of materials, supplies, and services used up in producing those goods and services. GDP, in this sense, is value added created through the production of goods and services in a country and time period. From a different perspective, GDP is a measure of national income, specifically the incomes that accrue to the primary factors of production – labor and capital – and the government (from the taxes levied on the goods and services). Disregarding exports and imports, the goods and services that constitute GDP are used for consumption and investment, where investment is understood as representing future consumption opportunities. GDP, therefore, can be construed as a measure of present and future consumption.

This chapter starts by summarizing the weaknesses of GDP as a welfare measure and proceeds by discussing recent efforts in academic and political spheres to overcome the exclusive identification of economic performance with income and GDP, the introduction into economics of subjective wellbeing (SWB; happiness) as a welfare measure, and the methodological and critical issues involved. The chapter describes the elicitation of happiness data through surveys, how such data can and have been used to track the progress of society at the national or regional level and as a tool for cost-benefit evaluation, and the advantages and limitations of using happiness data as a welfare measure and valuation tool. The chapter focuses on different conceptual dimensions of SWB (affective and evaluative) and on issues of measurability of happiness traditionally raised by economists.

DOI: 10.4324/9781003206163-3

New Measures of Welfare

While GDP is commonly understood as the single most important measure of economic development and progress, it is not a measure of social welfare or aggregate utility – and was not intended to be one. The deficiencies of GDP have spurred various efforts to create more adequate measures of welfare.

Limitations of GDP as a Welfare Measure

There are several reasons for a discrepancy between GDP and welfare. First, not everything that contributes to welfare is included in GDP because GDP comprises only market goods and services, provided by private firms, and nonmarket goods, provided by the state. Other goods and underlying production activities arguably contribute to welfare but are not included in GDP. Classic examples are unpaid housework and volunteering. With respect to the former, hiring someone to do the housework, instead of doing it oneself, raises GDP without creating additional welfare. More generally, the replacement of market activities for nonmarket activities implies an increase in GDP but not necessarily in welfare. Due to the neglect of potentially welfare-relevant production activities, GDP may understate national welfare.

A further reason why social welfare may differ from GDP is that some activities that contribute to GDP are not directly sources of utility themselves but are regrettably necessary inputs to activities that may yield utility. Some consumer outlays, for instance, are only instrumental, such as the costs of commuting to work. Some government expenditures are also of an intermediate or "defensive" nature, in that they serve to attenuate disutility (from pollution, say), rather than being a generic source of utility. Due to such intermediate items, GDP may overstate welfare.

Even disregarding instrumental, defensive, and intermediate consumption, the degree to which truly final consumption contributes to welfare may be ambiguous. With respect to privately provided final market goods, the price an individual pays for them in the market can be considered to be a measure of how much these goods contribute to the individual's utility. There are many instances, however, where the production and use of a good has negative impacts on third parties that are not accounted for in the market price. Examples of negative third-party impacts, so-called externalities, include the effects of air pollution and climate change that arise in the production and use of fossil fuels. Importantly, as in the case of climate change, externalities may be intertemporal, that is, they affect people in the future. In general, while the market value of goods may be taken to indicate their utility to those purchasing them, this private utility need not coincide with the social welfare created, particularly not in an intertemporal sense. Due to negative externalities arising in the creation or use of various GDP items, GDP may overstate national welfare.[1]

With respect to publicly provided goods, the situation is even worse than with respect to market goods. Not only may there be externalities that imply a discrepancy between private utility and social welfare, but, in addition, there are typically no market prices that indicate the utility individuals derive from those goods. Even though economists have developed valuation techniques to capture individuals' willingness to pay for nonmarket goods and the utility underlying it, such surrogate prices play no role in the computation of GDP. Instead, the contribution of publicly provided goods to GDP is calculated on the basis of the costs of providing them, which need not correspond to the utility created.

In addition to the issues mentioned so far, a more fundamental criticism maintains that the very focus on produced goods and services implies too narrow a concept of welfare. From this perspective, GDP fails to account for the leisure time foregone and the unpleasantness encountered in its creation. This view implies that in order to arrive at an adequate welfare assessment, an increase in GDP must be set off against the loss in leisure time. An increase in GDP therefore does not necessarily imply an increase in welfare.

The criticisms that were raised against GDP apply to GNP (gross national product) alike.[2]

An obvious approach to creating a more appropriate measure of social welfare is to try and fix the deficiencies of GDP (and GNP) just discussed. These efforts lead to several kinds of monetary measures of welfare that center around income and consumption. Other approaches involve broader conceptions of welfare and nonmonetary welfare measures.

Adjustments to GDP and the "Measure of Economic Welfare"

In view of the preceding discussion, efforts to correct the deficiencies of GDP (or GNP) aim at accounting for (a) leisure time, (b) unpaid activities, (c) instrumental activities and intermediate expenditures, (d) the benefits (net of costs) from publicly provided goods, and (e) the externalities arising from production and consumption. An early effort to address some of these issues was the computation by Nordhaus and Tobin (1973) of a "measure of economic welfare" (MEW), designed to be a comprehensive measure of the annual real consumption of households on the presumption that the ultimate goal of economic activity is consumption, present and future. In this approach, consumption is intended to include all goods and services, marketed or not, as well as leisure.

The computation of MEW involves adjustments to GNP that fall into three general categories:

- Imputation for leisure and for the product of household work
- Reclassification of GNP expenditures as consumption, investment, and intermediate, and removing the latter expenditure category
- Correction for some of the disamenities of urbanization

Through the former two adjustments, issues (a) through (c) were addressed. The "disamenities of urbanization" addressed by the third adjustment were meant to refer to disutility from living in localities with greater population density, or congestion. Correcting for such disamenities goes some way toward accounting for negative externalities more generally.

Applying the MEW framework to the United States, Nordhaus and Tobin (1973) found that, in 1965, the real economic value of leisure was about equal to GNP. The value of unpaid activities amounted to about 48 percent of GNP. Together, adding them to GNP implied an increase by close to 150 percent. On the other hand, instrumental, intermediate, and defensive expenditures amounted to 15 percent, whereas urban disamenities amounted to about 6 percent. Overall, MEW was about twice as large as GNP. Interestingly, MEW, as of 1929, had been only 67 percent larger than GNP, which implies that the discrepancy between GNP and welfare, as captured by MEW, increased substantially over the three and a half decades considered. The driver of the increasing divergence between MEW and GNP was that the former grew much more slowly than the latter.

Sustainable Income and Green Accounting

By deducting from GNP the value of "urban disamenities" and "defensive" expenditures, the Nordhaus-Tobin framework goes some way toward accounting for negative externalities and the costs of tackling them. Yet, their approach is far from systematically addressing large-scale environmental problems such as pollution and the effects of climate change and biodiversity loss that worry us today.

Addressing environmental externalities and the degradation and depletion of natural resources is the purpose of "green" accounting. Similar to Nordhaus and Tobin (1973), green accounting focuses on final consumption as the source of economic welfare, but ideally considers not only how environmental degradation and resource depletion affect current consumption but also how they impact future consumption possibilities.

The key focus of such approaches is on the role of capital as a source of future consumption, and a fundamental concept in this regard is Hicksian income, defined as that level of income that is compatible with keeping the stock of capital constant (Hicks 1946). While "capital" showing up in this definition was originally conceived of as produced capital, the concept of Hicksian income lends itself nicely to a "green" interpretation by extending the set of assets to be kept constant to natural assets or, likewise, natural capital.

"Green" Hicksian income is a theoretically attractive construct, but its empirical measurement is fraught with several difficulties, specifically with respect to the treatment of produced and natural capital. A key issue refers to the question whether and to what degree produced capital is a substitute for natural capital. If produced capital is a perfect substitute (in all relevant uses), it is admissible to run down natural capital, provided it is compensated by an increase in produced capital, such that the aggregate remains constant. Such a scenario gives rise to the notion of *weak sustainability*, which postulates the preservation of aggregate capital. If, conversely, the two components are completely non-substitutable, natural capital must be kept constant, an imperative known as *strong sustainability*. In reality, substitutability between produced and natural capital is likely to be neither perfect (infinite) nor nil.

In addition to the problem of aggregating produced and natural capital, depending on substitutability, similar issues exist with respect to the very concept of "natural capital". Considering that it involves such diverse items as mineral resources, biological resources, and the climate system, it is unclear how these items can be aggregated in a meaningful way. In particular, while prices for mineral and biological resources traded in markets could serve as weights in such an aggregation, prices do not exist for the services provided by biodiversity and the climate system. In addition, market prices, if existing, likely reflect the contribution of the respective resources to present, but not future, consumption (Fleurbaey 2009).

Such issues make it difficult to correct GDP or GNP for the depletion of assets. In SNA, the depreciation ("depletion") of produced capital is routinely deducted from GDP or GNP, thus arriving at net domestic product (NDP) or net national product (NNP), respectively. This is easy to do since market prices are available to value capital goods and make them commensurable to consumption goods. A "green" NDP or NNP, in addition, would have to deduct the depletion of natural assets, measured in monetary units that reflect their contribution to present and future consumption, but prices that achieve this are unlikely to be available.

Given the conceptual and practical problems involved, Hicksian income and related measures have not played a big role in real-world approaches to measuring social welfare. Yet, the idea of sustainability, in the sense of preserving natural assets, has spurred efforts to extend the SNA in appropriate ways. Rather than adjusting SNA and its key indicator, GDP, national statistical offices worldwide have introduced a System of Environmental and Economic Accounting (SEEA) that combines physical and monetary data in a manner compatible with economic transactions as presented in the SNA (United Nations 2014). SEEA includes not only *flows* between the economic and environmental systems (such as natural resource inputs and waste outputs of the economic system) but also *stocks* of environmental assets, that is, "the naturally occurring living and non-living components of the Earth, together constituting the biophysical environment, which may provide benefits to humanity" (United Nations 2014, p. 13). The natural assets included in SEEA are mineral and energy resources, land, soil resources, timber resources, aquatic resources, other biological resources, and water resources. By reporting these stocks over time, SEEA permits the tracking of important dimensions of sustainability. Complex natural assets like the climate system and biodiversity are not monitored in SEEA.

Accounting for Nonmarket Goods

The approaches to welfare measurement discussed so far aim at accounting for the benefits or utility stemming from items other than current consumption or income, as well as for the implied disutility through unaccounted third-party effects. In the Nordhaus-Tobin MEW framework, unaccounted benefits are those from leisure and housework, whereas unaccounted disutility is that from "urban disamenities". In contrast to the latter, the concepts of "green" NDP and NNP focus on *intertemporal* third-party effects and the associated disutility, that is, the restriction of future consumption possibilities through the depletion and degradation of assets.

A common problem of these approaches is the valuation of the items to be corrected for. This is easy with respect to leisure and housework (MEW), where market wages can be used, and produced capital (NDP/NNP), where market prices can be applied. Difficulties exist, however, with respect to nonmarket goods, such as environmental quality, health, education, law and order, and the like.

Nonmarket goods can be subdivided into those provided ("produced") by the state, for instance law and order, and those that are not produced at all, such as environmental quality or the services provided by biodiversity and the climate system. With respect to the produced goods, it is common to use the *costs* of production as a proxy for the welfare created by their provision. Indeed, this is how the "output" of the public sector is captured in the National Accounts. Nonmarket goods that are not produced, however, fail to show up in the National Accounts entirely. In both cases, an adequate measure of welfare is lacking.

There are several approaches to capturing the welfare afforded by nonmarket goods, some of which are intended to yield monetary welfare measures, whereas others are not. Social indicators belong in the latter category. They combine various domain indicators of economic, social, and environmental performance into a summary indicator (Gadrey and Jany-Catrice 2006). Probably the most prominent social indicator is the Human Development Index (HDI). The HDI is a composite index of life expectancy, years of schooling, and per capita income and is used to rank countries' levels of human development.

A common problem with such composite indicators is that the selection of domain indicators is arbitrary. With respect to the HDI, for instance, life expectancy is supposed to be a measure of health. To measure health, it might be better to use so-called quality-adjusted life years (QUALYs) rather than simple life expectancy. In addition, the domain indicators are typically incommensurate in terms of measurement units, which implies ambiguity with respect to the rankings derived from the summary indicators (Ebert and Welsch 2004). Finally, the weights of the various domain indicators in the general index are conventional, and the proponents of such indicators rarely formulate a framework for a rational discussion about what these weights should be (Ravallion 1997). While one can invoke the ethical preferences of the observer, there is little philosophical or economic theory that gives us clues about how to form such preferences (Fleurbaey 2009). In general, the assessment by Nordhaus and Tobin (1973) still seems to apply that the social indicators movement lacks a coherent, integrative conceptual and statistical framework.

The standard approach to integrating nonmarket goods into welfare analysis is to estimate their monetary value by using methods of nonmarket valuation. This permits aggregation of nonmarket and market goods into a measure of money-metric utility. Common techniques of nonmarket valuation are usually differentiated into *revealed preference* and *stated preference* approaches (Freeman et al. 2014). The former use complementarity or substitutability relationships between nonmarket goods and market goods to infer the value people attribute to the former from observed behavior with respect to the latter. Examples include the defensive behavior and damage cost method, hedonic price analysis, and the travel cost approach. In the stated preference approach, individuals are asked to directly value the nonmarket good in question or to make choices in appropriately designed choice experiments, from which their valuation can be inferred. The most prominent stated preference method is contingent valuation, which attempts to elicit the valuation of hypothetical changes in the availability of nonmarket goods.

The *defensive and damage cost method* refers to the actual costs induced by the degradation of amenities (environmental or other). While the defensive costs include those expenses that the affected individuals incur to protect themselves against worsening conditions, the damage costs represent the monetary value of the adverse effects that remain in spite of defensive behavior. Damage costs mostly refer to physical property or human health and lives lost but also include income forgone due to changed conditions. In spite of being based on costs, this valuation method differs from reporting the costs of publicly provided goods in the National Accounts because the latter leaves it open whether the amount or quality of those goods matches individuals' preference for them. The cost-based valuation method at hand, conversely, relies on what people's choice of defensive actions reveals about their preferences and implied valuations.

According to the *hedonic pricing approach*, housing prices and wage rates reflect the value of amenities in the respective locations or time periods: greater availability of amenities (e.g., better air quality or greater public safety) shows up in higher housing prices and lower wages. The corresponding differentials in housing prices and wage rates serve as implicit prices of differences in amenities and reflect, in equilibrium, the individuals' marginal willingness to pay for them. The hedonic pricing method is applicable to local amenities, since it relies on spatial variation in prices (wages) and local conditions.

The *travel cost method* uses the costs people incur to get to attractive locations as approximations of the underlying valuation. Costs include not only actual expenses but also the opportunity costs of the time spent. The travel cost method is typically applied to recreation sites.

The *contingent valuation method*, being the most widespread stated preference technique, asks people to state their willingness to pay for a hypothetical but well-defined improvement of given conditions or the monetary compensation they require to accept a well-defined deterioration (willingness to accept). The contingent valuation method can be applied to any kind of conditions, provided the hypothetical changes can be described with sufficient accuracy.

A *choice experiment* is a survey approach designed to elicit individuals' preferences based on hypothetical markets. Respondents are required to choose between multiple market and nonmarket goods or alternative situations. This choice is expected to occur by trading off the individual attributes of the different goods available, and choosing the good (or alternative) that provides the most utility. A series of observed choices is used to infer an underlying utility function, that is, utility weights for each attribute. Since one of the attributes typically is cost or price, it is possible to estimate willingness-to-pay or willingness-to-accept measures for changes in the attributes of nonmarket goods and to conduct welfare estimations. Since choice experiments involve stated choices in hypothetical markets rather than observed choices in real markets, they belong to the category of stated preference methods.

A major difference between revealed and stated preference methods is that the former typically refers to so-called use values of the nonmarket goods under consideration, as opposed to existence values; costs of traveling or taking defensive measures as well as house prices and wages reflect the benefits people derive from using those goods, for instance, enjoying clean air or a beautiful landscape. Existence value – the satisfaction of knowing that an endangered species, say, exists – is measurable by stated preference rather than revealed preference methods, for instance by asking people to state their willingness to pay for a wildlife or biodiversity conservation program. In contrast to use value, existence value may refer to nonmarket goods in faraway places, such as coral reefs and polar bears.

Assuming that the monetary value individuals attach to nonmarket goods has been established, it is possible to aggregate market and nonmarket goods into a monetary measure of utility or welfare, using market prices for the former and accounting (nonmarket) values for the latter. Performing such an exercise may proceed at the national or global level. While local and regional nonmarket goods yield utility within a nation and are components of *national* welfare, the utility from global nonmarket goods often cannot be allocated to nations but nevertheless is a component of *global* welfare. This applies, in particular, to some existence values.

It remains to note that the welfare so determined typically refers to a *change* in assets or wealth, not a stock. What is being valued is the improvement or deterioration of air quality, say, over a period of time. Since deterioration of nonmarket goods often results from third-party effects unaccounted for by market prices, accounting for nonmarket goods can often be interpreted as an adjustment for externalities from market transactions.

Beyond Consumption

The various criticisms of GDP discussed previously all rely on the idea that GDP fails to capture individuals' utility in some way or other, and so do the various approaches to addressing those criticisms. The fundamental notion of welfare underlying these approaches, hence, is utility, and the approaches can be referred to as varieties of *utilitarianism*. More specifically, the utilitarian approaches discussed can be termed "consumption focused", as they revolve around consumption – of market and nonmarket goods, present and future.

The focus on consumption, however broadly defined, involves a rather narrow conception of utility, as it disregards many items that arguably yield utility, such as health, social status, or family life, to name a few. The narrow conception can be defended on dogmatic or pragmatic grounds. The dogmatic defense maintains that sources of utility other than consumption are outside the scope of economics. The pragmatic defense maintains that utility beyond consumption is immeasurable – noting that proper measurement of consumption is difficult enough.

Modern economics has transcended consumption-focused utilitarianism in several ways. One is to abandon utilitarianism altogether and develop alternative conceptions of welfare. An important conception in this vein is the so-called capability approach. Another way of transcending the consumption focus is to conceptualize utility more broadly and use data on SWB (happiness and life satisfaction) to measure it.

The capability approach, developed by Sen (1985), rests on the central concepts of "functionings", understood as the "beings and doings" (states and activities) in the life of an individual, and "capabilities", understood as the functionings that are feasible for a person to achieve. By focusing on functionings, the capability approach transcends the focus on commodities or resources characteristic of traditional approaches to welfare. Focusing on capabilities highlights the importance of opportunities and freedoms, as opposed to achievements (income, consumption, and utility).

Freedom, in the sense of enhancing individuals' capability set, has been proclaimed to be the goal of economic and social development (Sen 1999). Examples of such substantive freedom, as opposed to mere freedom in the legal sense, include the ability to live to old age, engage in economic transactions, or participate in political activities. Freedom, ultimately, is people's ability to live a good life.

Being rather general, the capability framework needs to be specified in order to allow empirical application. While the body of empirical literature that takes inspiration from the capability approach is large, the empirical studies are in many cases similar to sociological studies of living conditions, except for terminology (Fleurbaey 2009).

Two central questions pervade the empirical applications. One is whether one should focus on functionings or on capabilities. The empirical literature mainly deals with functionings because they are more easily observable than pure potentialities. However, many functionings, such as income and health, also directly determine capabilities (to consume or to move around, say). In addition, some work has explored the possibility of using questionnaires to directly inquire whether individuals feel able to do certain things (e.g., Anand et al. 2005).

The other question concerns the construction of an aggregate welfare index. No matter whether it builds upon functionings or capabilities, the various dimensions of life must be aggregated, and the selection of weights involved faces the same criticisms as was discussed earlier with respect to composite social indicators (of which the HDI was actually inspired by the capability approach). In addition, if specified exogenously, there is no chance that the weights will respect individuals' own values about life, and the procedure will appear paternalistic.

To avoid paternalism, it may be useful to ask people about their weights, rather than specifying them exogenously. Still another approach to determining the various functionings' and capabilities' weights is to estimate their contribution to individuals' SWB, provided one is willing to accept the latter as a measure of welfare. In pursuing such an idea, it was found that a wide range of capabilities exhibit statistically significant relations to SWB (e.g., Anand et al. 2005).

Subjective Wellbeing and Economics

Psychologists started to study SWB in the late 1940s (Diener et al. 1999), and it was introduced into economic analysis in the 1970s in a paper investigating the relationship between income growth and self-rated happiness in the United States (Easterlin 1974). Since then, the field of wellbeing studies has seen a massive expansion and has developed into an interdisciplinary science. In parallel, SWB has received increasing attention not only in academic spheres but also in political spheres. The kingdom of Bhutan adopted "gross national happiness" as a policy target as early as the 1970s, and the Centre for Bhutan Studies began publishing the Bhutan Gross National Happiness Index in 2008. In 2014, the UK Office for Statistics launched its happiness and wellbeing statistics titled "Measures of National Wellbeing". In 2019, the Treasury of New Zealand published its first "Wellbeing Budget". At the international level, the United Nations started to release the annual World Happiness Report in 2011.

Concepts of Subjective Wellbeing

The term "SWB" refers to individuals' assessments of their own subjective experience of their lives (e.g., Diener and Suh 1997). SWB is a multidimensional concept that involves components such as pleasant affect, unpleasant affect, life satisfaction, fulfillment, and more specific states such as stress, affection, trust, and joy (Diener 2000). Yet, the various specific components can be grouped into affective and cognitive dimensions, that is, emotional states and evaluations of life, respectively (Diener 1984). While *happiness*, in the narrow sense, refers to the affective component, the cognitive (evaluative) component is usually referred to as *life satisfaction*.

Affective wellbeing involves a reference to mood, emotions, or affective states of an individual. This component is usually elicited with questions such as "How happy are you?" or via questions on positive and negative affect or the experience of mood states. In contrast to affective wellbeing, cognitive wellbeing is the outcome of a process where individuals reflect and then judge (and approve of) their lives. It is elicited, for instance, via the question "Overall, how satisfied are you with life as a whole these days?". In addition to satisfaction with life overall, domain satisfaction measures, where individuals reflect on specific domains of their lives (such as, e.g., their financial situation), also fall under cognitive measures of wellbeing.[3]

Affective and cognitive measures are thus conceptually distinct, and their determinants have been shown to differ as well. For example, income is no longer associated positively with affective wellbeing above a threshold of US$75,000, while still maintaining a positive relationship with life satisfaction (Kahneman and Deaton 2010). Yet affective and cognitive measures overlap to some extent and are highly correlated with each other. In a representative sample from 29 European nations, for instance, the correlation coefficient between happiness and life satisfaction amounts to 0.71 (European Social Survey, Round 9). In addition, the most important individual-level correlates of SWB (education, marital status, income, and labor-force status) were found to be correlated to affective and evaluative wellbeing (as well as to measures of eudaimonic wellbeing) in very much the same way in three different data sets (Clark 2016).

One approach to reconcile the differences in content with the positive correlation is the "mediator model of life satisfaction", which links cognitive to affective wellbeing. The mediator model maintains that people's evaluations of their lives partly rely on their prevailing affective states (Suh et al. 1998). In this sense, affect may be said to be just one domain of life that, in their life evaluations, people are willing to trade for objective achievements (Fleurbaey 2009). In addition, affective states typically are more volatile and may be influenced by the mood of the day, the current weather, or anecdotal events such as finding a dime a few minutes earlier. Uses of SWB in economics therefore focus on evaluative rather than affective wellbeing.

In spite of the differences, it is common in economics to use the terms SWB, happiness, and life satisfaction synonymously. Following common practice, the term happiness will henceforth be used in the wider sense, referring to SWB in general, unless stated otherwise.

Measuring Subjective Wellbeing

In 2013, the Organization for Economic Cooperation and Development (OECD) published its "Guidelines on Measuring Subjective Wellbeing"

(OECD 2013), which proposes to elicit life satisfaction in household surveys by means of the following "core question":

> The following question asks how satisfied you feel, on a scale from 0 to 10. Zero means you feel "not at all satisfied" and 10 means you feel "completely satisfied". Overall, how satisfied are you with life as a whole these days?
>
> (OECD 2013, p. 253)

This question is intended to capture the respondent's evaluative judgment of how their life is going while imposing the minimum level of respondent burden. It is envisaged that this question will serve as the primary measure of SWB when a single measure is required. The guidelines also propose questions for eliciting affective states, in particular happiness, but they explicitly refer to how respondents felt "yesterday". Given the volatility of affective states, they are arguably less relevant to welfare measurement than evaluative judgments.

A slightly more sophisticated life evaluation question relies on the so-called Cantril Ladder (Cantril 1965):

> Please imagine a ladder with steps numbered from 0 at the bottom to 10 at the top. The top of the ladder represents the best possible life for you and the bottom of the ladder represents the worst possible life for you. On which step of the ladder would you say you personally feel you stand at this time?

In comparison with the core life satisfaction question, the Cantril Ladder strives to enhance respondents' self-anchoring. According to OEDC (2013) it could be used in circumstances where a more in-depth understanding of SWB is required or to help understand methodological issues in measuring SWB.

Data on life satisfaction are routinely elicited in large-scale social surveys both at national and international levels. Important national data sources, among others, are the Keio Household Panel Survey (KHPS) from Japan, the German Socio-Economic Panel (SOEP), and the UK Household Longitudinal Study (UKHLS, also called *Understanding Society*). At the international level, SWB data are included, among others, in the Eurobarometer Surveys (covering the member countries of the European Union), the European Social Survey (covering 36 European countries), the World Values Survey (covering more than 80 countries worldwide) and the Gallup World Poll covering (156 countries). In these and similar surveys, people are regularly asked questions about their happiness or life satisfaction. The European Social Survey, for instance, asks representative samples of people "How happy are you?" (on a scale from 0 = extremely unhappy to 10 = extremely happy) and a version of the OECD's core life satisfaction question: "All things considered, how satisfied are you with your life as a whole nowadays?" (from 0 = extremely dissatisfied to 10 = extremely satisfied). The Gallup World Poll uses the Cantril Ladder to elicit life satisfaction scores. While the samples used in international surveys typically change over time, national surveys like the KHPS, SOEP, and UKHLS rely on fixed sets of people over several years, thus allowing longitudinal analyses of SWB and its correlates. The latter is important because it permits the separation of interpersonal differences in wellbeing levels that may stem from personality and do not change over time from changes in individuals' wellbeing that arise as a result of changed circumstances, for instance, getting laid off.

The *World Database of Happiness* (Veenhoven 2020) provides a useful archive of SWB data and findings.

Using Wellbeing Data for Nonmarket Valuation

Almost two decades after a pioneering study of the relationship between happiness and income growth in the United States (Easterlin 1974), the use of wellbeing data gained momentum in the 1990s. In addition to studying how economic, social, and environmental conditions affect wellbeing – to be discussed in the next two chapters – wellbeing data started to be used for valuation of nonmarket goods and for conducting cost-benefit analyses of public policy.

The basis for valuing nonmarket goods using wellbeing data is a wellbeing equation that models people's SWB (happiness or life satisfaction) as a function of their incomes and the level of the nonmarket good under consideration (usually controlling for a variety of socio-demographic variables). The nonmarket goods may include, for example, public safety or environmental amenities (measured, for instance, by crime rates and pollution levels, respectively) and many others. Once estimated with appropriate statistical methods, the coefficients of the wellbeing equation indicate how much an increase in income, on one hand, and a higher level of the nonmarket good, on the other, affect wellbeing. Dividing the coefficient on the nonmarket good by that on income then indicates how an "average" individual from the sample trades off one additional unit of the good for one additional unit of income, that is, how much money one would be willing to forego for a one-unit increase of the good while holding the level of wellbeing constant. This amount of money is an implicit indicator of one's willingness to pay for the nonmarket good in question.

The same kind of analysis can be conducted for subgroups of the population, by gender or age, say, to obtain the willingness to pay of individuals with the respective characteristics, rather than an average individual. In addition, it is possible (and often done) to specify the wellbeing equation with the logarithm of income instead of the absolute level. This takes account of the circumstance that one additional unit of money contributes less to the wellbeing of a wealthier individual than a less wealthy individual (diminishing marginal utility of income). Computing the willingness to pay based on such a specification implies that wealthier people have a higher willingness than those who are less wealthy to pay for the nonmarket good considered.

The SWB approach (or happiness approach) to nonmarket valuation differs from the revealed and stated preference approaches discussed earlier and has a number of advantages and disadvantages compared to them (Welsch and Kühling 2009). The happiness approach is much more direct than the revealed preference approach, in that it directly refers to the wellbeing attributable to the nonmarket goods in question, for instance environmental amenities, rather than to private goods – such as housing – whose value is assumed to be affected by them. However, it is not as direct as the contingent valuation approach, in that it does not ask people how they value amenities. Instead, wellbeing scores elicited in surveys are correlated with respondents' incomes and observed measures of environmental conditions, say, in the places where they live, and these correlations serve to estimate the trade-offs people are willing to make between money and amenities. The happiness technique avoids some of the specific difficulties of the standard approaches (especially, stringent assumptions concerning the rationality of agents and the functioning of markets in the revealed preference case, and the use of hypothetical scenarios, which may entail unreliable results and strategic behavior in the stated preference case). It also avoids a fundamental problem common to all standard approaches: while the standard methods rely on at least some knowledge of cause–effect relationships on the part of the individuals, the happiness approach is able to capture all effects of a change in environmental conditions, even if the affected individual may not be consciously aware of them. For instance, exposure to nuclear radiation can damage people's health through a process unnoticed by them but which nevertheless may affect SWB. Similar reasoning applies to the effects of air pollution.

The circumstance that less knowledge is required is one reason why the happiness approach is cognitively less demanding than the standard approaches. Another reason is that people are not requested to perform the unfamiliar task of actively placing monetary values on environmental conditions. Therefore a strong point can be made for the use of happiness (experienced utility) in environmental valuation, on the presupposition that goods have value by virtue of their capacity to create pleasurable affective states (Kahneman and Sugden 2005). While this assumption may be questionable in some cases of pure existence value, for most environmental goods, experienced utility is a source of value. Therefore, the happiness approach can capture several aspects of environmental conditions, ranging from nonmonetized health to aesthetic values, ecological effects, altruism, consequences of correlated pollutants, and income losses. In addition, since the preference function is estimated directly, the happiness approach permits not only marginal but also non-marginal effects to be valued in a straightforward manner. This is important since many environmental issues are non-marginal (e.g., a development next door, a hog farm nearby, an oil spill, air pollution episodes, climate change, and flood events).

Given its advantages, the happiness approach may serve as a valuable addition to the toolbox of nonmarket valuation. By treating income as potentially being affected by amenities (in the spirit of the hedonic valuation technique), effects of amenities on wages can be incorporated into the analysis. In addition, if housing prices depend on amenities, the happiness function can be extended to include these prices. Combining the extended happiness function with the hedonic housing price function then permits amenity values capitalized in housing prices to be differentiated from non-compensated ones. If the latter turn out to be significant, this suggests that the hedonic pricing technique underestimates overall amenity values.

While there are advantages of the happiness valuation approach, there are also a number of difficulties that require attention when applying it (Levinson 2020).

One problem is selection: people choose where to live, and those who care the most about pollution, say, presumably choose cleaner places. Survey respondents who have chosen polluted places might express no less happiness than respondents who chose less-polluted places. They chose the polluted places because they care less about pollution. But that doesn't mean that increasing pollution in the clean places wouldn't make their residents less happy. The selection by people into polluted and unpolluted places may mask any true direct effect of pollution on happiness for a representative person. A way of addressing this problem is to consider how changes in amenities change the happiness of people at given places, rather than to compare amenities and happiness across places.

Another problem is habituation: people become inured to, or habituated to, things like poor health, crime, corruption, and democracy (Graham 2011). That is, unhealthy people living in dangerous, corrupt, undemocratic places may be not less happy as a consequence, at least not in the long run. They become habituated to those problems, and the same may apply to pollution. To accommodate this concern, happiness valuation may focus on changes in amenities that are not long lasting enough for people to become habituated. An example is the happiness impact of day-to-day variation in air pollution (Levinson 2020).

The WELLBY Approach to Cost-Benefit Analysis

Building on several governments' efforts to create happiness and wellbeing statistics, it has recently been proposed to use SWB not only for valuing specific nonmarket goods but also for systematic policy evaluation and appraisal (Frijters and Krekel 2021). The idea is to ultimately move from using GDP to using SWB, specified as life satisfaction, as the primary metric for measuring economic and societal progress.

In an intermediate perspective, it is envisaged that life satisfaction be routinely used for cost-benefit or cost-effectiveness analysis of government policy, and the Treasury of the United Kingdom has issued pertinent guidelines in a supplement to their *Green Book: Central Government Guidance on Appraisal and Evaluation* (HM Treasury 2021). Areas where wellbeing appraisal of government policy is envisaged to be applied include changes in physical or mental health; reductions in loneliness, changes from employment to unemployment, changes in job quality, crime, cultural and heritage assets, changes in vacant land, changes in green space in surrounding areas, odor near sewage treatment works, noise, air quality, and several specific programs with respect to schooling and education (HM Treasury 2021, pp. 61–69). In addition to health and employment, considerable attention is thus paid to local and environmental issues but, remarkably, not to global environmental goods such as the climate and biodiversity.

The metric used in such appraisals is *wellbeing adjusted life year* (WELLBY), where a WELLBY equates to a one-point change in life satisfaction on a 0–10 scale, per person per year. The WELLBY methodology of measuring societal wellbeing follows the classical utilitarian understanding of the wellbeing of the population being the sum of the individual wellbeing of all citizens, where every individual counts equally and every point on the life satisfaction scale is equally valuable. Similarly, lifetime wellbeing can be estimated by summing up wellbeing in each year of life for any individual (with appropriate discounting of future years) into a "lifetime life satisfaction" number (What Works Centre for Wellbeing 2020).

For cost-benefit analysis, to make the WELLBY metric of benefits commensurate with the money metric of costs, a central value monetary equivalent of £13,000 of a WELLBY is suggested, with low and high values of £10,000 and £16,000, respectively (HM Treasury 2021). Raising life satisfaction by 0.4 for one year, for example, would have a value of 0.4 × £13,000 = £5,200, with a range of £4,000–£6,400. The same WELLBY value should be applied to all individuals regardless of income, and represents a population average willingness to pay. Cost-benefit policy appraisal will compare average willingness to pay, so obtained, with the policy's costs per person.

While adding up WELLBY across individuals and years is consistent with classical utilitarianism, modifications may respond to a number of outstanding research questions (Frijters and Krekel 2021):

- Valuing different effects on different groups: Should more weight be given to changes (up or down) in the wellbeing of people whose wellbeing is currently low?
- Valuing effects over time: Should future effects of policy changes be discounted and, if so, by how much? How should effects on people not yet born be treated?

Both of these questions refer to issues of distribution, intra-temporal and inter-temporal/inter-generational, respectively, which are controversial and notoriously difficult to handle.

Another issue is that, consistent with the neglect of global public goods noted earlier, WELLBY accounting of policy impacts, as currently envisaged in the United Kingdom, is restricted to the national population. In view of transnational or global impacts of many policy actions, the question arises of how to account for such spillover effects. For example, reducing greenhouse gases involves costs domestically, whereas benefits arise worldwide. Cost-benefit appraisal of greenhouse gas mitigation programs will yield more favorable assessment if global rather than domestic benefits are accounted for. Such issues are obviously of paramount importance in view of all the global challenges ahead. Adequately addressing them arguably would require international harmonization of WELLBY accounting.

Open questions notwithstanding, when asked about their views about the WELLBY methodology, 14 out of 16 experts in wellbeing research agreed or completely agreed to the following statement (while none disagreed)[4]: "The WELLBY cost-benefit methodology as it is now adopted by the UK and New Zealand bureaucracy will give a greater weight to mental health, social relations, and the environment in cost-benefit calculations than the classic economic methods it replaces." Reasons for agreement included the inherent breadth of factors that contribute to life satisfaction and hence to WELLBY calculations and the circumstance that – as will be seen in Chapters 3 and 4 – income and consumption play a less-important role for life satisfaction compared to social relations (including work) and the environment.

Subjective Wellbeing as a Welfare Measure

In spite of the conceptual and practical merits of the WELLBY concept and its ability to aid policy makers in prioritizing investments, questions remain as to its relation to traditional as well as alternative concepts of utility and welfare, and to methodological issues of measurement. These issues are important because, from the late 19th century onward, economists deemed utility to be a purely "metaphysical" concept and were skeptical with respect to the chances of pinning it down empirically. The question thus is whether, against this background, measures of SWB are meaningful measures of utility and welfare.

Subjective Wellbeing and Utility

It was already noted that the WELLBY cost-benefit methodology shows a formal similarity with classical utilitarianism in that welfare is conceived of as the sum of individuals' utility. To judge whether such summation is meaningful, some technical issues of measurability and comparability of wellbeing must be addressed.

Before proceeding to that, it is useful to discuss utility and wellbeing from a substantive point of view. As to utility, 20th-century economists deemed the concept not only to be immeasurable but also unnecessary for conducting important parts of economic analysis. To understand this, a distinction between two varieties of utility is helpful: experienced utility, which is the *ex post* hedonic quality associated with an (economic) outcome, and decision utility, which describes the *ex ante* expectation of experienced utility (Kahneman et al. 1997). While experienced utility is the key concept of utilitarianism, economists later focused on decision utility and showed that it is just a tool for describing preferences and choices, used solely for convenience. In this view, three statements concerning mutually exclusive (and feasible) options A and B are equivalent: (a) A yields greater utility than B. (b) A is preferred to B. (c) A is chosen. The assumed equivalence of statements (a) and (b) implies that (decision) utility is an ordinal, not a cardinal, concept: for A to be preferred to B, it does not matter by how much the (expected) utility of A exceeds that of B. The assumed equivalence of (b) and (c) implies that observed choices include all relevant information on underlying preferences. In particular, when the options in question are market goods, prices emerging in (undistorted) markets reveal individuals' preferences for and valuations of those goods.

Assuming that the value of a thing reflects the utility or enjoyment experienced by an individual (as posited by early neoclassical economists and fairly undisputed to the present day), inferring value from choices in markets presupposes that decision utility and experienced utility coincide. This proposition is at odds with mounting evidence in behavioral economics that found systematic failures in utility forecasting (Loewenstein and Adler 1995). In addition, when it comes to nonmarket goods, this method of inferring value is infeasible a priori. Measurement of experienced utility is thus anything but unnecessary, and SWB is a prime candidate for a measure of experienced utility.

Criticism of Wellbeing as a Welfare Measure

Criticism of positing SWB as a measure of welfare has been raised, in particular, by proponents of an "objectivist" approach to social welfare, notably the capability approach. Indeed, such criticism refers not just to specific measures of wellbeing, such as reported life satisfaction, but also to utilitarianism more generally (Sen 1985).

A key element of that criticism is the idea that subjective adaptation is likely to hide objective adversities and inequalities. While early discussions relied on anecdotal evidence, such as the example of the tamed housewife who accepts her impoverished condition and is happy about it (Sen 1985), recent evidence shows that people indeed adapt to many life events and changes (such as promotion, changes in income beyond "basic needs", disability, and divorce) so that the wellbeing impact can diminish over time (Graham 2011).

However, importantly, this does not apply to all aspects of life, and studies that have followed the same participants over time show that wellbeing can change significantly over the long term (HM Treasury 2021). For example, when people are in a stable partnership, their wellbeing ratings are higher than those of people not in such relationships, and they stay higher. People who are unemployed have lower ratings of wellbeing than others, and wellbeing stays low while they remain out of work and beyond. The same applies to living in poverty. Furthermore, people do not adapt to the negative impact of noise or disagreeable job conditions, and tend to adapt little to situations that regularly draw their attention.

In sum, it *cannot* be concluded that adaptation invalidates using SWB as a welfare measure. On the contrary, if alternative options differ in the degree to which people adapt, this can be an important factor in comparative cost-benefit appraisal. For example, a study of alternative power generation options (Von Möllendorff and Welsch 2017) found that the deployment of wind turbines negatively affected the life satisfaction of residents living nearby (through visual disamenity), but the effect disappeared in the second year after windmills were built. By contrast, the wellbeing effects of biomass-based power plants (through bad smell) were not only larger but also persisted throughout their lifetime. Wellbeing thus adapts differently to different circumstances, and such differences in adaptation are of obvious importance to policy makers' choice between competing options.

Another criticism of using wellbeing as a welfare measure concerns a focus on *average* wellbeing effects, which neglects inequalities. However, such criticism can easily be accommodated. One possibility is to give more weight to people whose wellbeing is currently low. Another is to use estimates of wellbeing effects differentiated by subgroups of the population. Criteria for differentiation may be socioeconomic variables, such as income, but it is also possible to differentiate effect sizes by the current level of wellbeing.

Overall, it appears that neither adaptation nor concern about inequality invalidate the use of SWB as a welfare measure and in cost-benefit appraisal. Rather, an attractive feature of cost-benefit appraisal based on wellbeing is that it permits giving more weight to projects with more durable positive and less durable negative effects, and to projects that benefit the less well-off.

Measurability and Comparability of Subjective Wellbeing

In addition to these substantive issues, criticism has focused on methodological issues of the measurement of SWB. Economists have traditionally taken a skeptical stance on subjective data elicited in surveys and asked, "Do people mean what they say?" (Bertrand and Mullainathan 2001). However, there is ample evidence that self-reports of SWB are in good agreement with results from methods such as experience sampling (mood declaration at random moments of the day) and day reconstruction (short recall mood declaration), physiological measures (hormone concentration, skin conductivity), neurological measures (brain activity), as well as behavioral observations (smiling). One can thus be confident that survey questions yield valid and reliable estimates of SWB (Fleurbaey 2009; Frey and Stutzer 2002).

In spite of this, estimating how various options and circumstances affect wellbeing poses some methodological issues. These issues concern whether wellbeing data elicited in surveys are to be treated as ordinal or cardinal data. For example, ordinal *measurability* means that a person is more satisfied when reporting a life satisfaction score of 8 than when reporting 4, but the numerical difference between 8 and 4 contains no meaningful information. It does not indicate that a person is twice more satisfied in the former than in the latter condition, as would be required for cardinal measurability. Similarly, when several persons are concerned, ordinal *comparability* means that a person reporting 8 is more satisfied than a person reporting 4, but the difference is again not meaningful, as would be required for cardinal comparability.

When survey data for many people are to be used to statistically estimate how wellbeing is "on average" related to given circumstances, ordinal comparability must be assumed. This is not a problematic assumption given ample evidence that interpersonal patterns of self-reports correspond to the physiological and neurological measures and behavioral observations mentioned before. Given ordinal comparability, appropriate statistical methods for estimation are available. It has, however, been found in a large number of studies that applying methods for cardinal data leads to very similar conclusions with respect to the determinants of wellbeing (Ferrer-i-Carbonell and Frijters 2004).

In sum, it is by now widely accepted that subjective data elicited in surveys are valid measures of wellbeing and can be used for inferring the determinants of wellbeing and the relative strength of their influence.

Conclusion

While economics was very much concerned with personal and social welfare until the late 19th century, the standard economics that emerged thereafter shifted the focus to more easily measurable objects. As consumption came to be viewed to be the single most important purpose of economic activity, there was no need to deal with the difficult-to-capture "metaphysical" notion of utility – in the sense of personal welfare – and to struggle with its measurement. In microeconomics, utility survived in a rudimentary form as ordinal utility, which served as a convenient description of preferences over alternative consumption options. In macroeconomics, the concepts of GNP and GDP were developed, and supposed to serve as measures of aggregate consumption at present and in the future.

While GNP and GDP were explicitly not intended to be measures of social welfare, it was clear that they did not even capture consumption in an adequate way, since they disregard important activities that contribute to consumption (such as housework) while including others that reduce it (through degradation of amenities and natural assets). Accordingly, measures were proposed that account for these deficiencies, such as sustainable income. As these measures involve aggregating produced and natural capital in a way that captures their respective ability to contribute to present and future consumption, it turned out that their implementation poses significant problems.

Departing from the focus on consumption, other approaches take a more holistic view. Objectivist approaches rely on exogenously specifying what the ingredients to welfare are, or they categorically dismiss the utility-focused approach by postulating to enhance individuals' capabilities, that is, the set of states and activities that are feasible for a person to achieve. Subjectivist approaches, by contrast, revert to the classical notion of individual welfare as SWB or experienced utility.

Over the past decades, SWB was increasingly found to be measurable in a valid and reliable way, and it was recently proposed to use wellbeing adjusted life years as a metric for benefit appraisal of public policy. This proposal rests on large-scale and robust evidence of how SWB relates to a variety of economic and noneconomic factors. The next two chapters summarize this evidence, placing a specific focus on how SWB may be affected by some of the important challenges facing societies worldwide.

Notes

1 Positive externalities from some GDP-relevant activity may imply that the welfare created by it is larger than its contribution to GDP. For instance, the activity of a tree nursery may yield utility not only to eventual buyers of the trees, which is measured by the trees' market price but also to third parties, by improving air quality. The market-based activities that make up GDP are likely to involve more negative than positive externalities.

2 While GDP measures the value of goods and services produced within a country's borders, by citizens and noncitizens alike, GNP measures the value of goods and services produced by only a country's citizens both domestically and abroad. GDP is the most commonly used measure of aggregate economic activity.

3 There is a third category of subjective wellbeing measures, "eudaimonic wellbeing" (Ryff 1989). Such measures tap into notions of what it means to lead a good life, but these are conceptually less well understood and sometimes also presuppose a more substantive definition of the good life, which is no longer left to the individual.

4 World Wellbeing Panel Survey December 2021 (https://bse.eu/research/world-wellbeing-panel/wellbys).

Bibliography

Anand, P., Hunter, G., Smith, R. (2005), Capabilities and Well-Being: Evidence Based on the Sen-Nussbaum Approach to Welfare, *Social Indicators Research* 74, 9–55.

Bertrand, M., Mullainathan, S. (2001), Do People Mean What They Say? Implications for Subjective Survey Data, *American Economic Review* 91, 67–72.

Cantril, H. (1965). *The Pattern of Human Concerns* (Vol. 4), New Brunswick, NJ: Rutgers University Press.

Clark, A.E. (2016), SWB as a Measure of Individual Well-Being. In: M. Adler, M. Fleurbaey (eds.), *Oxford Handbook of Well-Being and Public Policy* (pp. 518–552), Oxford: Oxford University Press.

Diener, E. (2000), Subjective Well-Being: The Science of Happiness and a Proposal for a National Index, *American Psychologist* 55, 34–43.

Diener, E. (1984), Subjective Well-Being, *Psychological Bulletin* 95, 542–575.

Diener, E., Suh, E. (1997), Measuring Quality of Life: Economic, Social, and Subjective Indicators, *Social Indicators Research* 40, 189–216.

Diener, E., Suh, E.M., Lucas, R.E., Smith, H.L. (1999), Subjective Well-Being: Three Decades of Progress, *Psychological Bulletin* 125, 276–302.

Easterlin, R. (1974), Does Economic Growth Improve the Human Lot? Some Empirical Evidence. In: P.A. David, M.W. Reder (eds.), *Nations and Households in Economic Growth: Essays in Honour of Moses Abramovitz* (pp. 89–125), New York: Academic Press.

Ebert, U., Welsch, H. (2004), Meaningful Environmental Indices: A Social Choice Approach, *Journal of Environmental Economics and Management* 47, 270–283.

Ferrer-i-Carbonell, A., Frijters, P. (2004), How Important Is Methodology for the Estimates of the Determinants of Happiness? *Economic Journal* 114, 641–59.

Fleurbaey, M. (2009), Beyond GDP: The Quest for a Measure of Social Welfare, *Journal of Economic Literature* 47, 1029–1075.

Freeman, A.M. III, Herriges, J.A., Kling, C.L. (2014), *The Measurement of Environmental and Resource Values: Theory and Methods*, 3rd edition, New York: Routledge.

Frey, B.S., Stutzer, A. (2002), What Can Economists Learn from Happiness Research, *Journal of Economic Literature* XL, 402–435.

Frijters, P., Krekel, C. (2021), *A Handbook for Wellbeing Policy Making: History, Theory, Measurement, Implementation, and Examples*, Oxford: Oxford University Press.

Gadrey, J., Jany-Catrice, F. (2006), *The New Indicators of Well-Being and Development*, London: Macmillan.

Graham, C. (2011), Adaptation Amidst Prosperity and Adversity: Insights from Happiness Studies from Around the World, *World Bank Research Observer* 26, 105–137.

Hicks, J.R. (1946), *Value and Capital*, 2nd edition, Oxford: Oxford University Press.

HM Treasury (2021), *Wellbeing Guidance for Appraisal: Supplementary Green Book Guidance*, London: HM Treasury.

Kahneman, D., Deaton, A. (2010), High Income Improves Evaluation of Life but Not Emotional Well-Being, *Proceedings of the National Academy of Sciences* 107 (38), 16489–16493.

Kahneman, D., Sugden, R. (2005), Experienced Utility as a Standard of Policy Evaluation, *Environmental and Resource Economics* 32, 161–181.

Kahneman, D., Wakker, P.P., Sarin, R. (1997), Back to Bentham? Explorations of Experienced Utility, *Quarterly Journal of Economics* 112, 375–405.

Levinson, A. (2020), Happiness and Air Pollution. In: D. Maddison, K. Rehdanz, H. Welsch (eds.), *Handbook of Wellbeing, Happiness and the Environment* (pp. 164–182), Cheltenham: Edward Elgar.

Loewenstein, G., Adler, D. (1995), A Bias in the Prediction of Tastes, *Economic Journal* 105, 929–937.

Nordhaus, W., Tobin, J. (1973), Is Growth Obsolete? In: M. Moss (ed.), *The Measurement of Economic and Social Performance, Studies in Income and Wealth*, (vol. 38, pp. 509–564), NBER.

OECD (2013), *OECD Guidelines on Measuring Subjective Well-Being*, Paris: OECD Publishing.

Ravallion, M. (1997), Good and Bad Growth: The Human Development Reports, *World Development* 25, 631–638.

Ryff, C.D. (1989), Happiness Is Everything, or Is It? Explorations on the Meaning of Psychological Well-Being, *Journal of Personality and Social Psychology* 57, 1069–1081.

Sen, A. (1985), *Commodities and Capabilities*, Amsterdam: North-Holland.

Sen, A. (1999), *Development as Freedom*, New York: Oxford University Press.

Suh, E., Diener, E., Oishi, S., Triandis, H.C. (1998), The Shifting Basis of Life Satisfaction Judgements Across Cultures: Emotions Versus Norms, *Journal of Personality and Social Psychology* 74, 482–493.

United Nations (1993), *System of National Accounts 1993*, New York and others: United Nations.

United Nations (2014), *System of Environmental and Economic Accounting 2012 - Central Framework*, New York: United Nations.

Veenhoven, R. (2020), World Database of Happiness: A 'Findings Archive'. In: D. Maddison, K. Rehdanz, H. Welsch (eds.), *Handbook of Wellbeing, Happiness and the Environment* (pp. 25–45), Cheltenham: Edward Elgar.

Von Möllendorff, C., Welsch, H. (2017), Measuring Renewable Energy Externalities: Evidence from Subjective Well-Being Data, *Land Economics* 93, 109–126.

Welsch, H., Kühling, J. (2009), Using Happiness Data for Environmental Valuation: Issues and Applications, *Journal of Economic Surveys* 23, 385–406.

What Works Centre for Wellbeing (2020), Wellbeing in Policy: Exploring Issues of Measurement and Methodology, Working Paper.

3 Economic Determinants of Wellbeing

Introduction

There is by now a large and expanding body of research that explores the factors that relate to, or determine, an individual's level of subjective wellbeing (Frijters and Krekel 2021). People with higher subjective wellbeing (SWB) generally

- Have higher income,
- Are employed,
- Have good health,
- Are partnered, and
- Are at either end of the age spectrum.

Out of these five major factors of wellbeing, two relate to the economic sphere: income and employment.

In spite of their importance, economic factors of SWB started to be investigated systematically relatively recently. While the question "Does economic growth improve the human lot?" was first studied in the mid-1970s (Easterlin 1974), it took about 20 years until the *economics of happiness* started to be established as a proper field of economic analysis. With the expansion of the literature on SWB came the recognition that SWB might work as a measure of economic performance and social progress (e.g., Stiglitz et al. 2009).

In addition to the individual-level (microeconomic) factors of wellbeing – income and employment – several contextual variables have been identified that influence SWB, in particular, the rates of unemployment, inflation, and growth, and the levels of economic inequality and poverty. This chapter reviews the findings on the relationships between those factors and SWB and discusses the relevance of the findings in relation to some of today's most pressing problems, as described in Chapter 1.

Microeconomic Factors of Wellbeing

The key microeconomic factors of SWB are individuals' income and employment status. Their relationship to wellbeing has been studied from several perspectives, including the affective and cognitive aspects of

DOI: 10.4324/9781003206163-4

wellbeing, the role of other individuals' income and employment status as reference values, and adaptation to changes.

Income and Wealth

Virtually all studies on the economics of SWB include personal or household income as major factors of wellbeing and find SWB to be positively and significantly related to income. Moreover, the relationships found are typically consistent with the idea of diminishing marginal utility of income, that is, the income–SWB relationship is weaker at high levels of income than at low levels. It is, however, not clear to what extent income *causes* wellbeing. In particular, there may be reverse causation, that is, personality-related "genuine" happiness may imply higher productivity (Oswald et al. 2015), or unobserved third factors, such as personality traits, may influence both happiness and productivity (Dolan et al. 2008).

As noted in Chapter 2, concepts of SWB can be grouped into affective and cognitive dimensions, that is, emotional states (happiness in the narrow sense) and evaluations of life (life satisfaction), respectively. While most studies of the income–SWB relationship are concerned with cognitive-evaluative wellbeing, some focus on affective-emotional wellbeing. A study from the United States that involves both aspects of wellbeing found that life evaluation rises steadily with household income, whereas emotional wellbeing also rises, but there is "satiation", that is, no further progress beyond an annual income of approximately $75,000 (Kahneman and Deaton 2010). The authors conclude from these results that increases in income beyond that threshold no longer improve individuals' ability to do what matters most to their emotional wellbeing, such as spending time with people they like, avoiding pain and disease, and enjoying leisure activities. Cognitive-evaluative wellbeing, which involves self-image and status concerns, continues to rise.

A similar study covering 164 countries around the world found "income satiation" to arise not only with respect to emotional wellbeing but also evaluative wellbeing (Jebb et al. 2018). Globally, satiation occurs at annual incomes of US$95,000 for life evaluation and US$60,000–US$75,000 for emotional wellbeing. However, there is substantial variation across world regions, with satiation occurring later in wealthier regions. The highest satiation incomes for life evaluation were found in North America and Australia/New Zealand, amounting to US$105,000 and US$125,000, respectively. In addition, in certain parts of the world, incomes beyond satiation were found to be associated with lower rather than stationary life evaluations.

In a cross-cultural perspective, it was found that the relationship between income and life satisfaction was stronger in people socialized in East Germany than in West Germany, which was interpreted as echoing the materialist education in the formerly communist East Germany (Van Hoorn and Maseland 2010). Remarkably, this difference still existed more than a decade after German reunification. Consistent with this finding, the relationship between income and life satisfaction (up to the satiation point) was found to be stronger in Eastern Europe than in any other world region, and similarly so for affective wellbeing. In addition, satiation occurred at a much lower income in Eastern Europe than in most other regions (Jebb et al. 2018). Steep income–SWB curves combined with low satiation incomes were also found in sub-Saharan Africa and Latin America, whereas relatively flat income–SWB curves with high satiation income prevail in Australia/New Zealand, North America, and Western Europe. Generally, satiation income by region was highly correlated with the regions' median income, that is, satiation income is high in rich regions and low in poor regions.

Whether an income–SWB curve that is steeper below the satiation level but satiates at lower income – as is the case in (postcommunist) Eastern Europe, sub-Saharan Africa, and Latin America – should be interpreted as more "materialistic" is not self-evident. Another explanation relies on the notion of relative income effects, that is, people evaluate their income relative to some reference value, where reference values may be an individual's own income in the past and/or the income of other individuals. The extent to which wellbeing depends on absolute and relative income, respectively, may explain differences in the shape of the income–SWB curve: when the well-being evaluation of income depends on the difference between one's own income and others' income (relative income) rather than the level of one's own income (absolute income), an increase in one's own income will buy little additional wellbeing if others' incomes rise as well, and high levels of income are required until satiation sets in.

Relative concerns have been found to influence individuals' economic behaviors in many ways, and accounting for relative concerns has been found to be important for a thorough understanding of the relationship between income and wellbeing. With respect to behavior, *Prospect Theory* (Kahneman and Tversky 1979) suggests that, in making economic choices, individuals "edit" the choice situation, which involves interpreting the outcomes of various options as changes from the status quo. The status quo thus serves as a reference point. Moreover, behavioral models involving other-regarding preferences (e.g., Bolton and Ockenfels 2000; Fehr and Schmidt 1999) assume that people's choices depend not only on the outcomes to themselves but also on those outcomes relative to the outcomes to other people.

Similar to such models of economic behavior, both intertemporal and interpersonal relativity play important roles with respect to the income–SWB relationship (Clark et al. 2008). Intertemporal relativity implies that people evaluate their current incomes relative to their incomes in the past. Income earned in the past creates an aspiration level for the income that an individual deems satisfactory, such that only increases relative to that prior level lead to additional wellbeing. The reason for this effect is hedonic adaptation. With hedonic adaptation, increases in income have mainly transient effects, because individuals become accustomed to their new circumstances. By triggering hedonic adaptation, higher past income negatively affects current SWB, an effect referred to as a negative intrapersonal externality or "internality" (Frank 1985). The negative internality implies that the long-term marginal utility of income is smaller than the short-term marginal utility. In quantitative terms, one study found that the effect of an income increase after four years is only about 42 percent of the effect after one year: the majority of the short-term effect of income vanishes over time (Di Tella et al. 2010).

Interpersonal relativity implies that people evaluate their income relative to the income of others. With respect to such relative evaluations, a distinction is usually made between relative deprivation and relative satisfaction. Relative deprivation is said to prevail if the income of the individual in question is lower than the relevant comparison income, whereas relative satisfaction prevails if the individual's income is higher than comparison income. In both cases, relative income is an indicator of social status. A standard finding in the income comparison literature is that higher comparison income reduces the individual's wellbeing (Clark and D'Ambrosio 2015) through either greater deprivation or lower satisfaction. Comparison income – the income of others – thus yields a negative interpersonal externality, sometimes referred to as envy or jealousy. Due to such mutual income externalities, the social marginal utility of income is smaller than the private marginal utility of income.

In contrast to one's own past income, the notion of *others'* income is ambiguous. Studies of interpersonal income comparisons have typically used the average income of individuals with similar characteristics (gender, age, education level, and place of residence) as comparison income. Using such an approach, the interpersonal income externality is usually found to be strong; it may be so large as to completely neutralize the effect of one's own income, which means that wellbeing is completely relative in income (Clark et al. 2008). However, perceived deservingness of others' income (in terms of ability and effort) may create the perception that others' high income is "justified" and, accordingly, was found to reduce the "envy" effect (Clark and D'Ambrosio 2015).

While interpersonal income externalities are typically negative in developed and stable economies, they may be positive in certain stages of economic development. When economic conditions are uncertain, individuals may take rising incomes of "similar" others as a signal that their own economic prospects will also improve. Consistent with this idea, it was found that the satisfaction of Russians in the 1990s was positively related to the income of their fellow citizens (Senik 2004). Similar positive relationships were obtained for East Germans in the same period, whereas they were negative for West Germans (Welsch and Kühling 2015a). Interestingly, both the positive and the negative relationships disappeared after significant labor market reforms were undertaken in Germany that tied individuals' income closer to their level of education and other productivity-relevant characteristics. An interpretation of this finding is that a closer relationship between income and productivity increased both the predictability of one's own future income and the perceived deservingness of others' income, such that both the "signaling" and the "envy" effect were reduced. Overall, positive income externalities due to signaling effects seem to be the exception rather than the rule.

The preceding discussion of income–SWB curves in different world regions suggests a strong income–SWB relationship at low income, which becomes weaker until satiation is reached. This is consistent with the idea that absolute income, which serves to satisfy basic needs (food, clothing, dwelling, heating), is the main concern at low income, whereas relative income, which serves to satisfy status concerns, becomes more important as incomes rise. This suggests that people living in poverty – understood as low absolute income – may benefit particularly strongly from an increase in income.

Considering that absolute poverty – defined by the World Bank as living on less than US$1.90 a day – is not a big issue in developed countries, the poverty concept typically adopted in the latter countries is a relative concept. For instance, the European Union follows the convention that individuals are considered as living in poverty if their income (adjusted for household size) is less than 60 percent of the median income (the so-called poverty line). The idea behind this convention is a relative understanding of the standard of living, which involves not just the satisfaction of basic needs but also an access to the goods and services that are deemed necessary for adequate social participation (EAPN 2022).

With respect to relative poverty, so defined, a number of remarkable findings exist. First, life satisfaction drops when people fall into poverty or when the intensity of poverty (distance from the poverty line) increases. When an individual falls into poverty, the individual's life satisfaction score drops by an amount of the same magnitude as the happiness boost from marriage. While the quantitative effects are different, the qualitative effects are robust to different definitions of the poverty line (40, 50, 70, and 80 percent of median income). Second, there is little adaptation within a poverty spell: poverty starts bad and stays bad in terms of SWB. Third, poverty scars: those who have been poor in the past report lower life satisfaction today, even when out of poverty. Finally, the order of poverty spells matters: for a given number of years in poverty, satisfaction is lower when the years are linked together (Clark et al. 2015, 2016). Thus, while there is a general tendency for adaptation to income (as discussed earlier), this does not apply to incomes below the poverty line.

In contrast to the income–SWB relationship, the relationship between wealth holdings (assets and debts) and SWB has been investigated relatively rarely, mainly because of a lack of representative data on wealth. In data for Germany it was found that individuals' life satisfaction is significantly positively associated with a household's wealth holdings even if income is controlled for. The relationship is positive for assets and negative for debt. It is, in particular, financial assets (rather than real assets) and non-mortgage debt (rather than mortgage debt) that affect life satisfaction. Similar to income, not only the absolute value of assets and debt matter for life satisfaction but also assets and debt relative to other households. Relative concerns imply that greater wealth goes with greater wellbeing only in non-wealthy areas (neighborhoods) because in wealthy areas co-movements of one's own wealth and that of others undermine any wellbeing benefit from rising wealth (Jantsch et al. 2022).

Unemployment

Regarding unemployment, practically every study of SWB that has considered the labor force status has found that people who are unemployed experience substantially lower levels of SWB than people who have a job. This holds even if the level of income is controlled for. The latter suggests that the effect on SWB of being unemployed relates to psychological and social factors rather than the income loss associated with unemployment (Feather 1990). Psychological costs are depression, anxiety, and a loss of self-esteem. At the societal level, these costs may be reinforced by the stigma that is often attached to being unemployed. While the psychological costs arise in addition to any drop in current income, they may also involve concern about one's future financial position.

In quantitative terms, one early study of unemployment and SWB (for Britain) concluded that "joblessness depressed wellbeing more than any other single characteristic, including divorce and separation" (Clark and Oswald 1994, p. 655). In data for 12 European countries over the period between 1975 and 1991, it was found that unemployed persons were 0.33 points less satisfied, on a 4-point scale, than people in employment (Di Tella et al. 2001). Similarly, in data for Germany, between 1990 and 2018, the corresponding difference was 0.84 points on an 11-point scale, again much larger than the wellbeing gap between separated or divorced individuals and married ones (Biermann and Welsch 2021). When people are laid off and simultaneously fall below the poverty line, the combined effect is more than twice that of becoming unemployed alone (Clark et al. 2016).

Similar to the case of income, there is the issue of causation: does unemployment make people unhappy or do unhappy people have a higher risk of being laid off? The latter may be the case, because unhappy people may not perform well, which makes it more likely that they lose their jobs. However, considering the evolution of life satisfaction over time shows that people who are later unemployed do not start out with low life satisfaction but experience a drop in satisfaction when they are laid off (Lucas et al. 2004). This suggests that the dominant causation runs from unemployment to unhappiness rather than the other way round. The drop in life satisfaction also refutes the proposition that unemployment is voluntary: if unemployment is chosen over employment, then it should yield a higher level of wellbeing.

Similar to the income–SWB relationship, it has been studied whether there are adaptation and comparison (context) effects in the relationship between unemployment and wellbeing. With respect to adaptation, it was found that individuals who are unemployed for more than a year experience a more negative reaction to unemployment, and previous unemployment experience does not reduce the harm of current unemployment. Moreover, there is a "scarring" effect, as individuals do not return to their pre-unemployment levels of life satisfaction once unemployment has ended (Clark et al. 2001). Rather, any period of unemployment over the last ten years has a negative impact on wellbeing (Louis and Zhao 2002). Men's drop in life satisfaction when becoming unemployed is not only larger than women's but also grows larger when unemployment lasts longer than three years (Clark and Georgellis 2013).

Turning to social comparisons over unemployment, the effect of context takes a rather different form than with respect to income. Social comparison here amounts to unemployment acting as a "social norm" (Clark 2003), such that the impact of unemployment on wellbeing is smaller in higher-unemployment regions. The negative effect of being unemployed would be neutralized at a regional unemployment rate of 24 percent. Moreover, having an unemployed partner is beneficial for the unemployed, while being detrimental for those working. These findings have been taken to suggest that the impact may be dependent upon the extent to which an individual can substitute other activities for work, belong to non-work-based social networks, is able to legitimize their unemployment, and lives in higher unemployment households (Dolan et al. 2008).

Another question pertaining to unemployment is to what extent the detrimental effects of unemployment or the risk thereof can be mitigated by labor market institutions, in particular employment protection and unemployment benefits. In studying these issues in a data set from ten European countries over the period 1975–2002, it was found that more employment protection and a higher benefit replacement rate increase the life satisfaction of the average citizen. At the subgroup level, different segments of the population are affected differently by the two categories of labor market institutions. While employment protection is valued especially by employed persons of intermediate age, more generous unemployment benefits are valued especially by older persons and by the unemployed. These results are consistent with the idea that "insiders" (the employed) and "outsiders" (the unemployed) have different preferences over the two types of labor market institutions. Longer benefit duration has no significant effect except for older individuals, presumably because they face a higher risk of long-term unemployment (Ochsen and Welsch 2012).

Macroeconomic Factors of Wellbeing

In addition to personal or household income and individuals' employment status, macroeconomic indicators such as the level and growth of per capita income and the rates of unemployment and inflation have been identified as correlates of SWB.

Conceptual Relationships

One of the most important findings in the economics of SWB is the so-called Easterlin paradox of substantial increases in per capita income or gross domestic product (GDP) without a corresponding rise in people's SWB (Easterlin 1974). Explanations of this finding are based on the concept and evidence of social comparison discussed earlier: due to social comparison, a person's SWB depends on the person's income relative to average income. Thus, when everybody's income rises, average relative income does not change, nor does the average level of SWB (Easterlin 1995). However, relative income concerns are more likely to dominate absolute income concerns in richer societies than in poorer societies – where the satisfaction of basic needs plays a larger role in the SWB function. As discussed earlier, there may even be a positive signaling effect from others' income when economic development starts, which later fades off. This suggests that economic development goes with decreasing gains in SWB due to increasing comparison effects relative to absolute income effects. Consistent with this view, plots of SWB against per capita income typically yield strongly concave functions, with a positive relationship at low income levels that become almost horizontal at high levels of income.

Another reason why higher per capita income – which represents a higher level of economic activity – need not go with greater wellbeing relates to the costs of higher activity levels, such as higher workloads and more pollution (Di Tella and MacCulloch 2007). This suggests that per capita income may even enter the wellbeing equation with a negative sign if such side effects are not accounted for.

In contrast to the (per capita) GDP *level*, GDP *growth* is likely to have a positive effect on SWB. The reason is that people get habituated to the level of riches they have attained (Clark et al. 2008). Due to habituation, wellbeing depends on current income relative to past income and, hence, on the change in income. To maintain a constant level of wellbeing, an increase in income is required. A decrease in the rate of GDP growth thus triggers a decrease in wellbeing.

Another important macroeconomic variable is the unemployment rate. In addition to personally being unemployed, people may be unhappy about unemployment in general even if they are not themselves put out of work (Frey and Stutzer 2002). They may feel bad about the unfortunate fate of those who are unemployed and they may worry about the possibility of becoming unemployed themselves in the future. They may also feel repercussions on the economy and society as a whole. They may dislike the increase in unemployment contributions and taxes likely to happen in the future, they may fear that crime and social tension increase, and they may even see the threat of violent protests and uprisings.

Turning to inflation, several reasons can be mentioned for why people are concerned about it (Easterly and Fisher 2001). In the first place, inflation reduces people's standard of living, as it erodes their purchasing power. This happens especially if people rely on income that is not indexed to inflation or in the case of non-indexed progressivity of the tax system. In addition, inflation may invalidate people's assets, in particular if they have a large share of cash and if they have little access to financial instruments that hedge in some way against inflation. High rates of inflation may trigger fear of political instability. It is obvious that these concerns may have an effect on SWB.

Evidence

Given these economic and psychological mechanisms that link personal wellbeing to growth, unemployment, and inflation, we now turn to the empirical evidence. The consequences of macroeconomic conditions for SWB were first studied empirically by Di Tella et al. (2001). Their regression analyses for 12 member countries of the European Union (EU12), 1975–1992, produced statistically significant inverse relationships between the life satisfaction of the citizens and the unemployment and inflation rates prevailing in their countries. Since the life satisfaction regressions control for the individual employment status, the evidence indicates that the general unemployment rate has effects on SWB beyond those of being personally unemployed. The effect size of unemployment was found to be considerably larger than that of the inflation rate. In the main specification of the SWB equation, the effect of a given rate of unemployment was found to be about one and a half times larger than that of an inflation rate of equal size. For the period 1992–2002, the life satisfaction of the citizens of EU12 was found to be negatively and significantly related to the unemployment and inflation rate and positively and significantly related to the annual GDP growth rate (Welsch 2011). Furthermore, it was shown that, in contrast to year-to-year changes in GDP, long-term increases of a country's income hardly affect wellbeing because of habituation (Easterlin et al. 2010).

While those studies mainly referred to the 1990s, analyzing data for 25 developed countries from 2002 to 2012 showed that life satisfaction was significantly negatively related to the rates of unemployment and inflation, where the effect of unemployment was somewhat larger than that of inflation (Welsch and Kühling 2016). In addition, life satisfaction was significantly positively related to the rate of annual GDP growth and significantly negatively related to the level of GDP per capita (as was also found by Proto and Rustichini 2013 in a set of rich countries). As noted earlier, the negative effect of GDP per capita may reflect some negative side effects of economic activity, such as workload or environmental degradation. Indeed, when the latter aspects are controlled for, the GDP level has a positive effect on wellbeing (Di Tella and MacCulloch 2007).

With respect to annual GDP changes, research covering more than 150 countries and multiple business cycles over four decades found that measures of SWB are more than twice as sensitive to negative changes (recessions) as compared to positive changes (De Neve et al. 2018). While some of this asymmetry is explained by the fact that unemployment typically increases during recessions, the asymmetry is not entirely wiped out when unemployment is accounted for. This suggests that the phenomenon of loss aversion (Kahneman and Tversky 1979) might play a role in the evidence found.

The finding of a stronger response of SWB to recessions as compared to upturns may contribute to explaining the Easterlin paradox: if long-term growth is understood as a sequence of business cycles, periodic recessions can rapidly undo the wellbeing gains from longer expansionary periods and lead to an insignificant relationship between national income and average wellbeing when considered in the long run (De Neve et al. 2018).

Estimated coefficients on the rates of GDP growth, unemployment, and inflation were used to investigate how changes in these variables during the macroeconomic crisis of 2008–2009 affected SWB (Welsch and Kühling 2016). It was found that the effects on an average citizen's wellbeing were of a similar magnitude as the effects of the most serious personal life events. To illustrate, in countries most strongly affected by the crisis, the effects were as strong as if every person got divorced. The main driver of these effects was the drop in GDP, whose impact was aggravated by the increase of unemployment. Though the inflation rate went down in several of the countries, the effect was too weak to significantly reduce the negative effect of the changes in GDP and unemployment. The results suggest that GDP fluctuations are important drivers of SWB, even if – due to habituation – long-term changes are not.

In addition to effects of the unemployment and inflation rates on the "average" individual, it is instructive to ask if and how the effects differ between socioeconomic groups. In particular, they may differ between the well-off and the less well-off in society, and this issue – referred to as social incidence – is often invoked in controversies over macroeconomic priorities: are anti-inflation and anti-unemployment policies "pro-poor" or "pro-rich"?

A number of studies addressed this issue using results of international surveys in which individuals were asked whether they think inflation is an important national problem and how important it is in comparison with unemployment and other problems (Easterly and Fischer 2001; Jayadev 2006, 2008; Scheve 2004). These studies suggest that inflation aversion *per se* decreases with income and education levels, whereas aversion toward inflation *relative* to unemployment is greater among the well-off than among the less well-off.

In contrast to such studies of stated preference, studying the relationship between countries' inflation and unemployment rates and citizens' SWB offers an alternative approach to the issue of social incidence. Using SWB data from 30 OECD (Organization for Economic Cooperation and Development) countries over the period 1990–2008, it was investigated how people's implicit aversion toward inflation and unemployment varies with income and education (Welsch and Kühling 2015b). While inflation aversion decreased with income and increased with education level, unemployment aversion was independent of income and decreased with the level of education. Less wealthy individuals were thus more averse to inflation than wealthy individuals, presumably because it affects their standard of living more than that of wealthier people. And the less well educated were more averse to higher unemployment levels than the better educated, presumably because they consider their risk of being laid off to be higher. In spite of income and education dependence, aversion toward inflation was less than aversion toward unemployment, not just on average but at all levels of income and education. This suggests that issues of social incidence are not a dominant concern for macroeconomic policy making when it comes to prioritizing anti-inflation or anti-unemployment policies.

In addition to social incidence, a further aspect of aggregate unemployment is its composition in terms of unemployment duration. As any given level of the annual unemployment rate can arise from a certain number of persons unemployed for a short period of time or a smaller number unemployed for a longer period, the unemployment rate incorporates not only the risk but also the (expected) severity of unemployment. The questions then arise whether the severity (expected duration) has a separate effect on wellbeing and whether the inclusion of such an effect influences the measured wellbeing consequences of general unemployment. If a separate effect exists, it indicates that the fear of losing (or not finding) a job is more detrimental when the prospect is to stay unemployed for a long time. With respect to the issue of adaptation, it would suggest that people, at least, do not expect to adapt to unemployment.

In studying these issues, it was found that the percentage of jobless people that are unemployed for more than one year (long-term unemployment) affected self-rated life satisfaction in a sizable and significant way, in addition to the impact of the general unemployment rate. When the indicator of long-term unemployment is included alongside the general unemployment rate, the estimated effect of the former amounts to more than one-fifth of the latter. The *quality* of unemployment in terms of duration thus matters a lot in addition to the *level* of unemployment. The effect of unemployment duration is rather uniform across people with different employment status. Thus, whether employed or unemployed, people worry not just about the risk of becoming (or staying) unemployed but also about the severity of the unemployment spell (Ochsen and Welsch 2011). This then suggests that – in addition to issues of human capital depreciation associated with long-term unemployment – reducing the share of long-term unemployment would be welfare increasing even if it did not affect the overall unemployment rate.

Inequality

Conceptual Background

Income inequality can be viewed from two perspectives, the comparative view and the normative-ethical view (Clark and D'Ambrosio 2015). In the comparative view, an individual compares her own income with that of relevant others. The comparative evaluation of inequality in terms of SWB and the pertinent evidence were discussed earlier in the chapter.

In the normative view, an individual evaluates the overall degree of income inequality without making any comparisons to individuals who are richer or poorer than she is. Normative evaluations of inequality can be understood as manifestations of ethical beliefs and values (Samuelson 1983), such as fairness, care, and empathy. From this perspective, income inequality may affect SWB because it is in disagreement with an individual's "moral sentiments" (Smith 1759).

Certain forms of inequality, in particular a high level of aggregate poverty, may not only contradict an individual's normative principles and intuitions but may also create several kinds of worries (Welsch and Biermann 2019). For instance, a high level of poverty may create fear of becoming poor in the future (personal worries) as well as concern about tax increases or social tension (political worries). Because such worries are neither comparative nor normative considerations, this suggests that a third perspective can be taken on the relationship between income inequality and wellbeing: a signaling view.

Considering the worries that underlie the signaling view, personal worries should mainly affect individuals living in uncertain conditions, due to age or family situation, say. Political worries should arguably be more salient among the rich than among the poor. Such reasoning is consistent with the theory of institutional reform, which explains the emergence of redistributive programs in Western societies by a desire of the elite to prevent social unrest (Acemoglu and Robinson 2000). It is also consistent with the finding that high-income earners' stated preference for income redistribution is related to their perceived degree of conflict between the rich and the poor (Yamamura 2016).

Evidence

With respect to normative evaluations of income inequality in terms of wellbeing, the evidence on the inequality–SWB relationship is mixed, and there seems to exist some cross-cultural heterogeneity. Studying income inequality across nations in Europe and federal states in the United States, inequality was found to reduce wellbeing among Europeans but not Americans, as far as the "average" citizen is concerned (Alesina et al. 2004). European's aversion to inequality is more concentrated in certain groups. In particular, those who define themselves as leftist show a strong distaste for inequality, while those who define themselves as right wing are unaffected by it. In addition, the happiness of the poor is strongly negatively affected by inequality, while the rich are unaffected. In the United States, the only group that is negatively affected by inequality are the rich leftists. The latter is consistent with a normative-ethical view of the inequality–SWB relationship: those Americans whose SWB responds to inequality are mainly those who are not personally affected by the comparative aspects of inequality (the rich) and who have a strong normative stance on the issue (the left). In Europe, the left–right difference is also present, but – in contrast to the Americans – it is the poor Europeans whose SWB negatively responds to inequality. This suggests that there may be some comparative element in Europeans' inequality–SWB relationship. An approach to explaining the apparent lack of the comparative element in the United States relies on higher perceived social mobility: due to upward social mobility, poorer people in the United States may perceive their current income deprivation to be less immutable than do Europeans. Richer Americans, by contrast, may not only feel uncomfortable about downward social mobility (personal worries) but also about political tension and social unrest that may be spurred by inequality (social worries).

Studies that considered the relationship between aggregate inequality and SWB have almost universally used a particular indicator to measure inequality: the Gini index. The *Gini index* is one measure from a wider class of *Gini measures*, all of which focus on individuals' or households' income *levels*. Aggregate inequality, measured this way, increases if a redistribution from a poorer to a richer person occurs and decreases if the redistribution is from a richer to a poorer person (other things equal). Varieties of Gini measures differ according to whether they place a greater weight on such (hypothetical) redistributions at the higher or lower end of the income distribution. Even more general inequality measures take account of whether redistribution affects not just the level but also the *rank* (position) of individuals within the distribution.

Considering a large set of such inequality measures and applying them to European data, it was found that both level and rank of inequality negatively affect wellbeing and that the overall degree of inequality aversion is greater than that which is found when the Gini index is used (Ebert and Welsch 2009). Moreover, the results indicate that inequality aversion focuses more on lower than on higher incomes. Overall, inequality-increasing (inequality-reducing) redistribution affects SWB of the average individual more negatively (more positively) if it occurs at the lower rather than the higher end of the income profile, and redistribution is particularly relevant to SWB if it is strong enough to change individuals' position in the income profile.

An inequality measure that plays a large role in public discourse but has only recently been studied in wellbeing research is the poverty ratio. The poverty ratio is the proportion of individuals whose income is below a predefined poverty line, and the latter is defined as a percentage of mean income (typically 60 percent). The poverty ratio is thus an indicator of the *relative* poverty prevailing in a society; as such it can be considered to be an inequality measure with special emphasis on the bottom part of the income distribution.

The effect of aggregate poverty on SWB was studied using the evolution of the poverty ratio in the federal states of Germany over nine years

(Welsch and Biermann 2019). It was found that German citizens' wellbeing is negatively correlated with the regional (state-level) poverty ratio while controlling for individual poverty status and poverty intensity, the individual unemployed status, and the state-level unemployment rate. The wellbeing repercussions from a 1 percentage point increase in aggregate poverty are about half as strong as the repercussions from a 1 percentage point increase in aggregate unemployment. While this applies to the "average" citizen, the negative relationship between aggregate poverty and SWB is more salient in the upper segments of the income distribution. In particular, the relationship is significant only for those whose income is greater than the median income, which implies that it is insignificant for those who live in poverty themselves (having an income less than 60 percent of the median income). Overall, the poor suffer from the individual poverty spell (and its intensity), whereas the non-poor suffer from the aggregate level of poverty. While the former is consistent with the comparative view of the inequality–SWB relationship, the latter is consistent with the normative-ethical view and the signaling view: the SWB of the non-poor is negatively related to aggregate poverty as they may fear to fall into poverty themselves or because they fear higher taxes or social unrest.

Though the results on aggregate poverty actually rely on data from Germany, the existence of wellbeing repercussions for the non-poor but not the poor are consistent with the finding that in the United States inequality affects only the wellbeing of the rich.

While Americans and Europeans seem to differ with respect to the role of comparative considerations in the inequality–SWB relationship, there may be cultural differences within Europe, which relate to different socialization histories. In particular, there may be differences between people socialized in liberal-democratic societies and those socialized in ex-communist societies. Indirect evidence comes from a study of satisfaction with democracy and the demand for redistribution policy in Germany (Welsch 2022): in West Germany, individuals' demand for redistribution was found to be shaped by both comparative concerns (relating to individuals' position in the income distribution) and normative-ethical concerns (relating to a desire for care and fairness), whereas it was shaped exclusively by normative-ethical but not by comparative concerns in the East. In addition, the effect of the normative-ethical concerns was stronger in the East than in the West.

While these findings are based on data collected almost 30 years after the collapse of the communist regime, the stronger role of care and fairness concerns in the East is consistent with the moral values of solidarity and equality being more strongly endorsed in former communist East Germany than in liberal-capitalist West Germany. The role of comparative concerns in the West and its absence in the East, conversely, are consistent with different attitudes toward competition. Cultural priming thus seems to have lasting effects on people's stance on issues of inequality.

Implications for Public Policy

As discussed in Chapter 2, indicators of SWB are serious candidate measures of social welfare. To the extent that SWB is considered relevant as a benchmark for designing public policies – as is the case in several countries now – findings from economic wellbeing research over the past close to five decades have considerable policy implications, particularly with respect to tax, redistribution, and labor market policies.

Important policy-relevant findings concern the issue of how wellbeing relates to income. In this regard, the most important insight is the paramount importance of relative income once absolute income has reached a level that allows for satisfying basic needs. Beyond that level, individuals' wellbeing mainly depends on their own income relative to the income of others (social comparison). In addition, individuals' wellbeing depends on their current income relative to their own past income, because people adjust their income aspirations to what they have already achieved (hedonic adaptation).

Social comparison and hedonic adaptation have long been discussed in the economic literature (Duesenberry 1949; Veblen 1899), but their actual importance for wellbeing has been rigorously established only recently, with the increasing use of SWB data. In parallel, the implications of the pertinent findings for welfare analysis and public policy were elaborated in recent decades. In a welfare economic perspective, the circumstance that one individual's income negatively affects other individuals' utility means that income yields negative externalities, defined as unpriced, unintended, and uncompensated side effects of one agent's actions that directly affect the welfare of another agent (Baumol and Oates 1988). Standard microeconomic analysis suggests that in the presence of negative externalities, individuals choose inefficiently high levels of the action that causes the externality, because people's choices do not take into account the negative effect they inflict on others. Individuals' choices are hence not socially efficient.

Similarly, the circumstance that an individual's past income negatively affects her current utility can be referred to as an "internality" (Frank 1985). In the case of income internalities (intrapersonal externalities), fully rational (forward-looking) decision making would internalize the intrapersonal externality, that is, individuals would anticipate the adaptation-related negative effect of higher income today on utility in the future and make income-leisure choices accordingly. However, an important finding from behavioral economics is that adaptation to higher income is largely unforeseen in an individual's decision making (projection bias), due to a failure in affective forecasting (Loewenstein et al. 2003; Wilson and Gilbert 2003). Individuals, in other words, tend to behave in a myopic rather than forward-looking way, disregarding the internality that their present income inflicts on future utility. Similar to classical (interpersonal) externalities, negative intrapersonal externalities then imply that the chosen level of work (income) is higher than the optimal level. More specifically, income-leisure choices do not only fail to be socially efficient (due to social comparison) but also fail to be individually efficient (due to unanticipated adaptation).

Implications of social comparison and hedonic adaptation for public policy were analyzed in a model of income-leisure choice (Layard 2006). Drawing on the additional insight that – in contrast to income – people do not compare their leisure with other people's (Solnick and Hemenway 1998), the analysis showed that in such circumstances people's income-leisure choice is biased to the disadvantage of leisure and that an income tax is not necessarily distortionary, as suggested by standard public economics, but is required to prevent distorted decision making. The required tax rate is one that "internalizes" the interpersonal and intrapersonal income externalities such that work effort will be reduced to a level where the "fruitless effort to raise income" (Layard 2006) is fully offset.

While adaptation to income makes people's effort to raise it beyond certain levels "fruitless", people do not adapt to every level of income. In particular, living in poverty – even in a relative sense – implies a large and lasting loss in wellbeing, and it disappears only partly even when the poverty spell has ended. One aspect of poverty's negative effect is that the poor are much more strongly affected by inflation than are the non-poor. The policy implication is clear: fighting poverty should be a key target of public policy. To fight poverty while at the same time preventing efforts to attain inefficiently high levels of income, a so-called negative income tax (Friedman 1962) may be useful, which should be calibrated such that everybody's after-tax income is above the poverty line. Such a schedule would involve a (progressive) tax on incomes above the poverty line and a transfer proportional to the gap between an individual's earned income and the income that defines the poverty line. The evident advantage of such a schedule is that it is incentive-compatible, that is, it encourages poor people to raise their earned income, since a portion of every increase in earned income will remain with the individual. This way, it helps people to escape the "welfare trap" often associated with lump-sum transfers.

Similar to poverty, another phenomenon with large and lasting ("scarring") repercussions on wellbeing is unemployment. Therefore, fighting unemployment is another public policy priority suggested by wellbeing research. While being unemployed was found to affect wellbeing in addition to any associated income loss, unemployment is, in reality, one major determinant of poverty. Unemployment and poverty combined have far larger wellbeing repercussions than any other phenomenon studied in wellbeing research. Policies to reduce unemployment may have the twin benefit of fighting the two most detrimental factors that impact wellbeing.

Fighting poverty and unemployment is important not only because of poverty's and unemployment's large and lasting effects on those personally affected by them. It is even more important because it was found that high levels of aggregate poverty and unemployment affect even the non-poor and the employed. In this sense, fighting poverty and unemployment is a pure public good: every instance of escaping poverty and/or unemployment benefits not just those personally involved but also everybody in society.

Social comparison (along with hedonic adaptation) provides an important reason why large increases of developed economies' per capita income over the long term were not accompanied by significant increases in average wellbeing (the so-called Easterlin paradox): if everybody gets richer in absolute terms but relative incomes do not change, wellbeing is largely stationary. The evidence on the wellbeing repercussions from poverty, however, suggests that increases in per capita income that are accompanied by increasing inequality at the lower end of the income distribution may indeed go with *lower* average wellbeing. This may be one reason why some studies found the level of per capita income to enter the wellbeing equation with a negative sign.

Another candidate explanation of this finding is that the costs of high income in terms of workload and environmental degradation may exceed the benefits, such that the *net* wellbeing benefit is negative. This explanation is supported by findings that the sign of per capita income in the wellbeing equation is positive when those factors are controlled for – consistent with a positive *gross* benefit. That costs related to work and pollution may exceed the benefits (rather than just balancing them) is consistent with the circumstance that not accounting for negative externalities from work and pollution implies distorted choice in favor of income.

While long-term changes in developed economies' per capita income have little effect on wellbeing, short-term (year-to-year) changes do have an effect. In particular, as was found with respect to the financial crisis of 2008–2009, a drop in per capita income implied a large loss in wellbeing. This loss occurred in addition to that caused by the rise in unemployment. These findings suggest that stabilization policy is another top priority for public policy. Moreover, with respect to a trade-off between stabilization policy and anti-inflation policy, wellbeing research suggests that the former is more beneficial than the latter, irrespective of individuals' level of income and education.

Conclusion

Over the past few decades, research has provided a rich body of findings on the economic determinants of wellbeing. Important insights refer to factors both at the individual and aggregate levesl. At the individual level, research has focused on income and found that it is mainly relative rather than absolute income that affects the wellbeing of people in developed economies. Moreover, there is psychological adaption to the level of income attained, such that ever-increasing income is required to yield wellbeing. While differing by culture, there is evidence of satiation, that is, wellbeing stops to increase when a certain threshold is passed. The maximum satiation income found in any world region is $125,000 per year.

An important exception to income adaptation applies to income below the poverty line. Living in poverty has a large and persistent effect on wellbeing, and this is true even if poverty is measured in relative rather than absolute terms. In addition to personally living in poverty, the aggregate level of poverty negatively affects wellbeing, even if measured as aggregate *relative* poverty. Considering that aggregate relative poverty is a form of inequality, these findings corroborate findings of negative wellbeing effects of inequality, particularly in Europe.

Similar to living in poverty, being unemployed has a large and lasting effect on wellbeing, and, similar to aggregate poverty, a high level of aggregate unemployment negatively affects the wellbeing of those who are not unemployed themselves. While inflation also affects wellbeing, the wellbeing effect of a given increase in the unemployment rate is larger than that of an equal increase in the inflation rate.

With respect to aggregate income (per capita income), short-term (year-to-year) changes considerably affect wellbeing, and negative changes (recessions) affect wellbeing much more strongly than do positive changes. By contrast, long-term growth has little effect in developed economies because people get habituated to it. In addition, any remaining positive wellbeing effects of rising income are partly neutralized by income externalities stemming from social comparison, and they may be reduced by environmental externalities that arise in the generation and consumption of income.

The findings on the economic determinants of wellbeing are in surprisingly great agreement with what students of economics worldwide think to be the most pressing problems economists should be addressing and what the United Nations' Sustainable Development Goals identified as major challenges to be addressed by the world community: poverty, inequality, and unemployment. The findings from wellbeing research strongly suggest that the issues that students and international institutions perceive to be the most pressing are in fact those that affect people's wellbeing most strongly.

The findings from wellbeing research have clear policy implications: given that poverty has not only large but also "scarring" effects on wellbeing, poverty alleviation is of paramount importance for social wellbeing. Poverty alleviation is even more to be recommended because high levels of aggregate poverty negatively affect the whole society, not just the poor. On the other hand, further increases in income yield only small increases in wellbeing when income is already high, and those increases in wellbeing vanish completely at a finite point of satiation. Together, these findings suggest a large potential for redistribution policy to raise social wellbeing. Similarly, labor market policies that reduce unemployment may greatly enhance social wellbeing, since being unemployed involves large and persistent wellbeing repercussions for the unemployed, and aggregate unemployment affects the wellbeing of the whole society. Policies designed to engineer economic growth, but carry a high risk of even relatively short recessions, are unlikely to improve wellbeing in the long run.

While this chapter has been concerned with economic determinants of SWB, the pertinent research discussed has also provided some preliminary insights on the roles of environmental factors and moral values. As noted earlier, wellbeing effects of rising national income are reduced by environmental degradation arising in the generation and use of income. With respect to moral values, it was found that the wellbeing repercussions from inequality and a demand for redistribution may involve normative-ethical concerns (for care and fairness). The role of environmental factors for wellbeing will be addressed in more detail in the next chapter, whereas ethical and moral concerns will be the subject of Chapters 5 through 7.

Bibliography

Acemoglu, D., Robinson, J.A. (2000), Why Did the West Extend the Franchise? Democracy, Inequality and Growth in Historical Perspective, *Quarterly Journal of Economics* 115, 1167–2000.

Alesina, A., Di Tella, R., MacCulloch, R. (2004), Inequality and Happiness: Are Europeans and Americans Different? *Journal of Public Economics* 88, 2009–2048.

Baumol, W.J., Oates, W.E. (1988), *The Theory of Environmental Policy*, 2nd Edition, Cambridge: Cambridge University Press.

Biermann, P., Welsch, H. (2021), An Anatomy of East German Unhappiness: The Role of Circumstances and Mentality, 1990–2018, *Journal of Economic Behavior and Organization* 181, 1–18.

Bolton, G.E., Ockenfels, A. (2000), ERC: A Theory of Equity, Reciprocity, and Competition, *American Economic Review* 90, 166–193.

Clark, A.E. (2003), Unemployment as a Social Norm: Psychological Evidence from Panel Data, *Journal of Labor Economics* 21, 323–351.

Clark, A.E., D'Ambrosio, C. (2015), Attitudes to Income Inequality: Experimental and Survey Evidence. In: A.B. Atkinson, F. Bourguignon (eds.), *Handbook of Income Distribution* (pp. 1147–1208), Amsterdam: Elsevier.

Clark, A.E., D'Ambrosio, C., Ghislandi, S. (2015), Poverty Profiles and Well-Being: Panel Evidence from Germany, *Research on Economic Inequality* 23, 1–22.

Clark, A.E., D'Ambrosio, C., Ghislandi, S. (2016), Adaptation to Poverty in Long-Run Panel Data, *Review of Economics and Statistics* 98, 591–600.

Clark, A.E., Frijters, P., Shields, M.A. (2008), Relative Income, Happiness and Utility: An Explanation for the Easterlin Paradox and Other Puzzles, *Journal of Economic Literature* 46, 95–144.

Clark, A.E., Georgellis, Y. (2013), Back to Baseline in Britain: Adaptation in the BHPS, *Economica* 80, 496–512.

Clark, A.E., Georgellis, Y., Sanfey, P. (2001), Scarring: The Psychological Impact of Past Unemployment, *Economica* 68, 221–241.

Clark, A.E., Oswald, A.J. (1994), Unhappiness and Unemployment, *Economic Journal* 104, 648–659.

De Neve, J.E., Ward, G., De Keulenaer, F., Van Landeghem, B., Kavetsos, G., Norton, M.I. (2018), The Asymmetric Experience of Positive and Negative Economic Growth: Global Evidence Using Subjective Well-Being Data, *Review of Economics and Statistics* 100, 362–375.

Di Tella, R., Haisken-De New, J., MacCulloch, R. (2010), Happiness Adaptation to Income and to Status in an Individual Panel, *Journal of Economic Behavior and Organization* 76, 834–852.

Di Tella, R., MacCulloch, R. (2007), Gross National Happiness as an Answer to the Easterlin Paradox? *Journal of Development Economics* 86, 22–42.

Di Tella, R., MacCulloch, R.J., Oswald, A.J. (2001), Preferences Over Inflation and Unemployment: Evidence from Surveys of Happiness, *American Economic Review* 91, 335–341.

Dolan, P., Peasgood, T., White, M. (2008), Do We Really Know What Makes Us Happy? A Review of the Economic Literature on the Factors Associated with Subjective Well-Being, *Journal of Economic Psychology* 29, 94–122.

Duesenberry, J. (1949), *Income, Saving, and the Theory of Consumer Behavior*, Cambridge and London: Harvard University Press.

EAPN. (2022), European Anti-Poverty Network: What is poverty?, available at: https://www.eapn.eu/what-is-poverty/, accessed 17 October, 2022.

Easterlin, R.A. (1974), Does Economic Growth Improve the Human Lot? Some Empirical Evidence. In: P.A. David, M.W. Reder (eds.), *Nations and Households in Economic Growth: Essays in Honour of Moses Abramovitz* (pp. 89–125), New York: Academic Press.

Easterlin, R.A. (1995), Will Raising the Incomes of All Increase the Happiness of All? *Journal of Economic Behavior and Organization* 27, 35–47.

Easterlin, R.A., Angelescu McVey, L., Switek, M., Sawangfa, O., Smith Zweig, J. (2010), The Happiness-Income Paradox Revisited, *Proceedings of the National Academy of Sciences of the United States of America* 107, 22463–22468.

Easterly, W., Fischer, S. (2001), Inflation and the Poor, *Journal of Money, Credit and Banking* 33, 160–178.

Ebert, U., Welsch, H. (2009), How Do Europeans Evaluate Income Distributions? An Assessment Based on Happiness Surveys, *Review of Income and Wealth* 55, 801–819.

Feather, N.T. (1990), *The Psychological Impact of Unemployment*, New York: Springer.

Fehr, E., Schmidt, K.M. (1999), A Theory of Fairness, Competition and Co-Operation, *Quarterly Journal of Economics* 114, 817–868.

Frank, R.H. (1985), *Choosing the Right Pond: Human Behavior and the Quest for Status*, New York: Oxford University Press.

Frey, B.S., Stutzer, A. (2002), What Can Economists Learn from Happiness Research? *Journal of Economic Literature* XL, 402–435.

Friedman, M., assisted by R. Friedman (1962), *Capitalism and Freedom*, Chicago, IL: University of Chicago Press.

Frijters, P., Krekel, C. (2021), *A Handbook for Wellbeing Policy Making: History, Theory, Measurement, Implementation, and Examples*, Oxford: Oxford University Press.

Jantsch, A., Le Blanc, J., Schmidt, T. (2022), Wealth and subjective well-being in Germany, Deutsche Bundesbank Discussion Paper No. 11/2022.

Jayadev, A. (2006), Differing Preferences between Anti-Inflation and Anti-Unemployment Policy Among the Rich and the Poor, *Economics Letters* 91, 67–71.

Jayadev, A. (2008), The Class Content of Preferences Towards Anti-Inflation and Anti-Unemployment Policies, *International Review of Applied Economics* 22, 161–172.

Jebb, A.T., Tay, L., Diener, E., Oishi, S. (2018), Happiness, Income Satiation and Turning Points Around the World, *Nature Human Behaviour* 2 (January), 33–38.

Kahneman, D., Deaton, A. (2010), High Income Improves Evaluation of Life but Not Emotional Well-Being, *Proceedings of the National Academy of Sciences of the United States of America* 107, 16489–16493.

Kahneman, D., Tversky, A. (1979), Prospect Theory: An Analysis of Decision Under Risk, *Econometrica* 47, 263–291.

Layard, R. (2006), Happiness and Public Policy: A Challenge to the Profession, *Economic Journal* 116, C24–C33.

Loewenstein, G., O'Donohue, T., Rabin, M. (2003), Projection Bias in Predicting Future Utility, *Quarterly Journal of Economics* 118, 1209–1248.

Louis, V.V., Zhao, S. (2002), Effects of Family Structure, Family SES, and Adulthood Experiences on Life Satisfaction, *Journal of Family Issues* 23, 986–1005.

Lucas, R.E., Clark, A.E., Georgellis, Y., Diener, E. (2004), Unemployment Alters the Set Point for Life Satisfaction, *Psychological Science* 15, 8–13.

Ochsen, C., Welsch, H. (2011), The Social Costs of Unemployment: Accounting for Unemployment Duration, *Applied Economics* 43, 3999–4005.

Ochsen, C., Welsch, H. (2012), Who Benefits from Labor Market Institutions? Evidence from Surveys of Life Satisfaction, *Journal of Economic Psychology* 33, 112–124.

Oswald, A.J., Proto, E., Sgroi, D. (2015), Happiness and Productivity, *Journal of Labor Economics* 33, 789–822.

Proto, E., Rustichini, A. (2013), A Reassessment of the Relationship between GDP and Life Satisfaction, *PLoS ONE* 8, e79358(2013).

Samuelson, P.A. (1983) *Foundations of Economic Analysis*, enlarged edition, Press, Cambridge, MA: Harvard University.

Scheve, K. (2004), Public Inflation Aversion and the Political Economy of Macroeconomic Policymaking, *International Organization* 58, 1–34.

Senik, C. (2004), When Information Dominates Comparison: Learning from Russian Subjective Panel Data, *Journal of Public Economics* 88, 2093–2123.

Smith, A. (1759), *The Theory of Moral Sentiments*, London: Andrew Millar(1967).

Solnick, S.J., Hemenway, D. (1998), Is More Always Better? A Survey on Positional Concerns, *Journal of Economic Behavior and Organization* 37, 373–383.

Stiglitz, J.E., Sen, A., Fitoussi, J.-P. (2009), Report of the Commission on the Measurement of Economic Performance and Social Progress (CMEPSP), available at http://www.stiglitz-sen-fitoussi.fr/en/documents.htm.

Van Hoorn, A., Maseland, R. (2010), Cultural Differences between East and West Germany after 1991: Communist Values Versus Economic Performance? *Journal of Economic Behavior and Organization* 76, 791–804.

Veblen, T. (1899), *The Theory of the Leisure Class*, London: Macmillan, George Allen and Unwin.

Welsch, H. (2011), The Magic Triangle of Macroeconomics: How Do European Countries Score? *Oxford Economic Papers* 63, 71–93.

Welsch, H. (2022), What Shapes Satisfaction With Democracy? Interests, Morals and the German East-West Divide, *Social Indicators Research* 163, 197–217.

Welsch, H., Biermann, P. (2019), Poverty is a Public Bad: Panel Evidence From Subjective Well-Being Data, *Review of Income and Wealth* 65, 187–200.

Welsch, H., Kühling, J. (2015a), Income Comparison, Income Formation, and Subjective Well-Being: New Evidence on Envy Versus Signaling, *Journal of Behavioral and Experimental Economics* 59, 21–31.

Welsch, H., Kühling, J. (2015b), Macroeconomic Preferences by Income and Education Level: Evidence from Subjective Well-Being Data, *Review of Economics and Finance* 5, 15–32.

Welsch, H., Kühling, J. (2016), How Has The Crisis Of 2008–09 Affected Subjective Well-Being? Evidence from 25 OECD Countries, *Bulletin of Economic Research* 68, 34–54.

Wilson, T.D., Gilbert, D.T. (2003), Affective Forecasting. In M. Zanna (ed.), *Advances in Experimental Social Psychology* (Vol. 35, pp. 345–411), New York: Elsevier.

Yamamura, E. (2016), Social Conflict and Redistributive Preferences Among the Rich and the Poor: Testing the Hypothesis of Acemoglu and Robinson, *Journal of Applied Economics* 19, 41–64.

4 Wellbeing and the Environment

Introduction

It was noted in the preceding chapter that rising pollution stemming from increasing economic activity is one candidate explanation of stationary wellbeing in spite of rising national incomes – the Easterlin paradox. While the co-movement of pollution with national income (gross domestic product, or GDP) diminished in many developed economies due to the use of pollution control technologies, for example, exhaust gas cleaning, such technologies are applicable to some types of pollution but not others. Specifically, the mitigation of climate-relevant gases (greenhouse gases) such as carbon dioxide (CO_2) cannot rely on large-scale application of end-of-pipe control devices but requires the reduction of activities that cause the respective emissions – the burning of coal, oil, and gas. Other than climate change, another form of ongoing degradation is the destruction of natural environments that provide important amenity values and ecosystem services and are a reservoir of biodiversity.

The past two decades have seen a steady increase of studies investigating the impact of environmental factors on subjective wellbeing. Major issues studied are air pollution, climate change, and environmental amenities. This chapter reviews the insights from the pertinent literature and discusses the wellbeing relevance of the natural environment relative to economic wealth as well as implications for public policy.

Air Pollution

One of the environmental issues most thoroughly studied in the wellbeing literature is air pollution. Air pollution can affect subjective wellbeing, as it leads to a wide range of respiratory and cardiovascular problems that negatively affect subjective wellbeing (Gouveia and Maisonet 2005). Some of the studies on air pollution and subjective wellbeing were among the first to put a monetary value on the wellbeing costs of environmental degradation by calculating the hypothetical amount of money (income) that would compensate an individual for the wellbeing loss arising from pollution.

DOI: 10.4324/9781003206163-5

Evidence from Aggregate Data

Studies of the relationship between air pollution and wellbeing began two decades ago. Early studies used national average levels of air pollution and wellbeing in a multi-country framework. The first paper of this type studied the impact of average levels of ambient sulfur dioxide, nitrogen dioxide, and total suspended particles on country-average happiness in a cross-section of 54 countries in the mid-1990s (Welsch 2002). The paper found that larger nitrogen dioxide concentrations are statistically associated with lower average happiness, whereas higher per capita income is associated with higher average happiness. Nitrogen dioxide stems mainly from power generation and car traffic. It leads to respiratory illness and lung damage and is a precursor of photochemical smog and low-level ozone, which are forms of air pollution most damaging to human health.

Since air pollution has a negative effect, while income has a positive effect, on wellbeing, it can be calculated from the estimated coefficients how much additional income a representative person would need to compensate for the loss of wellbeing caused by air pollution. These hypothetical compensation payments – which can be interpreted as a monetary value of better air quality – turned out to be large. To illustrate, in the data studied, pollution loads in Japan were larger than those in Germany by 27 kilotons per capita, and compensating a representative German citizen for the unhappiness caused by the excess pollution would cost about US$1,900 per year (at prices of 1995). The marginal happiness costs were found to be about US$70 per kiloton nitrogen dioxide. This figure is similar to common estimates of the monetary equivalent of health damage from nitrogen dioxide. Since the figure is much larger than the marginal abatement costs (from installing denitrification devices in power stations and cars), abatement of nitrogen dioxide has a positive net value in terms of wellbeing (Welsch 2002).

That analysis was extended to a comprehensive welfare analysis by estimating not only the monetary benefits of air pollution abatement but also the associated costs in terms of national income foregone (Welsch 2007). The idea was that – different from the partial-analytical perspective that focuses on specific pollution control technologies – the appropriate notion of pollution control costs is the loss in national income that results from reducing pollution. The (macroeconomic) costs conceptualized this way may differ from the (microeconomic) costs of installing pollution control equipment because those latter costs may have wider economic consequences, for example, in terms of the general price level.

To capture macroeconomic costs of abatement, one can treat pollution as a quasi-input to production, as is common in environmental economics (Ebert and Welsch 2007). The idea is that more final output (value added) can be produced if fewer resources are used for pollution abatement. Following this approach, national income was modeled as a function of nitrogen dioxide (along with physical and human capital), and a concave production function for national income was estimated (that is, a function exhibiting decreasing marginal product of pollution). Using the same data as in Welsch (2002), it turned out that at observed pollution levels, the monetized gain in wellbeing from reducing pollution by one unit (kiloton) was larger than the associated loss in income in most of the 54 countries studied. To bring the marginal monetized benefit from abatement and marginal income losses in line with each other – which is the condition for optimal abatement levels – large reductions of pollution were found to be justified (Welsch 2007). The optimal abatement levels were found to be particularly large in some countries where the pollution-income ratio was still very large by the time of analysis (mid-1990s), in particular some of the East European economies in transition.

From a methodological point of view, a challenge involved in multi-country cross-sectional studies is to control for country characteristics that may be correlated with both national pollution and national wellbeing levels, since their omission may lead to biased results. To better address the problem of omitted country characteristics, a further study used a combined cross-section time-series framework comprising annual data (1990–1997) for ten European countries (Welsch 2006). This kind of panel structure permits country fixed effects to be used to control for omitted factors at the country level. Except for using country fixed effects, the macro design of relying on averages of pollution and wellbeing is retained in this study. Pollution variables are ambient levels of nitrogen dioxide, total suspended particles, and lead. The wellbeing function is specified in a multiplicative fashion (Cobb–Douglas function), which allows for synergies among the pollutants.

In this study, nitrogen dioxide and lead were found to be significantly negatively related to wellbeing, whereas national income was positively related to wellbeing. The latter is remarkable because the countries studied were relatively rich member states of the European Union, for which the Easterlin paradox would predict that higher national income has no appreciable effect on wellbeing. The Easterlin paradox, however, refers to national income net of any impairments associated with its production. The results on national income together with those on pollution thus suggest that the gross wellbeing effect of higher national income is positive even though the net effect need not be – a very plausible scenario.

The estimation results were used to value the pollution reductions achieved in West European countries in the period considered (1990–1997) through the mandated use of denitrification devices (such as catalytic converters in cars) and a ban on leaded gasoline. The value of those reductions amounts to, on average, US$750 per capita per year in the case of nitrogen dioxide and about US$1,400 per capita per year in the case of lead. The figures for nitrogen dioxide vary between US$442 in the United Kingdom (where the bulk of pollution reduction programs had already been completed before the period considered) to US$1554 in the case of Spain (where reduction rates in the period considered were larger). Due to synergies among the pollutants, the value of simultaneously reducing nitrogen dioxide and lead is slightly higher than the sum of the respective values. Since total suspended particles are insignificant in the life satisfaction regression but correlated to the two other pollutants, the value of reducing them is captured implicitly by these estimates.

Evidence from Individual-Level Data

While most of the early studies of air pollution and wellbeing used average levels of pollution and wellbeing by country and year, more recent work is characterized by a higher spatial and temporal resolution of pollution data and by focusing on the wellbeing of the individuals affected by the pollution.

Most of the recent studies that have analyzed the impact of air pollution on individual-level wellbeing have relied on sub-national (regional or local) data. Using such an approach, a negative and significant relationship between life satisfaction and sulfur dioxide (SO_2) concentrations at the regional level in Europe was found (Ferreira et al. 2013), whereas a significant negative association between life satisfaction and concentrations of particulate matter (PM10) at the collection-district level (similar to a US census block group) was found in South East Queensland, Australia (Ambrey et al. 2014). Another study combined individual-level wellbeing data with high resolution SO_2 data at the county level for Germany (Luechinger 2009). Since the data used comes from a longitudinal panel survey, which follows individuals over several years, it was possible to control for individual fixed effects and to focus on changes in the pollution an individual was exposed to rather than focusing on differences between individuals. Moreover, using so-called instrumental-variable techniques, it was possible to rule out that results were biased by people's deliberately moving to less polluted places. Overall, the study thus established a causal effect of air pollution on wellbeing, rather than just a correlation.

In addition to the spatial dimension, an important issue is the temporal dimension of the link between wellbeing and environmental quality. While this is of less importance in the case of environmental amenities that do not change over a longer period of time, it may be highly relevant for air pollutants, especially if their amounts are volatile. By merging data on local air quality and individual-level wellbeing data, a significantly negative relationship was found between wellbeing and the daily concentration of PM10 on the day the wellbeing question was asked (Levinson 2012).

The studies using spatially and temporally disaggregated individual-level data confirm the findings from macro-level studies of negative relationships between air pollution and subjective wellbeing, even if not all of them are able to rule out biases stemming from people selecting into places with less pollution. While the cross-national macro-level studies are cruder in several ways, they can be said to deal with selection implicitly since people are probably unlikely to migrate cross-nationally to avoid pollution.

Assessment of the Evidence

While dozens of studies have found a negative impact of air pollution on subjective wellbeing, this body of research is characterized by substantial heterogeneity with respect to countries considered, wellbeing measures, pollution indicators, and empirical strategies. Against this background, questions arise as to general conclusions that can be drawn with respect to the size of effects and how they compare to other effects of air pollution that have been the focus of more traditional economic analysis (Levinson 2020).

General conclusions with respect to the size of effects are difficult to draw. Because all the studies use different units, the coefficients on pollution cannot be compared directly. What does it mean that in one study, a one-day increase in the number of days particulate matter exceeds 50 micrograms per cubic meter ($\mu g/m^3$) reduces life satisfaction by 0.0005 on an 11-point scale (García-Mainar et al. 2015), while another study finds that a 1 $\mu g/m^3$ increase in sulfur dioxide decreases happiness by 0.07 units on a four-point scale (Menz and Welsch 2012)?

Since all studies include income as a covariate, one way of comparing the pollution coefficients across different studies is to examine how they each relate to the income coefficient within the same studies. The ratio of the pollution and income coefficients indicates the amount of extra money (typically annual income) an average respondent needs to compensate for a one-unit increase in pollution, that is, the respondent's implicit marginal willingness to pay (MWTP) for clean air. Multiplying that by the standard deviation in the pollutant, dividing by 365 days per year, converting to US dollars, and adjusting for inflation to 2016 yields a measure of effect size that is comparable across studies (Levinson 2020). By applying this method, it was found that – disregarding outliers (US$0.01 and US$171) – the results typically fall into a reasonable range, from US$4 to US$40 for a day of cleaner air (Levinson 2020).

Interestingly, even the earliest, methodologically least sophisticated study (Welsch 2002) yielded a fairly reasonable result according to this standard, US$7.70, which gives the policy conclusion of large pollution reductions being justified (Welsch 2007) considerable credibility.

In addition to the size of air pollution's effect on wellbeing, a further question is whether the measured willingness to pay derived from wellbeing studies comports with other negative effects of pollution. A large body of research studies the effect of pollution on outcomes more tangible than subjective wellbeing, in particular health, mortality, and productivity.

It turns out that these disparate methods of valuing air quality match up well. The dollar value of willingness to pay for air quality derived from wellbeing studies looks remarkably similar to the dollar value typically assigned to decreased mortality or to the increased productivity from that air quality. Specifically, dividing MWTP estimates from wellbeing studies (dollar/pollution) by recent estimates of the mortality from pollution (deaths/pollution) gives estimates of the value of a statistical life (dollar/death) that are similar to ones used by policy makers and that come directly from hedonic wage regressions or contingent valuation questions. In the same way, combining the MWTP from wellbeing studies to recent studies of the effect of pollution on productivity shows that the monetary value of people's lost wellbeing from pollution is comparable to the value of lost productivity. Well-crafted studies of air pollution and wellbeing thus provide estimates of willingness to pay for air quality that are consistent with outcomes economists have more experience and comfort measuring, like health and productivity (Levinson 2020).

Climate Change

While the impairments from air pollution are of a regional and relatively immediate nature, the bulk of climate change's effects are global and expected to happen in the future. Climate-related effects are therefore less likely to affect individuals' current wellbeing than the more direct and contemporaneous effects of pollution.

In spite of this, wellbeing effects of climate change can be captured in two ways. One is by studying how wellbeing varies with spatial and temporal variation in climate parameters that are likely to change in the future, such as levels and seasonal patterns of temperature or precipitation. The other approach is by studying how wellbeing is affected by extreme events whose intensity and frequency are expected to increase due to climate change, such as storms, floods, droughts, or wildfires.

Climate Parameters

The first study on the relationship between subjective wellbeing and climate parameters refers to Russia (Frijters and Van Praag 1998). This country is suitable for such an investigation because the climate parameters show a large interregional spread due to the geographical extent of the country. In the study, data for temperatures, precipitation, wind speeds, and humidity in 35 regions were combined with data on general life satisfaction from representative population surveys in 1993 and 1994. Among other things, the study shows that people in regions with a higher average temperature in summer and in regions with a lower average temperature in winter have lower life satisfaction than people in regions with a more moderate climate. In particular, it was found that a one degree Celsius increase in average July temperature is associated with a loss of wellbeing as is a decrease in income by 16 percent.

A negative association between extreme temperatures and subjective wellbeing has also been found on a global scale. One study found for a data set of 67 countries and the period 1997–2000 that the lower the minimum temperatures and the higher the maximum temperatures in the country or year in question, the lower the wellbeing (Rehdanz and Maddison 2005).

From these results, the authors extrapolated that the expected changes in the frequency of cold winters and hot summers due to climate change will make people in cold and temperate latitudes "climate winners" and people in hot regions "climate losers" on balance. In a later study, they showed that climate is the second most important explanatory factor for differences in subjective wellbeing between countries, after per capita income (Maddison and Rehdanz 2020). They also emphasize that these are only direct effects on wellbeing, since possible influences on income are not included in the analysis (Maddison and Rehdanz 2011). Possible indirect effects due to changes in income (e.g., changes in harvest quantities) can amplify the direct effects. In addition, a case study for Australia found that experiencing increasing heat causes many people to worry about their future wellbeing (Zander et al. 2019).

Climate-Related Extreme Events

So-called attribution research has shown that global warming contributes to an increase in extreme weather events (Otto 2020). As a result of increasing climate change, extreme events such as droughts, forest fires, storms, and floods are expected to become more frequent and more severe.

The most obvious consequence of global warming is an increase in droughts and forest fires. With regard to droughts, a case study for Australia found significant effects on the subjective wellbeing of the population in rural areas (Carroll et al. 2009). The correlations found imply that the decrease in satisfaction from the projected doubling of the annual frequency of droughts in the future corresponds to the effect of a 1 percent decrease in annual national income. Impairments in life satisfaction due to drought have not only been found in Western "modern" societies but also for traditional communities, for example, in Papua New Guinea (Lohmann et al. 2019).

Another study for Australia focused on the impact of forest fire risk on life satisfaction, with the risk of a forest fire being measured by an index from 0 to 100 (Ambrey et al. 2017). The study found that a one-unit increase in the risk index was associated with a decrease in wellbeing equivalent to a US$10 loss of income. The impact of actual forest and bush fires on life satisfaction has been studied for France, Italy, Portugal, and Spain (Kountouris and Remoundou 2011). As expected, these were found to be greatest in more widespread fires and in rural areas. Furthermore, a study for the United States found that smoke pollution from forest and bush fires alone affects life satisfaction, again more in rural than in urban regions (Jones 2017).

With regard to storms, a first relevant case study found that subjective wellbeing in the United States plummeted after the extent of the damage caused by Hurricane Katrina on the US Gulf Coast became known (Kimball et al. 2006). Although the decline was strongest in the areas affected by the devastation, it was by no means confined to those areas but was nationwide. A multi-country study found a negative correlation between the frequency of hurricanes and general life satisfaction in both industrialized and developing countries (Berlemann 2016). The association was found to be stronger in poorer countries, where people have fewer resources to take protective action.

Other studies have looked at the impact of flooding on life satisfaction. In a multi-country study for Europe, it was found that flooding reduces wellbeing on average as much as a loss of annual income of around US$6,500 (Luechinger and Raschky 2009). A case study for Bulgaria found that the impact on wellbeing exceeds the purely material damage and that even minor floods have such an impact (Sekulova and Van den Berg 2016).

In a study for Germany, storm and hail events as well as floods were considered (Von Möllendorff and Hirschfeld 2016). Both types of events had a negative impact on life satisfaction. These were lower if those affected had appropriate insurance coverage. Furthermore, the impact of storms and hail proved short-lived, while satisfaction took several months to return to previous levels after a flood.

A study for the United States matched 31 billion-dollar disasters with individual survey data for more than 1.7 million people to estimate the effect of extreme weather events on the subjective wellbeing of US residents. The study contrasts and compares the effect of different types of extreme weather events, including tropical cyclones (mainly hurricanes), severe storms (mainly tornadoes), flooding, drought, wildfire, and freeze from 2005 to 2010. The results indicate that natural disasters have a negative and robust impact on subjective wellbeing in the affected communities, and that, on average, this impact peaks six months after the event, and then decays over time. Effects are large and significant for severe storm and drought, but insignificant for tropical cyclones. The study finds an attenuating impact of health care access, flood insurance, and governmental assistance programs as well as of stronger emotional and social support (Ahmadiani and Ferreira 2021).

Environmental Amenities and Land Use

There are several reasons for thinking that experiences of natural environments will be positively related to subjective wellbeing (MacKerron and Mourato 2013). First, there appear to be direct pathways by which such experiences affect the nervous system, bringing about stress reduction and restoration of attention. Second, natural environments are typically lower in environmental disamenities and pollution, such as noise and air pollution, which negatively affect wellbeing. Third, natural environments might increase wellbeing by facilitating and encouraging physically and mentally beneficial behaviors, such as physical exercise, recreation, and social interaction.

A growing body of research has studied the relationship between people's subjective wellbeing and environmental amenities near their place of residence. While some studies have focused on the extent of (e.g., size, total area cover) or proximity to vegetated areas (e.g., natural areas, urban parks) and water bodies (e.g., lakes, rivers), also termed green or blue space (World Health Organization 2017), more recent work has explored links between human wellbeing and the level of biodiversity in those places as well as between actual experiences of natural environments and wellbeing.

Environmental Amenities

In 2005, the United Nations stated that ecosystem services generated on cultivated and natural land areas, such as food and bioenergy provisioning, climate regulation, and landscape amenities, are essential for the wellbeing of mankind (Millenium Ecosystem Assessment 2005). Since then, a variety of studies at different spatial scales (cities, nations, and whole continents) have investigated the impact of environmental assets on subjective wellbeing.

With respect to cities, a study on urban land use in Germany found that subjective wellbeing is positively related to lower degrees of soil sealing, larger shares of vegetation, and a more heterogeneous configuration of urban fabric that reduces perceptions of density, especially in areas with high average population density (Bertram et al. 2020).

On a national level, differences in environmental amenities were found to explain considerable fractions of the spatial variation in subjective wellbeing within countries. With respect to Ireland, for example, an early study showed that, in addition to the usual individual-level factors, consideration of climate and environmental and urban conditions is critical when analyzing subjective wellbeing. Location-specific factors were found to have a direct impact on wellbeing, and the explanatory power of the wellbeing function substantially increased when the spatial variables were included (Brereton et al. 2008).

Similarly, a recent study for the United States found that (controlling for people's socio-demographic characteristics) average subjective wellbeing is higher in those counties that have more recreational land while being lower in counties with a higher percentage of urban area (leaving aside the more specific characteristics of urban land use) and those classified as a metropolitan area. Those relationships are stronger if the levels of housing prices and wages are controlled for than when they are not, but still significant in the latter case. This suggests that the (gross) utility from local/regional amenities (recreational land, non-urban and non-metropolitan area) is partly but not completely compensated by higher housing prices and lower wages, such that a positive net utility from those amenities remains (Ahmadiani and Ferreira 2019).

These findings refute the idea of locational equilibrium according to which people systematically move to more attractive places, thus bidding up house values and bidding down wages, until any spatial variation in average wellbeing is eliminated (Ahmadiani and Ferreira 2019). The findings corroborate previous results for Ireland that suggest that the equilibrium condition implicit in the hedonic pricing approach to nonmarket valuation does not hold (Ferreira and Moro 2010).

On a multi-country (continental) level, one study investigated the relationship between subjective wellbeing and the shares of 12 different types of land cover (4 artificial and 8 natural) in 283 regional units in 30 European countries. Except for wetlands, higher shares of all categories of natural areas in people's region of residence had a positive effect on residents' wellbeing, with agro-forestry and agriculture on natural areas having the highest positive effect, natural grassland and scrubland having the lowest positive effect, and pasture and natural forests lying in between. However, the effects were likely to be nonlinear, that is, positive effects are larger if the existing share of the respective category is smaller than if the share is larger. In other words, natural areas become more valuable in terms of wellbeing as they become scarcer through land use changes (Kopmann and Rehdanz 2013).

Access to Green Spaces

Focusing on green spaces, it was noted that access to them may affect wellbeing through the enhancement of physical activity; the provision of psychological relaxation and recreational opportunities; the stimulation of social cohesion; and the reduction of air pollution, noise, and heat (Markevych et al. 2017). Access to green spaces has been found to go with greater subjective wellbeing in data from China, Australia, and Britain (Ambrey and Fleming 2014; Smyth et al. 2011, and White et al. 2013a, respectively). Studies for Germany show that access to green urban areas, such as gardens and parks, is positively associated with subjective wellbeing. The wellbeing benefit from access to green urban areas translates into an average willingness to pay of about 45 euros per year for increasing the coverage of green urban areas by one hectare within a radius of 1,000 meters around people's place of residence (Bertram and Rehdanz 2015). The effects are strongest for residents who are older. For those, the effect of increasing the distance to a green area by 100 meters amounts to one-third of the effect of being unemployed. In contrast to access to green areas, proximity to abandoned areas, such as waste or leftover land, is negatively associated with wellbeing (Krekel et al. 2016).

A multi-country study covering 27 member states of the European Union investigated the role for subjective wellbeing of the ease of access to and the actual utilization of green and recreational areas. The study found that a higher degree of perceived access was associated with significantly higher subjective wellbeing. Furthermore, users of green areas show significantly greater wellbeing than nonusers (8 percent of individuals), but it is unclear to what extent not using green areas was due to a lack of access or people deliberately abstaining from use (Ruckelshauß 2020).

One way of assessing the wellbeing effects of green spaces is to study the impacts of deforestation and afforestation. A study focusing on deforestation due to the spreading of forest-attacking invasive species in the United States found that the emergence of the invasive emerald ash borer in a county within the past five years was associated with a decline in subjective wellbeing equivalent to a US$176 loss in annual household income and that the wellbeing loss was increasing in time as more trees died due to infestation (Jones 2020). On the other hand, a study focusing on an urban afforestation project found positive wellbeing effects. Specifically, the MillionTreesNYC afforestation program in New York City was found to be associated with a wellbeing gain equivalent to a US$505 (6.5 percent) increase in average per capita monthly household income. While the wellbeing impacts were growing in magnitude as more trees were planted, no impacts existed during the months when deciduous trees have no foliage. The latter finding is consistent with a pathway that involves both aesthetic and air quality considerations (Jones 2021).

Biodiversity

As discussed in Chapter 1, biodiversity loss is an aspect of land use that poses one of the most severe nature-related challenges currently and in the future, but relatively few studies of the relationship between land use and wellbeing focus specifically on biodiversity. In particular, few studies have made use of ecological measures of species diversity (e.g., based on field sampling and monitoring) as indicators for biodiversity.

Using such species diversity measures, a recent study demonstrated that faunal and floral species richness (number of species) is positively related to the subjective wellbeing of residents in the state of Victoria, Australia (Mavoa et al. 2019). Similar findings were obtained on a national level with respect to the United Kingdom (Wheeler et al. 2015).

At a continental level, a large-scale study related subjective wellbeing scores and socioeconomic data of more than 26,000 European citizens from 26 countries with macroecological data on the regional level for species diversity and other nature characteristics. Species diversity was measured as the species richness of birds, mammals (including megafauna), and trees. In addition, indicators were used for other nature and climate characteristics such as landscape and topographic heterogeneity, the area of green and blue space, and protected land cover. The study found that bird species richness is positively and strongly associated with subjective wellbeing across Europe. Possible pathways for this relationship may be the direct multisensory experience of birds, and beneficial landscape properties that promote both bird diversity and people's wellbeing (Methorst et al. 2021). The study corroborates previous evidence of a significant impact on wellbeing of the number of bird and mammal species in the respondent's country and reasoning that bird species seem to be a better indicator for biodiversity (Rehdanz 2007).

Experiences of Natural Environments

While the research discussed so far has related wellbeing measures to aggregate environmental characteristics between geographical regions or compared individuals' wellbeing with the proximity of their homes to natural environments, some recent studies have focused on actual experiences of natural environments. How visits to and experiences of natural environments (forests, parks, protected areas, lakes, rivers, and beaches) affect subjective wellbeing was investigated by asking people about their visit-related subjective wellbeing shortly after the visit (White et al. 2013b; Wyles et al. 2019) or their general subjective wellbeing while they are on-site (MacKerron and Mourato 2013).

The latter approach has been applied using a smartphone app that signals participants at random moments, presenting a brief questionnaire while using satellite positioning (GPS) to determine geographical coordinates. The app was used to collect over one million responses from more than 20,000 participants in the United Kingdom. Associating GPS response locations with objective spatial data, within-individual variation in momentary reported subjective wellbeing was related to land cover, while controlling for weather, daylight, activity, companionship, location type, time, day, and any response trend.

On average, study participants showed significantly and substantially greater wellbeing outdoors in all green or natural habitat types than in urban environments. Specifically, when outdoors, every habitat type except inland bare ground is associated with significantly higher wellbeing levels than the urban type. Marine and coastal margins are by some distance the happiest locations, with responses approximately 6 points (or 0.28 standard deviations) higher than urban environments on the 0–100 scale. This is a magnitude similar to, for instance, the difference between attending an exhibition and doing housework. All other green or natural environment types – "mountains, moors, and heathlands", "freshwater, wetlands and flood plains", "woodland, grasslands, and farmland" – score between 2.7 and 1.8 wellbeing points higher than urban environments. With respect to activities, birdwatching and nature watching are significantly positively related to subjective wellbeing (MacKerron and Mourato 2013).

Locally Undesired Land Use

The air pollution discussed earlier stems to a considerable extent from fossil fuel power plants. Emissions of sulfur dioxide, nitrogen oxides, and particulate matter are generically related to fossil fuel power generation because they are the chemical result of burning fossil fuels (coal, oil, and gas). Because of the air pollution they release, fossil fuel power plants are categorized as a locally undesired land use (LULU).

In addition to the general evidence on air pollution and subjective wellbeing discussed previously, a more specific piece of evidence on fossil fuel power plants' local and regional wellbeing effects is the finding that people's wellbeing is lower when they live downwind from the respective plants, unless the plants are equipped with scrubbers (Luechinger 2009).

Fossil fuels affect local wellbeing not only through their use but also by the mining of coal and the drilling of oil and gas. With respect to coal mining, a study focused on the Shanxi province of China, an area that holds 27 percent of

China's coal resources, with coal mining typically co-located with coal stockpiling and coal washing. Differentiating survey respondents into several categories of distance between their place of residence and the nearest coal mines, the study found that nearby residents scored significantly lower on satisfaction with air and water quality than did respondents in the more distant category (Li et al. 2017).

With respect to oil and gas development, a study examined the regional wellbeing effects across Texas, USA, by considering data on county level oil and gas drilling for 2005 through 2010, a period of heightened oil and gas development. The study differentiated between conventional and horizontally drilled wells because horizontal drilling implies increased environmental concerns, as the hydraulic fracturing process requires massive injections of water and chemicals into wells to free the oil and gas trapped in shale. In addition, it implies a much larger footprint due to the storage of water and increased surface disturbance due to the construction of access roads. The study found significant deleterious effects of horizontal drilling on wellbeing, but no significant effects of conventional drilling. Effects are concentrated in the Dallas-Fort Worth metropolitan area, an area that contains both very high levels of horizontal drilling and a large urban population (amounting to six million people). This suggests that for the typical resident, the costs of drilling in the area exceed the (economic) benefits and reduce their subjective wellbeing. The results suggest that a one standard deviation increase in horizontal drilling implies that about 1.7 percent of the sample would be moved to a lower wellbeing category on the 4-point scale (Maguire and Winters 2017).

Undesired local or regional wellbeing effects may stem not only from the extraction and use of fossil fuels but also from the presence of nuclear and renewable energy facilities. With respect to nuclear power stations, perceptions of nuclear risk may be thought to impact the wellbeing of nearby residents. In a case study for Japan, no wellbeing variation with proximity to the nuclear power plant at Fukushima-Daiichi existed before the nuclear meltdown on March 11, 2011, but a significant negative relationship between wellbeing and proximity after the disaster. For nuclear power stations other than Fukushima-Daiichi, a wellbeing variation with proximity to the nearest nuclear plant was found neither before nor after the Fukushima disaster (Rehdanz et al. 2015). In contrast to Japan, a study for Switzerland found a significant negative relationship between subjective wellbeing and proximity to the nearest nuclear plant at fixed income and housing costs. The gradient is smaller for those who may feel protected by wind direction and mountains. It remains significant when incomes and housing costs are omitted from the wellbeing equation, which indicates a violation of the condition for locational equilibrium – that is, differences in wages and housing costs do not compensate for differences in local amenities (Welsch and Biermann 2016).

While fossil fuel power generation has negative wellbeing effects in terms of air pollution, renewable energies (wind and solar power and power generation from biomass) have local undesired effects of their own, in particular visual impairments (wind and solar power) and odor nuisance (biomass). In the case of biomass, there may be additional impairments from noise caused by deliveries of fuel (mostly maize) and visual impacts from the large-scale growing of maize in areas where biomass plants are located.

A study that investigated the relationship between German citizens' subjective wellbeing and the presence of wind turbines in their vicinity found wellbeing to be significantly lower in individuals who live within 4 kilometers of wind turbines. The monetary equivalent of the presence of one wind turbine amounts to up to 59 euros per year, but the effects were found to be transitory due to hedonic adaptation, vanishing after five years at the latest (Krekel and Zerrahn 2017).

A similar study, also for Germany, found that a 1 megawatt (MW) increase in installed wind power capacity in people's postcode district creates a wellbeing loss equivalent to 5.8 euros per month, but the effect was (again) found to be short-lived (Von Möllendorff and Welsch 2017). The same study investigated the relationship between German citizens' subjective wellbeing and the presence of solar and biomass facilities in their neighborhoods (along with the presence of wind turbines). With respect to solar power, no significant wellbeing effects of solar panels in residents' own postcode districts were found. In contrast to this, the presence of biomass plants negatively affects the wellbeing not only of individuals in the same postcode district but also in adjacent ones. In monetary terms, a 1 MW increase in installed biomass capacity in one's own district and the adjacent districts is associated with a drop in life satisfaction corresponding to 20.5 euros and 6.6 euros per month, respectively. In contrast to wind power, the wellbeing effects from biomass remain significant over time and do not decrease in magnitude.

While these findings suggest a clear preference of wind power and, especially, solar power over biomass-based power generation, there do not seem to be studies that compare the respective local disamenities to those of fossil fuel plants. At a more aggregate level, however, there is some evidence on the relationship between subjective wellbeing and the share of several electricity generation technologies in countries' electricity mix. A study using representative wellbeing data for individuals in 25 European countries yielded a clear preference (in terms of wellbeing) for solar and wind power as well as power generation from natural gas over power generation from coal and oil. This result is consistent with not only solar and wind power but also natural gas being less polluting than coal and oil. Solar and wind power as well as electricity from natural gas are also preferred to nuclear power, consistent with concern over nuclear risk. Electricity from biomass is the least preferred type of electricity (Welsch and Biermann 2014).

Pro-Environmental Behavior

While the bulk of the literature on wellbeing and the environment has focused on objective environmental factors, a number of studies have explored the relationship between wellbeing and pro-environmental behaviors.

Some Evidence

Studies exploring the relationship between wellbeing and pro-environmental behaviors have been conducted in single-country and multi-country settings.

An early study investigated the relationships between subjective wellbeing and three pro-environmental behaviors (buying green products, recycling/reuse, water conservation) in data for more than 23,000 individuals from over 80 nations, both developed and developing, and found those relationships to be significantly positive (Videras and Owen 2006).

More recently, a study involving more than 2,000 individuals in Canada and the United States considered 39 pro-environmental behaviors. The study found that 37 behaviors were significantly positively related with wellbeing and only two non-significantly so. This finding suggests that a positive relationship between subjective wellbeing and acting pro-environmentally is detectable across a wide range of behaviors and thus is not limited to any particular type(s) of behavior. The size of the relationship displayed a considerable range, the strongest relationship (participate in local environmental activities) being seven times as large as the weakest (run washer/dryer only when full). Using ratings of the behaviors in terms of observability, costs, and socialness, it was found that the strength of the estimated relationships was significantly correlated with all three factors, the correlations with observability, costs, and socialness amounting to $r = 0.37$, $r = 0.74$, and $r = 0.50$, respectively (Schmitt et al. 2018).

Discussion

With respect to the relationship between subjective wellbeing and pro-environmental behavior, three issues deserve to be discussed: causality, motivation, and rationality (Welsch 2020).

The relationship between wellbeing and pro-environmental behavior differs from that between wellbeing and pollution, climate, and environmental amenities in that the latter relationship refers to given circumstances that are not influenced by individuals' choices (except for locational choices). With respect to environmental conditions, it is therefore reasonable to assume that those conditions affect wellbeing and not the other way round. Pro-environmental behaviors, by contrast, may affect wellbeing, but it is also possible that people who are happier have a higher propensity to behave pro-environmentally (Kasser 2017). While this issue of causation is not completely settled with respect to pro-environmental behavior, related experimental evidence on pro-social behavior (e.g., donations to charity) suggests that there is a causal influence from behavior on wellbeing (Dunn et al. 2008).

With respect to the motives for pro-environmental behavior, it should be noted that any single individual's acting pro-environmentally typically has virtually no impact on the environment. Rather than impact-related motives, other motivations are thus likely to play a role. That the strength of the various relationships is positively correlated with observability of the respective behaviors suggests that considerations of prestige and reputation may be relevant (Harbaugh 1998). The correlation with costs may reflect that costly behaviors are more prestigious, or it may indicate that contributing one's own resources enhances one's self-image as being a generous person (Aknin et al. 2013; Batson and Weeks 1996; Binder and Blankenberg 2017). The correlation with socialness is consistent with findings that people report the highest levels of wellbeing when socializing or connecting with other people (Kahneman et al. 2004). In addition to prestige, self-image, and socialness, pro-environmental behaviors may yield wellbeing in terms of moral satisfaction (Kahneman and Knetsch 1992).

In interpreting the evidence discussed, it should further be noted that the pertinent findings suggest a wellbeing benefit of acting pro-environmentally *net* of the associated costs in terms of money and effort. This is inconsistent with the idea that people make rational, utility-maximizing choices between consumption and environmental goods, as this would require benefits and costs to be equalized at the margin. Rather, it is consistent with people making choices between consumption and environmental goods that are biased to the disadvantage of the latter: when making choices, people overestimate the costs of behaving pro-environmentally in terms of consumption foregone, as those choices fail to foresee future hedonic adaptation to higher consumption levels (Chapter 3). Therefore, ex-post, the wellbeing benefit from behaving pro-environmentally exceeds the associated costs, resulting in a positive net benefit (Welsch and Kühling 2011).

Conclusion

As discussed in Chapter 2, economists have identified welfare with income and consumption over much of the 20th century, with occasional proposals to make adjustments for negative effects of production and consumption that affect people through the degradation of environmental amenities. It was not until the emergence of the field of environmental economics in the 1970s that the importance for welfare of environmental amenities was recognized, but exactly how various environmental characteristics relate to welfare and how they trade off against income and consumption remained largely ambiguous.

As also discussed in Chapter 2, the stated and revealed preference methods traditionally used to quantify those trade-offs have recently been complemented by the subjective wellbeing or happiness approach to environmental valuation. By relating people's subjective wellbeing to the environmental conditions they are exposed to and to their income, the importance of those conditions for wellbeing can be determined both in absolute terms and relative to income. The importance relative to income provides a measure of environmental conditions' monetary value.

Against this background, this chapter has reviewed the evidence on the relationship between subjective wellbeing and the environment. By focusing on climate change and green spaces, in addition to air pollution, the review has responded to global warming and biodiversity loss being perceived as major challenges the world is currently facing (Chapter 1).

The review showed that air pollution and climate change have large negative effects on wellbeing, whereas access to and experience of natural environments are associated with significant wellbeing benefits. In addition, comparing a large number of studies on air pollution showed a high degree of consistency of findings both with each other and with findings on mortality and productivity. Together, the evidence substantiates the assumption maintained by environmental economists that the environment is highly important for social welfare.

With respect to climate change, the large wellbeing impairments from heat waves, droughts, and severe storms, and their high monetary equivalents complement and corroborate previous insights on the detrimental effects of global warming obtained with more traditional methods of economic analysis and underscore the need for climate change mitigation.

With respect to biodiversity, the strong positive association between bird species richness and subjective wellbeing is intriguing, as it suggests that bird diversity may be an important indicator of more general landscape properties that promote people's wellbeing. The policy conclusion from this is that management actions for the protection of birds and the landscapes that support them may have considerable ancillary benefits. Moreover, regarding economic analysis, the finding that environmental amenities near people's place of residence fail to be capitalized in wages and housing values suggests that the idea of spatial equilibrium may need to be revised.

With respect to air pollution, the pertinent studies not only consistently document the importance of clean air for wellbeing but are also able to shed light on the Easterlin paradox of the insignificance of higher national income for wellbeing. The macro-level studies unanimously show significantly positive wellbeing effects of national income (GDP) once pollution is accounted for. The reason is that by controlling for the pollution associated with the generation of national income, GDP's *gross* wellbeing effect is obtained, whereas most studies of the Easterlin paradox (discussed in Chapter 3) omit pollution, thus showing GDP's wellbeing effect *net* of the effect of pollution and finding it to be insignificant or negative. This suggests that pollution associated with GDP growth is an important factor in understanding why growth may go with stationary wellbeing.

In spite of GDP's positive gross wellbeing effect, the size of the effect is typically small in developed economies, due to the social comparison and adaptation effects discussed in Chapter 3. As adaptation also applies to increases in *individual* income, the wellbeing effects of income are small, except at the low end of the income distribution. It is the small wellbeing effect of higher income in rich countries that explains findings reviewed earlier that the hypothetical increases in income required to compensate the wellbeing losses from environmental degradation are large.

While the bulk of the literature on wellbeing and the environment has focused on objective environmental phenomena (in particular air pollution, the climate, and terrestrial environmental amenities), a number of studies have explored the relationship between wellbeing and pro-environmental behaviors and typically found people who behave pro-environmentally to show higher levels of wellbeing. More specifically, the pertinent findings suggest a wellbeing benefit of acting pro-environmentally *net* of the associated costs in terms of money and effort. This is difficult to square with the idea that people make utility maximizing choices between consumption and environmental goods, as this would require benefits and costs to be equalized at the margin. Rather, it is consistent with people making choices between consumption and environmental goods that are biased to the disadvantage of the latter, as those choices fail to foresee future hedonic adaptation to higher consumption levels.

In sum, the literature reviewed in this chapter reveals that (a) environmental factors have a large impact on subjective wellbeing, (b) important assumptions of standard economic analysis (spatial equilibrium and rational choice) do not hold with respect to environmental goods, and (c) engaging in pro-environmental behaviors is associated with greater wellbeing. Since behaviors of single individuals have a negligible impact on the state of the environment, finding (c) begs the question of whether moral concerns may provide a better explanation of such behaviors than impact-related considerations. Moral values and concerns are the subjects of the following chapters.

Bibliography

Ahmadiani, M., Ferreira, S. (2019), Environmental Amenities and Quality of Life Across the United States, *Ecological Economics* 164, 106341.

Ahmadiani, M., Ferreira, S. (2021), Well-being Effects of Extreme Weather Events in the United States, *Resource and Energy Economics* 64(C), DOI: 10.1016/j.reseneeco.2020.101213.

Aknin, L.B., Dunn, E.W., Williams, A.V., Grant, A.M., Norton, M.I. (2013), Making a Difference Matters: Impact Unlocks the Emotional Benefits of Prosocial Spending, *Journal of Economic Behavior and Organization* 88, 90–95.

Ambrey, C.L., Fleming, C.M. (2014), Public Greenspace and Life Satisfaction in Urban Australia, *Urban Studies* 51(6), 1290–1321.

Ambrey, C.L., Fleming, C.M., Chan, A.Y.C. (2014), Estimating the Cost of Air Pollution in South East Queensland: An Application of the Life Satisfaction Non-market Valuation Approach, *Ecological Economics* 97, 172–181.

Ambrey, C.L., Fleming, C.M., Manning, M. (2017), Forest Fire Danger, Life Satisfaction and Feelings of Safety: Evidence from Australia, *International Journal of Wildland Fire* 26, 240–248.

Batson, C.D., Weeks, J.L. (1996), Mood Effects of Unsuccessful Helping: Another Test of the Empathy-Altruism Hypothesis, *Personality and Social Psychology Bulletin* 22, 148–157.

Brereton F., Clinch, J. P., Ferreira, S. (2008), Happiness, Geography and the Environment. *Ecological Economics* 65, 386–396.

Berlemann, M. (2016), Does Hurricane Risk Affect Individual Well-Being? Empirical Evidence on the Indirect Effects of Natural Disasters, *Ecological Economics* 124, 99–113.

Bertram, C., Goebel, J., Krekel, C., Rehdanz, K. (2020), Urban Land Use Fragmentation and Human Wellbeing, Kiel Working Paper No. 2147.

Bertram, C., Rehdanz, K. (2015), The Role of Urban Green Space for Human Well-Being, *Ecological Economics* 120, 139–152.

Binder, M., Blankenberg, A.K. (2017), Green Lifestyles and Subjective Well-Being: More About Self-Image Than Actual Behavior? *Journal of Economic Behavior and Organization* 137, 304–323.

Carroll, N., Frijters, P., Shields, M. (2009), Quantifying the Costs of Drought: New Evidence from Life Satisfaction Data, *Journal of Population Economics* 22, 445–461.

Dunn, E.W., Aknin, L.B., Norton, M.I. (2008), Spending Money on Others Promotes Happiness, *Science* 319, 1687–1688.

Ebert, U., Welsch, H. (2007), Environmental Emissions and Production Economics: Implications of the Materials Balance, *American Journal of Agricultural Economics* 89, 287–293.

Ferreira, S., Akay, A., Brereton, F., Cuñado, J., Martinsson, P., Moro, M., Ningal, T.F. (2013), Life Satisfaction and Air Quality in Europe, *Ecological Economics* 88, 1–10.

Ferreira, S., Moro, M. (2010), On the Use of Subjective Well-Being Data for Environmental Valuation, *Environmental and Resource Economics* 46, 249–273.

Frijters, P., Van Praag, B. (1998), The Effects of Climate on Welfare and Well-being in Russia, *Climate Change* 39, 61–81.

García-Mainar, I., Montuenga, V.M., Navarro-Paniagua, M. (2015), Workplace Environmental Conditions and Life Satisfaction in Spain, *Ecological Economics* 119, 136–146.

Gouveia, N.C., Maisonet, M. (2005), Health Effects of Air Pollution: An Overview. In: *Air Quality Guidelines: Global Update 2005* (pp. 87–109). Regional Office for Europe, Denmark: World Health Organization.

Harbaugh, W.T. (1998), What Do Donations Buy? A Model of Philanthropy Based on Prestige and Warm Glow, *Journal of Public Economics* 67, 269–284.

Jones, B.A., (2020), Happiness and Forest-Attacking Invasive Alien Species. In: D. Maddison, K. Rehdanz, H. Welsch (eds.), *Handbook on Wellbeing, Happiness and the Environment*, Cheltenham: Edward Elgar.

Jones, B.A. (2017), Are We Underestimating the Economic Costs of Wildfire Smoke? An Investigation Using the Life Satisfaction Approach, *Journal of Forest Economics* 27, 80–90.

Jones, B.A. (2021), Planting Urban Trees to Improve Quality of Life? The Life Satisfaction Impacts of Urban Afforestation, *Forest Policy and Economics* 125, 102408.

Kahneman, D., Knetsch, J.L. (1992), Valuing Public Goods: The Purchase of Moral Satisfaction, *Journal of Environmental Economics and Management* 22, 57–70.

Kahneman, D., Krueger, A.B., Schkade, D.A., Schwarz, N., Stone, A.A. (2004), A Survey Method for Characterizing Daily Life Experience: The Day Reconstruction Method, *Science* 306, 1776–1780.

Kasser, T. (2017), Living Both Well and Sustainably: A Review of the Literature, with Some Reflections on Future Research, Interventions and Policy, *Philosophical Transactions of the Royal Society A* 375, 20160369.

Kimball, M., Levy, H., Othake, F., Tsutsui, Y. (2006), Unhappiness after Hurricane Katrina, Working Paper 12062, National Bureau of Economic Research.

Kopmann, A., Rehdanz, K. (2013), A Human Well-Being Approach for Assessing the Value of Natural Land Areas, *Ecological Economics* 93, 20–33.

Kountouris, Y., Remoundou, K. (2011), Valuing the Welfare Cost of Forest Fires: A Life Satisfaction Approach, *Kyklos* 64, 556–578.

Krekel, C., Kolbe, J., Wüstemann, H. (2016), The Greener, the Happier? The Effect of Urban Land Use on Residential Well-being, *Ecological Economics* 121, 117–127.

Krekel, C., Zerrahn, A. (2017), Does the Presence of Wind Turbines have Negative Externalities for People in their Surroundings? Evidence from Well-Being Data, *Journal of Environmental Economics and Management* 82, 221–238.

Levinson, A. (2012), Valuing Public Goods Using Happiness Data: The Case of Air Quality, *Journal of Public Economics* 96, 869–880.

Levinson, A. (2020), Happiness and Air Pollution. In: D. Maddison, K. Rehdanz, H. Welsch (eds.), *Handbook on Wellbeing, Happiness and the Environment*, Cheltenham: Edward Elgar.

Li, Q., Stoeckl, N., King, D., Gyuras, E. (2017), Exploring the Impact of Coal Mining on Host Communities in Shanxi, China – Using Subjective Data, *Resources Policy* 53, 125–134.

Lohmann, P., Pondorfer, A., Rehdanz, K. (2019), Natural Hazards and Well-Being in a Small-Scale Island Society, *Ecological Economics* 159, 344–353.

Luechinger, S. (2009), Valuing Air Quality Using the Life Satisfaction Approach, *The Economic Journal* 119, 482–515.

Luechinger, S., Raschky, P.A. (2009), Valuing Flood Disasters Using the Life Satisfaction Approach, *Journal of Public Economics* 93, 620–633.

MacKerron, G., Mourato, S. (2013), Happiness is Greater in Natural Environments, *Global Environmental Change* 23, 992–1000.

Maddison, D., Rehdanz, K. (2011), The Impact of Climate on Life Satisfaction, *Ecological Economics* 70, 2437–2445.

Maddison, D., Rehdanz, K. (2020), Cross-Country Variations in Subjective Wellbeing Explained by the Climate. In: D. Maddison, K. Rehdanz, H. Welsch (eds.), *Handbook on Wellbeing, Happiness and the Environment*, Cheltenham: Edward Elgar.

Maguire, K., Winters, J.V. (2017), Energy Boom and Gloom? Local Effects of Oil and Gas Drilling on Subjective Well-Being, *Growth and Change* 48, 590–610.

Markevych, I., Schoierer, J., Hartig, T., Chudnovsky, A., Hystad, P., Dzhambov, A.M., de Vries, S., Triguero-Mas, M., Brauer, M., Nieuwenhuijsen, M.J., Lupp, G., Richardson, E.A., Astell-Burt, T., Dimitrova, D., Feng, X., Sadeh, M., Standl, M., Heinrich, J., Fuertes, E. (2017), Exploring Pathways Linking Greenspace to Health: Theoretical and Methodological Guidance', *Environmental Research* 158, 301–317.

Mavoa, S., Davern, M., Breed, M., Hahs, A. (2019), Higher Levels of Greenness and Biodiversity Associate with Greater Subjective Wellbeing in Adults Living in Melbourne, *Australia. Health Place* 57, 321–329.

Menz, T., Welsch, H. (2012), Life-cycle and Cohort Effects in the Valuation of Air Quality: Evidence from Subjective Well-being Data, *Land Economics* 88, 300–325.

Methorst, J., Rehdanz, K., Mueller, T., Hansjürgens, B., Bonn, A., Böhning-Gaese, K. (2021), The Importance of Species Diversity for Human Well-being in Europe, *Ecological Economics* 181, 106917.

Millenium Ecosystem Assessment (MA) (2005), *Ecosystems and Human Well-Being: Synthesis Report*, Washington DC: Island Press.

Otto, F. (2020), *Angry Weather: Heat Waves, Floods, Storms, and the New Science of Climate Change*, Vancouver: Greystone Books.

Rehdanz, K. (2007), Species Diversity And Human Well-Being: A Spatial Econometric Approach, Working Papers FNU-151, Research Unit Sustainability and Global Change, Hamburg University.

Rehdanz, K., Maddison, D. (2005), Climate and Happiness, *Ecological Economics* 52, 111–125.

Rehdanz, K., Welsch, H., Narita, D., Okubo, T. (2015), Well-Being Effects of a Major Natural Disaster: The Case of Fukushima, *Journal of Economic Behavior and Organization* 116, 500–517.

Ruckelshauß, T. (2020) The Effect of Green Areas on Life Satisfaction: A Comparison of Subjective and Objective Measures. In: D. Maddison, K. Rehdanz and H. Welsch (eds.), *Handbook on Wellbeing, Happiness and the Environment*, Cheltenham: Edward Elgar Publishing.

Schmitt, M.T., Aknin, L.B., Axsen, J., Shworm, R.L. (2018), Unpacking the Relationships Between Pro-environmental Behavior, Life Satisfaction, and Perceived Ecological Threat, *Ecological Economics* 143, 130–140.

Sekulova, F., Van den Bergh, J.C.J.M. (2016), Floods and Happiness: Empirical Evidence from Bulgaria, *Ecological Economics* 126, 51–57.

Smyth, R., Nielsen, I., Zhai, Q., Liu, T., Liu, Y., Tang, C., Wang, Z., Wang, Z., Zhang, J. (2011), A Study of the Impact of Environmental Surroundings on Personal Well-Being in Urban China Using a Multi-Item Well-Being Indicator, *Population and Environment* 32, 353–375.

Videras, J.R., Owen, A.L. (2006), Public Goods Provision and Well-Being: Empirical Evidence Consistent with the Warm Glow Theory, *B.E. Journal of Economic Analysis and Policy* **5**(1).

Von Möllendorff, C., Hirschfeld, J. (2016), Measuring Impacts of Extreme Weather Events Using the Life Satisfaction Approach, *Ecological Economics* 121, 108–116.

Von Möllendorff, C., Welsch, H. (2017), Measuring Renewable Energy Externalities: Evidence from Subjective Well-Being Data, *Land Economics* 93, 107–124.

Welsch, H. (2002), Preferences over Prosperity and Pollution: Environmental Valuation based on Happiness Surveys, *Kyklos* 55, 473–494.

Welsch, H. (2006), Environment and Happiness: Valuation of Air Pollution Using Life Satisfaction Data, *Ecological Economics* 58, 801–813.

Welsch, H. (2007), Environmental Welfare Analysis: A Life Satisfaction Approach, *Ecological Economics* 62, 544–551.

Welsch, H. (2020), Happiness and Green Lifestyle. In: D. Maddison, K. Rehdanz, H. Welsch (eds.), *Handbook on Wellbeing, Happiness and the Environment*, Cheltenham: Edward Elgar.

Welsch, H., Biermann, P. (2014), Electricity Supply Preferences in Europe: Evidence from Subjective Well-Being Data, *Resource and Energy Economics* 38, 38–60.

Welsch, H., Biermann, P. (2016), Measuring Nuclear Power Plant Externalities Using Life Satisfaction Data: A Spatial Analysis for Switzerland, *Ecological Economics* 126, 98–111.

Welsch, H., Kühling, J. (2011), Are Pro-Environmental Consumption Choices Utility Maximizing? Evidence from Subjective Well-Being Data, *Ecological Economics* 72, 75–87.

Wheeler, B.W., Lovell, R., Higgins, S.L., White, M.P., Alcock, I., Osborne, N.J., Husk, K., Sabel, C.E., Depledge, M.H. (2015), Beyond Greenspace: An Ecological Study of Population General Health and Indicators of Natural Environment Type and Quality, *International Journal of Health and Geography* 14, 1–17.

White, M.P., Alcock, I., Wheeler, B.W., Depledge, M.H. (2013a), Would You Be Happier Living in a Greener Urban Area? A Fixed-Effects Analysis of Panel Data, *Psychological Science* 24, 920–928.

White, M.P., Pahl, S., Ashbullby, K.J., Herbert, S., Depledge, M.H. (2013b), Feelings of Restoration from Recent Nature Visits, *Journal of Environmental Psychology* 35, 40–51.

World Health Organization (2017), Urban Green Space Interventions and Health: A Review of Impacts and Effectiveness, WHO Regional Office for Europe, Copenhagen.

Wyles, K., White, M.P., Hattam, C., Pahl, S., Austin, M. (2019), Are Some Natural Environments More Psychologically Beneficial than Others? The Importance of Type and Quality on Connectedness to Nature and Psychological Restoration, *Environment and Behaviour* 51, 111–143.

Zander, K.K., Moss, S., Garnett, S.T. (2019), Climate Change–Related Heat Stress and Subjective Well-Being in Australia, *Weather, Climate, and Society* 11(3), DOI 10.1175/WCAS-D-18-0074.1

Part II

Economics, Morality, and the Challenges Ahead

5 Ethics and Economics

Introduction

The preceding two chapters discussed how economic and environmental circumstances, respectively, shape individuals' wellbeing. While some of those circumstances exist independent of the affected individuals' behaviors, others are the result of people's aggregate choices and those made by policy makers. The present and the following two chapters are concerned with choices through which individuals and policy makers affect (other) individuals' wellbeing.

Individuals' choices – acts and/or intentions – can positively or negatively affect other individuals' wellbeing, both intentionally (e.g., by donating to charity or stealing others' money) or unintentionally (e.g., by fighting the spread of an infectious disease through vaccination or polluting the air). As is well-known, unintentional effects on others' wellbeing that are not compensated by prices are referred to as externalities. Similarly, policy makers' choices potentially affect all citizens' wellbeing intentionally or unintentionally (through choices' unforeseen and undesired consequences). Choices that affect the wellbeing or interests of human (or nonhuman) beings different from the decision maker can be said to be *morally relevant*.

This chapter is concerned with normative principles that moral philosophy (also referred to as ethical theory or ethics) has developed in order to deal with morally relevant choices, and with applications of those principles to economic issues. Such applications have often focused on the allocation of a given amount of an asset to a set of individuals in a given period of time (e.g., the distribution of gross domestic product, GDP) or across time (e.g., the time path of depletion of a given mineral resource stock). Accordingly, with respect to economic issues, this chapter will mainly be concerned with distribution and the normative issues pertaining to it: inequality and fairness.

As suggested by the examples just mentioned – donations, vaccinations, and pollution – morally relevant choices need not refer to the distribution of a given amount of an asset (such as GDP or a mineral resource) but may involve the cooperative creation of a larger amount of an asset – charity, public health, and clean air. The moral aspects of the cooperative creation (or preservation) of public assets will be discussed in Chapters 6 and 7.

DOI: 10.4324/9781003206163-7

This chapter, by contrast, discusses ethics and economics with a focus on distribution, and it does so mainly from a normative (prescriptive) perspective, that is, by asking how people and policy makers *should* behave in morally relevant situations. Different from the normative perspective, morally relevant behavior has been studied from a positive (descriptive) perspective, that is, by asking (a) how people behave in such situations and (b) what specific moral frameworks they apply in making morally relevant choices. Issues (a) and (b) are the subjects of Chapters 6 and 7, respectively, with a focus on the cooperative creation or preservation of public assets, notably the climate.

Consequentialism and Deontology

Consequentialism considers human behaviors by focusing on their (expected) outcomes (consequences), whereas deontology considers behaviors by focusing on their inherent nature. Consequentialist and deontological approaches can be found both in positive and normative analysis, that is, in accounts of how people *do* behave and how they *should* behave in morally relevant situations.

Consequentialism and Deontology in Positive Analysis of Choice

Before discussing normative (ethical) issues it is useful to briefly consider consequentialism and deontology in the context of the positive analysis of choice.

The standard economic model of choices and behaviors is based on a consequentialist paradigm, which assumes that individuals choose among alternative actions solely based on how actions' expected outcomes will affect individuals' interests. Actions, in other words, have only instrumental value, no value *per se*. For instance, people work to earn income (outcome), not because work may convey a sense of purpose and fulfilment independent of monetary benefits.

Some of the evidence discussed in Chapter 3 suggests that the purely instrumental view of work may be flawed: the unemployed display substantially lower levels of subjective wellbeing than the employed even controlling for the loss in income that may go with unemployment. Working (being employed or self-employed) thus seems to have a wellbeing benefit in itself.

Further evidence that actions may be taken for their own sake comes from observed behavior with respect to public goods. In settings of voluntary public good provision that involve many independent actors, a major prediction of consequentialist economics is that – due to free rider incentives – voluntary contributions are virtually zero. Importantly, this prediction does not rely on assuming self-regarding preferences but is obtained even with other-regarding (altruistic) preferences: even if potential contributors care for the benefits that others derive from a public good, the effect of any individual's contribution on the overall level of the public good is negligible, and so is an individual's predicted consequence-related contribution. Yet, as famously noted with respect to charitable giving, people systematically make substantial contributions to public goods even in large economies (Andreoni 1988). To explain such behavior, it has been proposed that people experience a "warm glow" from the very act of contributing (Andreoni 1990). The evidence discussed in Chapter 4 of people deriving subjective wellbeing from engaging in pro-environmental behaviors is consistent with this view.

The systematic violation of consequentialist predictions has led economists to consider behavioral frameworks that complement the traditional consequentialist view with deontological considerations. While consequentialism assumes that people evaluate actions – and choose among alternatives – based on actions' expected outcomes, the deontological approach assumes that people evaluate actions themselves.

As suggested by the example of charitable giving and other contributions to public goods, the distinction between consequentialist and deontological behavior should not be confused with the distinction between egoistic (self-regarding) and altruistic (other-regarding) behavior. In particular, altruistic and deontological behaviors are not the same. While altruistically motivated behaviors are undertaken in the interest of some favorable outcomes to others, deontological behaviors are undertaken regardless of outcome-focused considerations.

Consequentialist and Deontological Ethical Theories

Consequentialist and deontological behavioral (that is, positive) theories correspond to two traditions in ethical (that is, normative) theory: consequentialist ethics (Sinnott-Armstrong 2019) and deontological ethics (Alexander and Moore 2021). Consequentialist ethics includes Utilitarianism (in the tradition of John Stuart Mill) whereas deontological ethics includes (and is sometimes equated with) duty ethics (in the tradition of Immanuel Kant). According to consequentialist ethics, moral evaluation of some action should be based on the expected outcome of that action. In contrast, deontological ethics focuses on the duty to take the morally right action, irrespective of outcomes.

The remainder of this section discusses consequentialism and deontology as general ethical theories, whereas the next sections discuss applications of consequentialism to normative economic issues.

Consequentialist Ethics

Consequentialist ethics holds that choices – acts and/or intentions – are to be morally assessed solely by the states of affairs they bring about. Consequentialists thus must specify initially the states of affairs that are intrinsically valuable – often called, collectively, "the Good." They then are in a position to assert that whatever choices increase the Good, that is, bring about more of it, are the choices that morality demands to make and to execute. The Good in that sense is said to be prior to "the Right."

Consequentialists differ widely in terms of specifying the Good. An important variety of consequentialism, Utilitarianism, for example, identifies the Good with "utility", that is, pleasure, happiness, desire satisfaction, or well-being in some other sense. While conventional Utilitarianism merely adds or averages each person's share of the Good to achieve the Good's maximization (see more on this later), other consequentialists believe that how the Good is distributed among persons (or all sentient beings) is itself partly constitutive of the Good. Moreover, there are some consequentialists who hold that the assurance of rights, including property rights, belongs to the state of affairs constitutive of the Good to be maximized – the so-called Utilitarianism of rights (Nozick 1974).

Consequentialism is frequently criticized on a number of grounds. One is that it may be difficult to foresee the consequences of one's actions. Another criticism refers to what consequentialism seemingly permits or demands. It seemingly demands that, in certain circumstances, innocents be killed, beaten, lied to, or deprived of material goods to produce greater benefits for others. Consequences – and only consequences – can conceivably justify *any* kind of act, for it does not matter how harmful it is to some so long as it is more beneficial to others.

Deontological Ethics

While consequentialist ethics focuses on the Good, deontological ethics focuses on the Right: Some choices are demanded, permitted, or forbidden not because of their good or bad consequences, but because they are deemed intrinsically right or wrong, irrespective of consequences.

What makes a choice right is its conformity with a moral norm. Based on which individuals a moral norm is centered on, deontological theories can be differentiated into agent-centered and victim-centered (or "patient-centered") theories. Agent-centered theories focus on the obligations or *duties* agents have, whereas patient-centered theories are premised on people's *rights*. A core right is the right against being used only as means for producing good consequences without one's consent. Such a core right is to be distinguished from more discrete rights, such as the right against being killed, or being killed intentionally (Alexander and Moore 2021).

Deontological and consequentialist ethics may imply conflicting prescriptions as to which actions are to be taken, and a conflict between deontological and consequentialist prescriptions is often at the heart of *moral dilemmas*. For example, the so-called trolley problem involves stylized ethical dilemmas of whether to kill one person to save a larger number (Jarvis Thomson 1985) – which (considering the act) is ruled out by deontology, but (considering the outcome) seems to be demanded by (Utilitarian) consequentialism. Other examples involve situations where compliance with deontological norms will bring about disastrous consequences. For instance, suppose that unless a decision maker violates the deontological duty not to torture an innocent person, ten, or a thousand, or a million other innocent people will die because of a hidden nuclear device.

In spite of the possibility that compliance with deontological norms may bring about consequences that common sense would deem intolerable, some typical justifications of deontological norms suggest that consequences are not irrelevant to deontological ethics. Kant's insistence that the maxims on which one acts be capable of being willed as a universal law (Kant 1785) is a case in point: if compliance with those maxims (moral norms) would systematically lead to inappropriate consequences, it could hardly be "willed as a universal law". Justification of a moral norm in terms of the societal consequences of its adoption or dismissal may be viewed as consequentialism of the second order.

A similar link between deontological norms and the consequences of complying with them comes from the functionalist view of human morality (Tomasello 2016), which maintains that precisely those moral norms have evolved in (human) natural history which – by facilitating and enhancing cooperation – are beneficial to the survival of those groups whose members comply with them (see Chapter 7). Such an evolutionary advantage from acting morally will arise as a statistical tendency, irrespective of single instances where consequences may be bad. In addition, acting morally, according to norms "approved by evolution", may be a useful way of dealing with uncertainties regarding the consequences of actions in particular situations. Acting according to moral norms may reduce the mental costs of decision making.

Normative Accounts in Economics

The remainder of this chapter discusses the ethical (normative) branch of economic theory, applications thereof to the economics of natural resources and the climate, and some empirical evidence on ethical behavior with respect to economic choices.

Welfare Economics

Welfare economics is the normative branch of economic analysis. While positive economics deals with how an economy works and what outcomes it brings about, welfare economics is concerned with the normative evaluation of outcomes from the point of view of societal wellbeing, and the characterization of those outcomes that are desirable against the relevant normative standards. By focusing on outcomes, welfare economics relies on consequentialist ethics and applies it to economic issues.

The fundamental normative principle of welfare economics is efficiency. A configuration of economic outcomes – an allocation – is said to be efficient if there exists no feasible alternative allocation such that at least one economic agent is better off while no agent is worse off. A change of affairs (reallocation) such that at least one agent is better off and no agent is worse off is called a Pareto improvement. A way of describing an efficient state is thus by saying that no Pareto improvement is feasible. Accordingly, efficiency so defined is often referred to as Pareto efficiency.

The notion of Pareto efficiency seems intuitively appealing and uncontroversial: a situation in which it is possible to make one agent better off without making anyone worse off seems unsatisfactory (inefficient), and making use of the possibility of Pareto improvement can be supposed to lead to a more satisfactory and, hence, preferred state of affairs in most people's view. Whether this is indeed the case will be discussed further later in this chapter. For now, the adequacy of the Pareto criterion for evaluating economic outcomes will be taken for granted.

While Pareto efficiency seems to be a convincing concept, it provides a weak criterion for discriminating between alternative allocations because the set of efficient allocations may be large. For example, if a fixed amount of 100 dollars is to be allocated to two persons, any split that sums up to 100 is efficient because any re-allocation would make one person better off while making the other worse off relative to the initial state. All feasible allocations are thus efficient in this example. Deciding whether one allocation is "better" than another is not possible on efficiency grounds, but requires additional, stronger criteria.

In contrast to this example, more complex economic settings may involve efficient as well as inefficient outcomes, such that efficiency is a useful criterion for the screening of outcomes. Yet, the example is suggestive of the fact that the efficiency criterion often implies indifference with respect to many outcomes and needs to be complemented by stronger normative criteria that allow the ranking of several efficient outcomes.

The tool used by welfare economists in order to rank and evaluate alternative economic outcomes is the *social welfare function*. Considering an economy composed of a given set of agents (individuals), a social welfare function aggregates the various agents' individual utilities into a measure of social welfare. Utility, in this conception, is "experienced utility" (Kahneman et al. 1997), that is, hedonic experience or subjective wellbeing. In ethical terms, social welfare is the Good against which actions, policies, or rules are to be evaluated. Each individual's utility may, in principle, depend, via her *utility function*, on the entire configuration of outcomes. In particular, it may depend not just on the individual's own personal circumstances but also on the circumstances of others.

Properties of the social welfare function can either be postulated on the basis of some general normative considerations and axioms – the prescriptive approach – or be derived from individuals' ethical stance on their own and others' utility – the descriptive approach. An axiom typically invoked in the prescriptive approach is impartiality: individual utilities are to be evaluated from the point of view of an impartial external subject (which does not rule out utility weighting, if justified by some ethical principle). Since much of welfare economics has pursued the prescriptive approach, the following discussion will start from a prescriptive perspective.

A question that arises in welfare analysis, as in consequentialist ethics more generally, concerns the set of entities over whom consequences count, that is: who qualifies as an "agent", with utility to be included in the social-welfare function? Some have argued that not just human beings but all sentient beings – beings capable of experiencing pleasure and pain – should be included (Singer 1993). In this view, utility is a characteristic of sentience, not only humanity. The typical view taken by welfare economists, however, is human-focused (anthropocentric), restricting the set of relevant agents to human beings. Importantly, this does not by itself imply irrelevance of nonhuman beings for social welfare. Animal welfare, for example, may well be among the set of outcomes that enter humans' utility functions.

The concepts of individual utility and social welfare used in welfare economic frameworks are unobserved notional constructs. An important question is whether measures of utility are to be treated as ordinal or cardinal variables. A merely ordinal interpretation takes a decrease in utility to indicate that some change in circumstances makes an individual worse off, but the quantitative extent of the deterioration is indeterminate. The latter implies, in particular, that a decrease in an individual's utility that results from redistributing some asset from her to another individual cannot be quantitatively compared to the increase in utility that the other individual experiences as a result of redistribution. Consequently, it is impossible to decide whether a redistribution leads to an outcome that is better or worse from a societal point of view. The aim of ranking and evaluating economic outcomes is thus missed if a utility measure has only ordinal significance.

If we want to aggregate over measures of individual utility in order to rank and evaluate economic outcomes (other than those that can be ranked in terms of the Pareto criterion), utility measures must thus be cardinal, rather than merely ordinal. That means: numerically larger changes of a utility measure within an individual or larger differences between individuals affect social welfare more than do smaller changes or differences. In particular, an increase in one individual's utility that is larger than the associated decrease in another individual's utility is welfare increasing (other things equal).

While cardinality has been considered by some to be an unrealistic assumption, the discussion in Chapter 2 suggests that self-assessed wellbeing may be a reasonably valid measure of experienced utility to permit meaningful welfare analysis. In addition, some evidence discussed in Chapter 4 suggests that subjective measures of wellbeing depend on aspects of the nonhuman biosphere such as species richness. This aligns well with the idea that concern for the welfare of nonhuman beings may be included in (human) individuals' utility functions.

In sum, welfare economics is a variety of consequentialist ethics applied to normative economic issues. Welfare economics conceives of the Good as *social welfare* specified as an aggregate of individual utilities, which depend on outcomes irrespective of any inherent properties of the choices whose consequences those outcomes are. Utility-relevant outcomes may be not just an individual's personal circumstances but also those of other human and nonhuman beings.

Varieties of welfare economics differ in how they specify the aggregation of individual utilities into social welfare. The most prominent varieties are the Utilitarian and the Rawlsian approaches.

Utilitarian Welfare Economics

Welfare economics, as discussed up to this point, is often referred to as Utilitarianism, as it uses utility as its key concept. A more specific view takes as the defining characteristic of Utilitarianism a particular way of aggregating individual utilities into a measure of social welfare. Building on Bentham's "fundamental axiom" that welfare is "the greatest happiness of the greatest number" (Bentham 1789), Utilitarianism, in this sense, conceives of social welfare as a sum of individual utilities. Those individual utilities may enter either as such or, alternatively, multiplied by weighting factors (weights). Moreover, as is common in standard economics, the individual utility functions are assumed to show diminishing marginal utility with respect to the sources of utility. For example, if the only source of an individual's utility is her level of income, the increase in utility from an (arbitrarily small) increase in income (referred to as marginal utility of income) is smaller at higher levels of income than at lower levels of income. Conversely, a requirement that the marginal utility of income be large implies that the corresponding *level* of income be small.

Utilitarian welfare economics, as such, does not carry any implications with respect to the distribution of income between the members of a society, in particular considering that, rather than being exogenously given, aggregate income (GDP) is the result of economic activities that may be discouraged by the "threat" of redistribution. Disregarding the latter aspect for a moment, however, it is instructive to consider how a fixed total quantity of income should be distributed if total welfare is to be maximized.

Consider the case that welfare is the unweighted sum of individual utilities. Allocating a fixed total amount of income to the various agents, such as to maximize social welfare, then requires that marginal utilities be equalized across agents. To see this, assume that the marginal utility of one agent was smaller than that of another agent. It would then be possible to increase social welfare by reallocating some income from the first to the second agent, because the second agent's gain in utility would exceed the first agent's loss in utility. Whenever marginal utilities differ between agents, there is thus a potential for welfare-increasing reallocations.

The implications for the levels of income to be allocated to the various agents are clear if the agents' utility functions are identical: equalization of agents' marginal utilities implies equalization of their levels of income. With social welfare being the unweighted sum of identical utility functions, welfare maximization implies an equal distribution of income. With social welfare being a weighted sum of identical utility functions, welfare maximization implies equalization of agents' *weighted* marginal utilities. Smaller weights then imply larger (unweighted) marginal utilities, which (by virtue of diminishing marginal utility) requires that the corresponding level of income be smaller. A smaller weight on an agent's utility thus implies that less income is allocated to her, whereas a larger weight implies more income being allocated to her.

Things are more complicated if utility functions differ between individuals. With unweighted utilities, equalization of marginal utilities continues to be required for a welfare maximum, but this condition can only be satisfied if agents' levels of income differ. Specifically, assume that agent A enjoys a higher level of utility than agent B for any level of income, because A is more efficient at turning income into utility than B. This means, in other words, that A's marginal utility is greater than B's if both have the same level of income. In order to equalize marginal utilities (by decreasing A's and increasing B's marginal utility), the property of diminishing marginal utility implies that income be reallocated from B to A. In the end, equalization of marginal utilities, as required for a welfare maximum to obtain, implies less income being allocated to the less efficient agent.

This result may be considered paradoxical and ethically undesired. Not only does it imply less income being allocated to less-efficient individuals, but the difference in efficiency implies that this income inequality to the disadvantage of less efficient individuals translates into even greater inequality of utilities. Suppose an individual is less efficient than another because she suffers from depression. Would we then want to say that this result is fair?

This is the first example of an intuitively attractive ethical principle leading to a questionable outcome: striving for the greatest sum of happiness may work at the expense of the happiness of some. It is indicative of a potential tension between level-focused and distribution-focused normative criteria.

One way of addressing the apparent unfairness of Utilitarianism with unweighted individual utilities is by defining welfare as a weighted sum of utilities with more weight given to the less efficient individuals. Another is to replace the Utilitarian idea of additive welfare with a more distribution-focused (justice-focused) scheme.

Rawlsian Welfare Economics

An alternative to Utilitarianism that can fix the deficiency just discussed is Rawls' *Theory of Justice* (Rawls 1971). While Utilitarianism has been the most common welfare-economic application of consequentialist ethics over much of the 19th and 20th centuries, Rawlsian welfare economics has gained considerable prominence since it was developed in the early 1970s.

Rawls' intention was to identify principles of justice and social order that would be agreed on by everyone if we could impartially consider alternative social arrangements. To ascertain impartiality, he employed the device of imagining a hypothetical state of affairs prior to any ethical principles and social arrangements – the original position. In the original position, individuals exist behind a "veil of ignorance": each person has no knowledge of her inherited characteristics (such as intelligence, personality traits, physical and mental health), nor of the position she would take in any agreed social structure. He asserts that, behind the veil of ignorance, (risk-averse) individuals would opt for an arrangement that implies the best result – the maximum possible utility – for the least advantaged (because everybody considers the least advantaged could be them).

The focus of social arrangements on the least advantaged – derived this way – can be cast into a social welfare function that identifies welfare with the minimum across individuals of individual utilities. To illustrate, if society consists of just two individuals, A and B, social welfare is equal to whichever is the smaller, the utility of A or B.

The distributional implications of maximizing a Rawlsian social welfare function can be seen as follows. Assume that A's utility is greater than B's. Then welfare equals B's utility, and it can be increased by raising the latter – but only to the point where B's utility does not exceed A's utility (otherwise, welfare would become equal to A's utility). The only configuration of utilities where welfare cannot be increased through interpersonal transfers of utility is that where A's and B's (and everybody else's) utilities are equal.

Returning to the scenario in which the only source of utility is income and the total level of income is fixed, Rawlsian welfare maximization implies a distribution of income that yields equality of utilities. With identical utility functions, this means that income should be distributed equally – just as in the case of a Utilitarian social welfare function. With nonidentical utility functions, it means that individuals who are less efficient in deriving utility from income should get more income than more efficient individuals – the opposite to what the Utilitarian framework (without utility weights) implies.

In sum, the Rawlsian *Theory of Justice* implies that a state of affairs is just if it provides all individuals with equal utility. In terms of policy, this suggests, in particular, that public policy should strive to compensate for all differences in utility that come from differences in inherited characteristics.

While the principle of equal utility can be derived as just described, Rawls makes an important qualification to the equal-utility principle. He observes that the least-advantaged individuals' utility that is *attainable* may depend on the social arrangements in place, notably redistribution policy. If striving for equalization of utility – by income redistribution – discourages some individuals from working, such that the total redistributable amount of income gets reduced, the least advantaged might attain a higher level of *absolute* utility if some *difference* in utilities were admitted. Accordingly, the so-called difference principle takes account of a potential trade-off between equality and social efficiency: striving for equality of utility should stop at a point where it implies a loss in efficiency so large as to reduce the utility of the least advantaged.

The difference principle, as applied to income, relies on the assumption that individuals' utility depends exclusively on their own (absolute) income. It gets less relevant the more utility depends on relative, rather than absolute, income. As discussed in Chapter 3, concern for relative income and income inequality seems to be an important feature of individuals' utility (wellbeing) functions. The question, then, is whether admitting greater inequality in the interest of potentially higher aggregate income implies wellbeing benefits for the least advantaged.

Ethics and Natural Resource Utilization

Since the 1970s, welfare economic analysis has routinely been applied to normative issues of natural resource utilization: how should natural resources be used from the point of view of social welfare? The pertinent analyses have differentiated between nonrenewable resources and renewable resources. Nonrenewable resources, such as coal, mineral oil, and natural gas, are available in fixed total quantities, whereas renewable resources, such as fish or forests, are subject to inherent dynamic change due to biological processes. The climate system can also be regarded as a renewable resource, as it is governed by dynamic processes, though not biological but physical ones.

In contrast to the welfare economic issues discussed so far, the normative analysis of natural resource utilization necessarily involves a time dimension. With respect to nonrenewable resources, the issue is how to allocate a fixed resource stock across time; with respect to renewable resources, the issue is to find time paths of utilization that are consistent with the preservation of the respective natural asset. In both cases, the standard approach has been human-focused (anthropocentric). The anthropocentric view implies that nonrenewable resources are of *use value* to humans. Renewable resources may, in addition, have *existence value*: people may derive a psychological benefit from the existence of the Siberian tiger and its habitat. Use value and existence value may involve a trade-off.

Given that a key issue of normative resource economics is allocation across time (intertemporal allocation), issues of resource allocation *within* time periods will be neglected in this section. The approach is thus to ask how an impartial decision maker, who acts on behalf of the present and future "generations", should act such as to maximize intertemporal (intergenerational) welfare. The latter is understood as an aggregate of the various generations' utilities, and the pertinent utility functions are typically assumed to be identical to that of the "first" generation, as it is difficult to come up with meaningful assumptions as to precisely how future generations' utility functions might differ from the present generation's utility function.

The Cake-Eating Problem

A straightforward application of the preceding section's discussion to the use of nonrenewable resources is the so-called cake-eating problem (Perman et al. 2011). It involves the assumption that the consumption of a natural resource, whose total amount is fixed and finite, is a direct source of utility. The issue, then, is to allocate the fixed resource stock (the cake) to the various generations so as to maximize intergenerational social welfare.

Given the assumption of identical utility functions of the various generations, it is clear that both the Utilitarian approach without utility weighting and the Rawlsian approach imply an equal distribution of the resource stock across generations. This prescription, however, is infeasible to execute if the number of generations is infinite – which is more reasonable to assume than the alternative of extinction of mankind in a known future time period. The issue simply is that a finite "cake" cannot meaningfully be divided into infinitely many pieces of equal size.

A meaningful solution to the cake-eating problem with infinitely many generations exists if one assumes a Utilitarian welfare function with a particular kind of utility weighting. In this approach, welfare is specified as the sum of *discounted* generation-specific utilities, that is, utilities multiplied by generation-specific discount factors that are smaller for more distant time periods. For example, defining the length of a generation to be 30 years and assuming a constant annual discount *rate* of 0.02 (2 percent), the discount *factor* (weight) for the next generation's utility is $(1/(1.02))^{30} = 0.55$ while being 1 for the present generation's utility. Maximization of the sum of discounted (that is, present-value) utilities, which implies that the various generations' discounted marginal utilities be equal, then requires the resource stock to be allocated in such a way that the next generation's current-value marginal utility be $1/0.55 = 1.82$ times larger than the present generation's marginal utility.

Given the property of decreasing marginal utility, the requirement that the next generation's marginal utility be larger than the present generation's translates into a smaller portion of the resource stock being allocated to the next generation than to the present generation. As the discount factor gets smaller for more distant generations, so does the portion of the resource stock allocated to them. The welfare maximizing path of resource use is thus steadily decreasing over time and approaches zero as time goes to infinity. Its level can be calibrated in such a way that cumulative resource use over an infinite time horizon just matches the finite stock.

While discounting future utility solves the cake-eating problem, it is a controversial issue from the point of view of moral philosophy: why should future generations' utility have less value than the present generation's utility in a measure of welfare that respects the axiom of impartiality? One reason for using ever-decreasing utility weights for the more distant future (in spite of impartiality) may be the risk of extinction of mankind as time passes, for example, due to meteorite impacts or new viruses. Maximization of a discounted sum of utilities would then come down to maximization of expected utility.

The numerical value of the annual utility discount rate that can be justified by such reasoning – the risk of extinction per year – arguably is much smaller than 2 percent, as was assumed above for the purpose of illustration. Assuming it to be 0.001 (0.1 percent) instead would mean that the present value of utility arising 30 years (one generation) from now is 97 percent of the value of utility arising now.

Natural Resources and Sustainability

While the cake-eating problem may serve to illustrate some fundamental normative issues in the utilization of natural resources across time, it is not very realistic in that it assumes natural resources to be consumption goods that serve as direct sources of utility. More realistically, natural resources serve as production inputs together with a non-natural asset, that is, a production input that has been produced previously and accumulates over time (capital). In such a framework, the analysis of nonrenewable resource use involves the following elements: (a) a production function that shows how aggregate output is produced using the natural resource and capital inputs; (b) an accounting equation that says that output can either be used for investment or consumption; (c) an accumulation equation that shows how the capital stock evolves as a result of investment and depreciation; (d) a natural resource constraint that says that the sum across time of the natural resource inputs cannot exceed a fixed total amount; and (e) a social welfare function that aggregates the utilities of the various "generations". In the case of nonrenewable resources, the utilities are functions solely of the levels of consumption available to those generations. In the case of (some) renewable resources, utility may, in addition, depend on the size and quality of resource stocks. The dependence of subjective wellbeing on species richness, discussed in Chapter 4, is a case in point.

The ethical issues of the intergenerational allocation of natural resources continue to be captured by the intergenerational social welfare function, which the social decision maker is assumed to maximize. The solution to the maximization problem depends not only on details of the welfare function, in particular if and how future utilities are discounted, but of the production function, in particular the ease with which natural resources can be substituted by capital (including human capital, that is, knowledge). Therefore, a variety of results can arise, depending on circumstances (Perman et al. 2011).

One issue to be discussed in this context is *sustainability*. In the welfare economic analysis of natural resource use, sustainability is taken to mean non-declining utility over time. If the only source of utility is consumption, non-declining utility is equivalent to non-declining consumption. Two questions arise: (a) is a sustainable consumption path feasible in the framework just described, and (b) is it welfare maximizing?

The answer to question (a) is yes, provided that it is sufficiently easy to substitute capital for the natural resource, that is, to use the two inputs in variable proportions. Then it is possible to use ever smaller quantities of the resource while using ever greater quantities of capital, keeping output (as well as investment and consumption) constant. If the degree of substitutability is below a critical value, constant output cannot be sustained this way. In particular, if the two inputs can only be used in fixed proportions, constant output (and hence constant utility) requires a constant level of the resource input, which, as discussed earlier, is not possible with a finite nonrenewable resource stock and an infinite time horizon.

Assuming that the degree of substitutability between capital and the natural resource is large enough to allow for a constant level of consumption and utility, question (b) arises: is such a path welfare-maximizing? Considering the Utilitarian notion of welfare, the welfare-maximizing time path of consumption depends on the discount rate. Under the high-substitutability assumption, a solution to the welfare-maximization problem exists whether future utilities are discounted or not. If they are not, it turns out – maybe surprisingly – that a welfare maximum implies an *increasing* time path of consumption (Perman et al. 2011). The logic is that, without discounting, the present generation accumulates "too much" capital to its own disadvantage (through foregoing consumption) and the advantage of future generations (allowing them to produce and consume more).

This is another example of an intuitively attractive ethical principle – abdication of utility discounting – leading to an unexpected and possibly undesired result. In the Utilitarian framework, if increasing consumption levels are deemed undesired, some discounting of future utility is required to prevent "excessive" capital accumulation. Similar to the case of (intra-temporal) income distribution discussed earlier, a Rawlsian intertemporal (or intergenerational) welfare function will deliver a constant level of utility as the welfare maximum.

Ethics and Climate Change

The discussion up to this point focused on nonrenewable natural resources, and the pertinent ethical issues were seen to be rooted in their availability in finite quantities, to be allocated across time. This issue does not exist in the case of renewable resources; they can be used at a constant rate forever, provided that rate does not exceed those resources' regenerative capacities.

Typical examples are biological resources, such as forests and fisheries. However, while not a biological resource, the global atmosphere has some characteristics of a renewable resource. Similar to biological resources being diminished (harmed) by harvesting, the atmosphere is harmed by the deposition and accumulation of certain gases that arise from economic activities – mainly energy use; and similar to biological resources regenerating through biological processes, the atmosphere regenerates by chemical processes through which those gases decay over time.

These similarities notwithstanding, there is an important difference: the "impairment" of biological resources, through harvesting, mainly refers to their quantity (biomass), whereas the impairment of the atmosphere is of a qualitative nature: the gases in question, so-called greenhouse gases, change parameters of the global climate, notably the global temperature, which has adverse effects on human activities and human wellbeing (Chapter 4). Since the emissions of greenhouse gases (measured in terms of carbon dioxide) have exceeded the regenerative capacity for many decades, the atmospheric greenhouse gas concentration has risen, and so has the global temperature (global warming). Unless emissions are reduced from their current level, global warming is expected to continue.

Intertemporal Issues

A major ethical issue in releasing greenhouse gases into the atmosphere stems from the fact that the associated economic benefit (from the activities that cause the emissions) arises at present, whereas the adverse effects from global warming arise predominantly in the future. Likewise, the benefits from reducing greenhouse gases arise mainly in the future, whereas the costs arise at present.

In this situation, questions to be asked are: What time path of greenhouse gas mitigation maximizes intertemporal welfare? Or what is the net benefit or cost, in welfare terms, of pursuing a given mitigation target? In both cases, the specification of the welfare function and the choice of a discount rate, if any, are crucial.

The question as to the welfare consequences of pursuing a given mitigation target was studied in the Stern Review (Stern 2007), commissioned by the British government. The approach was to use a so-called integrated assessment model, which models the interaction between the global economic system and the climate system. Welfare was specified in terms of an intertemporal Utilitarian social welfare function, in which utility depends on consumption, which, in turn, depends on the use of fossil energies. Future utilities were discounted at an annual rate of 0.1 percent to account for a hypothetical risk of extinction, as discussed earlier. Small as the figure may appear, it means to assume that there is a 10 percent chance of extinction within the next 100 years. The analysis considered a business-as-usual scenario and a mitigation scenario. In the mitigation scenario it was assumed that the global greenhouse gas concentration was to be stabilized at 550 parts per million, which climate science said would require that by 2050 global emissions be 25 percent lower than in 2000. Given projected population growth, emissions per capita would need to fall to half of 2000 levels.

It was found that the damage in terms of money-metric present-value welfare of following a business-as-usual emission path was equivalent to a 10.9 percent reduction in global per capita consumption, whereas in the mitigation scenario damage would amount to 1.1 percent. This reduction of damage by almost 10 percent far exceeded the associated costs, which were estimated at 1 percent. Results are, however, sensitive to the choice of the discount rate. In answering to critics of the Stern Review, it was found that increasing the discount rate from 0.1 percent to 0.15 percent implies that the present value of damage, which mainly occurs in the future, gets reduced from 10.9 to 3.1 percent of per capita consumption (Dietz et al. 2007). Whether an extinction probability of 0.15 percent per year (equivalent to 14 percent per century) is more realistic than the already disquietingly high assumption of 10 percent per century is an open question.

As this example illustrates, the utility discount rate is of paramount importance for any assessment of the damage from global warming. Its importance can further be demonstrated in terms of the implied welfare costs to current and future generations of an additional ton of greenhouse gases, referred to as the social cost of carbon (SCC). While, using the model of Nordhaus (2008), SCC is estimated to be US$120 (at 2007 prices) under Stern's assumption (0.1 percent), the assumption, made in the work of Nordhaus, of a utility discount rate of 1.5 percent leads to an estimate of US$30 (Heal and Millner 2014, Figure 1).

When it comes to welfare-maximizing climate policy, the Nordhaus assumption leads to "optimal" global emissions by 2050 that are fairly similar to those in 2000 (rather than being 25 percent lower, as assumed in the Stern mitigation scenario), with an associated peak of global average temperature (arising around 2100) well above the 2°C limit postulatedt in the Paris climate agreement of 2015 (Nordhaus 2019).

It is clear that a utility discount rate of 1.5 percent per year is inconsistent with an interpretation in terms of extinction probabilities. However, while it was assumed that – given the postulate of impartiality – future utilities should be discounted only to reflect the likelihood of extinction, another view is that its choice represents a person's ethical judgment of how much she cares about the welfare of future generations. "As such, it is a parameter that is unique to each person; much like the moral legitimacy of the death penalty or abortion rights, it is the kind of thing reasonable people may reasonably disagree about. Once we adopt this position, it becomes clear that the economist's role is not to impose his or her own preferences on society, but rather to adopt a welfare framework that aims to represent the distribution of ethical views" (Heal and Millner 2014, 3695).

This view clearly follows a descriptive rather than prescriptive approach to intergenerational welfare. Instead of postulating the ethical position to be an impartial one, what matters is the ethical stance of the present generation. The weight attached to future generations' utility then captures the degree of the current generation's intergenerational altruism. The weight on future generations' utility thus may be lower than that on the current generation's utility, and it may be decreasing with respect to temporal distance.

It may be noted that, in spite of the explicitly descriptive nature of the aforementioned reasoning, utility weights that decrease in distance may nevertheless be interpreted against a prescriptive ethical background: they can be viewed as capturing decreasing moral obligations toward more distant individuals. This is consistent with Adam Smith's prescriptive view, taken in *The Theory of Moral Sentiments*, that moral obligations toward more distant people are less than those to people close (see Chapter 1).

Intra-Generational Issues

While the time path of global emissions is one ethical issue in the normative economics of climate change, another is the allocation of the global emission budget (or global reduction requirements) to the nations of the world.

There are two main focal principles for such allocation (Grubb 1995): egalitarianism, which implies an equal-per-capita allocation, and sovereignty, where allocation is based on status quo. The equal-per-capita allocation corresponds to the justice principle of "equality of resources", suggesting that all human beings should be entitled to an equal share of the atmospheric resource. Similar to an equal distribution of income discussed earlier, equality of emissions can be derived both from a Utilitarian framework with identical utility functions and a Rawlsian framework, where utility is modeled as a function of emissions in both cases. At the opposite end of the spectrum, a strict status quo allocation – proportionate to current emissions – has been considered. According to this view, current emissions would constitute a status quo right established by past usage and custom. Sovereignty suggests that an equal percentage emission reduction from the status quo is equitable.

A pragmatic argument against egalitarianism refers to the circumstance that per capita emissions in the status quo are very different across countries. By 2000, for example, carbon emissions per capita ranged from 0.21 tons in sub-Saharan Africa to 5.23 tons in North America. An instantaneous transition to equal emissions per capita – at a level consistent with global mitigation requirements – would therefore come at tremendous costs in high-emission nations. This speaks in favor of equal percentage reductions in the short term.

A natural way of reconciling the opposing approaches is implementing a steadily decreasing global emission pathway by a gradual transition from sovereignty to egalitarianism, a concept known as *contraction and convergence*. This would involve a gradual adjustment from current emission patterns toward a terminal point where future entitlements to emit will have become proportional to population. In a scenario where global per capita emissions would have to be reduced by half between 2000 and 2050, such a schedule would permit current (poor) low-emission nations to even increase their emissions per capita, whereas those of (rich) high-emission nations would be reduced (Böhringer and Welsch 2006).

While a compromise between alternative normative positions seems feasible and attractive, participants in real-world climate negotiations have endorsed those equity principles whose application would benefit the respective parties most. Specifically, the perceived support of equity criteria appears to be the stronger the less costly this criterion is to a nation compared to alternative criteria. This applies, in particular, to the United States' endorsement of the sovereignty principle. Contrary to the tendency to use equity principles in a self-serving manner, the EU is seen as supporting a criterion that favors poor countries expected to suffer strongly from climate change (Lange et al. 2010).

In addition to conflicts between alternative equity principles, the allocation of an emission budget to countries may involve a conflict between equity, however defined, and efficiency. Efficiency, in this context, means cost effectiveness, that is, the minimization of the overall costs of staying within the global emission budget. Some equity principles may imply large emission abatement requirements for countries where abatement is expensive, thus driving up overall costs. A solution to possible equity-efficiency conflicts consists of tradable emission rights. In this approach, shares in the global budget are allocated to countries on the basis of some equity criteria, but high-cost countries can buy additional emission rights from low-cost countries. In this way, legal abatement duties are decoupled from actual abatement action. As a result of the trade in emission rights, abatement then will take place in countries where it is relatively inexpensive. Combining the *contraction and convergence* approach with the tradability of emission rights was found to lead to a considerable estimated reduction in global abatement costs and significant financial flows from rich to poor countries (Böhringer and Welsch 2006).

Ethical Behavior and Fairness Preference: Some Evidence

As noted earlier, the fundamental normative criterion employed in welfare economics, Pareto efficiency, appears intuitively attractive. It seems natural to consider an economic outcome (allocation) as unsatisfactory if an alternative allocation is feasible in which (at least) one agent is better off without anyone else being worse off. Only if such improvements – Pareto improvements – cease to be feasible is an appropriate state of affairs reached. Hence, with given constraints on feasibility, efficient allocations – those that do not allow for Pareto improvements – are preferred over inefficient ones, irrespective of any other characteristics of those allocations.

Using Pareto efficiency as a normative criterion involves the tacit assumption that characteristics of allocations other than Pareto superiority/inferiority are irrelevant to the evaluation of outcomes. A question that has been studied in recent decades is whether this assumption is descriptively valid with respect to people's evaluation of alternative allocations of income. A possibility that has been considered is that Pareto efficiency may be in conflict with another ethical value: distributive fairness. While standard – prescriptive – welfare economics postulates a preference of Pareto efficient allocations over Pareto inefficient ones irrespective of distributive concerns, the question is whether such a preference exists in a descriptive sense.

In studying fairness preferences, it is necessary to specify the meaning of fairness. The notion usually considered is that of fairness as absence of (excessive) inequality. From an inequality perspective, fairness concerns are closely related to positional, or relative, concerns, in particular deprivation. Chapter 3 has considered inequality and relative concerns from the point of view of subjective wellbeing and has shown that income inequality (on the societal level) and income deprivation (on the individual level) are associated with lower wellbeing. Those results are consistent with a preference for fairness.

Another way of studying fairness preferences is by using economic choice experiments. Such experiments are designed such that people's choices reveal their ethical preferences with respect to fairness and efficiency. The approach is to allow individuals to make choices over hypothetical states of the world in order to understand how important relative and absolute outcomes are to them. In addition to studying relative-absolute and fairness-efficiency trade-offs, choice experiments can be taken to reveal people's degree of altruism, an issue relevant to choices that impact future generations.

Fairness versus Efficiency

While some experiments, to be discussed later, address the importance of the relative income position, others focus on people's willingness to accept unfair outcomes to themselves or to make fair/unfair offers to others.

Such issues of fairness, as opposed to efficiency, preferences were studied in the context of so-called ultimatum games, first proposed by Güth et al. (1982). An ultimatum (or bargaining) game is a two-stage experiment where two people, a proposer and a responder, bargain over a fixed amount of money. In the first stage, the proposer offers a split of the money, and in the second stage, the responder decides to accept or reject the offer. If accepted, each player receives money according to the offer; if rejected, each player receives nothing. Typical findings in such experiments are that the majority of offers are in the range of 25 to 50 percent of the fixed amount. Few offers are below 5 percent. Responders frequently reject offers below 20 percent of the fixed amount.

The behavior of the responders is easy to interpret. Even if the offer were zero, acceptance would be Pareto better than rejection: if responders accepted, rather than rejected, one individual (the proposer) would be better off without anybody being worse off. And more than that: the finding that responders reject offers as high as 20 percent at the cost of getting nothing indicates that getting "more" is not always better if the offer is deemed to be unfair. Relative concerns (for fairness) may trump absolute concerns.

With respect to the proposers, making sizeable offers may indicate a distaste for unfairness. It may, however, just as well reflect proposers' strategic concern that making a low offer carries the risk of rejection, in which case they would get nothing. Notably, making such strategic considerations presupposes that proposers expect responders to have a preference for fairness.

Relative and Absolute Concerns

A choice experiment used to study relative and absolute concerns without proposer-responder interaction involves asking individuals to choose between states A and B as follows (Solnick and Hemenway 1998):

A. Your current yearly income is $50,000; others earn $25,000.
B. Your current yearly income is $100,000; others earn $200,000.

It is specified that "others" refers to the average of other people in the society.

The key issue in this hypothetical-choice experiment is that subjects choose between one state in which they are better off in absolute terms (B) and another in which they are better-off compared with others (A). It is typically found that individuals are willing to give up absolute income in order to improve their relative position (choosing A over B). The percentage who exhibit "relative" preferences (preferring A to B) can be large: half of the respondents said that they preferred to have 50 percent less real income but higher relative income (Solnick and Hemenway 1998, 2005).

While these types of experiments often refer to rich countries, a useful extension is to compare rich and lower-income countries. Following such an approach, it was found that individuals in high-income countries are more concerned by relative standing than are those in lower-income countries (Corazzini et al. 2012).

Fairness and Altruism

In a variant of the ultimatum game, first proposed by Kahneman et al. (1986), strategic concerns are absent as the proposer simply states what the split will be and the responder has no veto power, rendering the proposed split as effective. This setting – the dictator game – permits interpretation of the proposer's behavior in terms of fairness preferences, such as inequality aversion. Typical findings in the dictator game are that usually more than 60 percent of subjects pass a positive amount of money, with the mean transfer roughly 20 percent of the endowment. Considering that the majority of offers in the ultimatum game are in the range between 25 and 50 percent, it may be concluded that the offers in the ultimatum game in fact reflect some strategic considerations.

Results from dictator games (and choice experiments more generally) depend on details of the experimental design (Levitt and List 2007). One factor is anonymity. If subjects know that their behavior is scrutinized by other subjects and the experimenter, observed behavior may be due not to a taste for fairness but rather to a social concern for what others may think, and for being held in high regard by others. Accordingly, lower offers arise in experiments that involve anonymity than in those that don't. Another factor is the size of the endowment. While relatively small changes in stakes (from \$10 to \$40) do not seem to make a difference, a large increase in stakes (from \$10 to \$100) generally leads to a less-than-proportionate increase in money transferred. Stakes effects have also been found in second-mover play in ultimatum games, in which the acceptance rate is generally increasing in the amount offered, conditional on the share offered – that is, a \$1 offer in a \$5 game is rejected more often than a \$100 offer in a \$500 game. Overall, the fairness preference of proposers (dictators) and responders (in the ultimatum game) seems to be lower when stakes are higher.

While findings from dictator games are consistent with a fairness interpretation, they may just as well reflect altruism. The difference is subtle, but important. While a fairness interpretation would focus on the inequality aspect of alternative distributions of the endowment, an interpretation in terms of altruism would rather focus on the "dictator's" concern for others' wellbeing. Still another interpretation would be that it is not (or not entirely) concern for outcomes that guides the dictators' choice but some intrinsic value of or "warm glow" from the act of giving – a deontological rather than consequentialist interpretation.

While the issue of deontological motives cannot be further pursued in the present setting, deontological "warm glow" behavior will be the focus of Chapter 6.

Deservingness

In addition to the size of the endowment, another critical issue of the experiments used to test inequality aversion is that they often neglect the procedure that is behind the money to be allocated. The roles of proposer/dictator are randomly assigned to participants, and the amount of money they can dispose of does not depend on any effort on their part. Accordingly, having more money than others is not seen as being deserved. However, in many real-world applications individuals likely believe that they earn more than others because they deserve to do so. As might be imagined, when income is considered to reflect effort rather than luck the results do change. For example, when the role of proposer in the ultimatum game is earned, rather than being randomly assigned, proposers offer less and respondents are more likely to accept an unequal offer (Hoffman et al. 1994). Similar results are found when the asset of the dictators reflects some effort (Cherry et al. (2002).

The Expanse of Moral Concern

An important issue in experimental tests of fairness preferences is to whom people feel obliged to be fair and by how much. Consistent with Adam Smith's normative view that moral obligations to people close are stronger than those toward more distant people (Smith 1759) as well as with psychological intuition, one would expect that people give less if the social distance between themselves and the recipient is greater. In a meta study of

616 experimental treatments, this conjecture was confirmed. In particular, the likelihood that the dictator gives everything (as opposed to making a different choice) is strongly positively related to social proximity. In addition to proximity, another strong predictor of this kind of behavior is that the recipient is in need, whereas the fact that there are multiple recipients acts as a weak predictor of such behavior (Engel 2011).

In extending the notion of social distance/proximity, recent research has started to explore the "expanse of the moral circle" (Waytz et al. 2019). The idea was to differentiate not just between people close and more distant people, but between moral regard directed toward socially closer and structurally tighter targets – parochial morality – and moral regard directed toward socially more distant and structurally looser targets – universalist morality. Specifically, a set of increasingly large "moral circles" (Singer 1981), one encompassing the other, was devised, which comprised 16 categories (Waytz et al. 2019): (a) all of your immediate family; (b) all of your extended family; (c) all of your closest friends; (d) all friends including more distant friends; (e) all acquaintances; (f) all people you have ever met; (g) all people in your country; (h) all people on your continent; (i) all people on all continents; (j) all mammals on all continents; (k) all amphibians, reptiles, mammals, fish, and birds; (l) all animals on earth, including paramecia and amoebae; (m) all animals in the universe, including alien lifeforms; (n) all living things in the universe, including plants and trees; (o) all natural things in the universe, including inert entities such as rocks; (p) all things in existence. In a choice experiment, subjects were asked to allocate 100 "moral units" among those 16 categories in order to indicate their degree of moral regard (their capacity to show empathy and be generous) toward the various targets. The categories were used to create composite moral allocation scores for humans only (average of units allocated to the first nine categories) and for nonhumans (average of units allocated to the last seven categories).

As might be expected, fewer moral units were allocated to more distant entities. On average, participants allocated 8.49 units to each of the nine human categories (totaling 76.4 units for the human categories) and 3.37 units to each of the seven nonhuman categories (totaling 23.6 units for the nonhuman categories). The allocation of moral units differed between political liberals (the more politically left) and conservatives (the more politically right). Those who declared to be "very liberal" allocated approximately 56 units to the human and 44 units to the nonhuman categories, whereas for those who declared to be "very conservative" the proportion was about 90 to 10. The choice to allocate moral units to *humans only* was significantly positively related to the degree of conservatism. Conversely, the more liberal people were, the more they allocated equally to humans and nonhumans. In addition, when asked to indicate the extent of their moral circle, that is, the outmost category for which they felt moral concern, liberals selected more outer categories, whereas conservatives selected more inner categories. Liberals thus displayed a wider moral circle than did conservatives.

Conclusion

Individuals are regularly faced with choices that affect other individuals' wellbeing without economic compensation through prices. Similarly, policy makers' choices potentially affect all citizens' wellbeing. Choices that affect the wellbeing or interests of human (or nonhuman) beings different from the decision maker can be said to be *morally relevant*.

Over many centuries, moral philosophy has developed normative principles in order to deal with morally relevant choices. Approaches to moral philosophy – or ethics – are categorized as either consequentialist or deontological. While consequentialist ethics evaluates choices by asking whether their *outcomes* are good or bad, deontological ethics evaluates choices by asking whether the choices *themselves* – actions and/or intentions – are right or wrong in terms of some moral norms of behavior.

The study of economic choices from a normative (evaluative) point of view and the derivation of prescriptions for action – welfare economics – has traditionally taken a consequentialist perspective. The approach of welfare economics is to focus on choices' effects on the relevant individuals' utility (wellbeing) and to aggregate individual utilities into a measure of societal welfare that is to be maximized. The social welfare function used to perform the aggregation can take various forms. While conventional Utilitarianism adds each person's utility, the Rawlsian approach is to identify social welfare with the minimum of utilities across individuals.

Application of the Utilitarian and Rawlsian approaches to important issues of public concern leads to different conclusions as to what outcomes are welfare maximizing, and some conclusions may be more intuitively appealing than others. When the issue is the distribution of income, maximization of the Utilitarian welfare function implies equalization of incomes and utilities across individuals, provided that individuals' utilities enter in an unweighted fashion and individuals' utility functions are identical. If utility functions are not identical, individuals who are less efficient in transforming income into utility end up with less income and lower levels of utility. The Rawlsian approach, by contrast, always leads to an equalization of utilities.

Similar to the issue of income distribution, different welfare economic approaches lead to different conclusions with respect to the intertemporal allocation of natural resources and with respect to the mitigation of climate change. An important ethical aspect of the Utilitarian approach to these intertemporal – or intergenerational – issues is utility discounting: should the utilities of future generations count less than the utility of the present generation? Taking a prescriptive view and postulating impartiality, utility discounting seems justified only insofar as it reflects a risk of extinction of mankind in the future due to external forces. As a rule, intertemporal welfare maximization leads to less of a natural resource being allocated to future generations and less aggressive climate change mitigation being undertaken the more future utilities are discounted.

Different from a prescriptive view, a descriptive view can be taken on utility discounting: instead of postulating the ethical position to be an impartial one, what matters is the ethical stance of the present generation. The weight attached to future generations' utility then captures the current generation's sense of fairness and altruism.

Fairness preferences and altruism have been much studied in countless choice experiments over the past few decades, and a preference for distributive fairness has unequivocally been found, such that a concern for equality and relative standing often dominates the concern for absolute payoffs. The degree of concern for others was typically found to decrease in social distance. In addition to concern for other humans, evidence suggests that individuals display considerable moral regard toward nonhumans.

The findings from experimental economics concerning equality and fairness preferences corroborate the evidence of a detrimental effect of inequality on subjective wellbeing (Chapter 3), whereas those on concern for nonhumans are consistent with the evidence on beneficial wellbeing effects of biodiversity (Chapter 4). Evidence from experimental economics thus provides a cross-validation of evidence from wellbeing research.

While deontological considerations have been largely absent in the economics discussed in this chapter, they will play an important role in the following ones. As will be seen, fairness and altruism, being outcome-focused, are not sufficient to solve the large-scale cooperation dilemmas that characterize some of the real-world challenges facing economics now and in the future.

Bibliography

Alexander, L., Moore, M. (2021), Deontological Ethics. In: Edward N. Zalta (ed.), *The Stanford Encyclopedia of Philosophy* (Winter 2021 Edition), https://plato.stanford.edu/archives/win2021/entries/ethics-deontological/.

Andreoni, J. (1988), Privately Provided Public Goods in a Large Economy: The Limits of Altruism, *Journal of Public Economics* 35, 57–73.

Andreoni, J. (1990), Impure Altruism and Donations to Public Goods: A Theory of Warm-Glow Giving, *Economic Journal* 100, 464–477.

Bentham, J. (1789), *An Introduction to the Principles of Morals and Legislation*, Chestnut Hill, MA: Elibron Classics (2005).

Böhringer, C., Welsch, H. (2006), Burden Sharing in a Greenhouse: Egalitarianism and Sovereignty Reconciled, *Applied Economics* 38, 981–996.

Cherry, T.L., Frykblom, P., Shogren, J.F. (2002), Hardnose the Dictator, *American Economic Review* 92, 1218–1221.

Corazzini, L., Esposito, L., Majorano, F. (2012), Reign in Hell or Serve in Heaven? A Crosscountry Journey into the Relative vs. Absolute Perceptions of Wellbeing, *Journal of Economic Behavior and Organization* 81, 715–730.

Dietz, S., Hope, C., Stern, N., Zenghelis, D. (2007), Reflections on the Stern Review: (1) A Robust Case for Strong Action to Reduce the Risks of Climate Change, *World Economics* 8, 121–168.

Engel, C. (2011), Dictator Games: A Meta-Study, *Experimental Economics* 14, 583–610.

Grubb, M. (1995), Seeking Fair Weather: Ethics and the International Debate on Climate Change, *International Affairs* 71, 463–496.

Güth, W., Schmittberger, R., Schwarze, B. (1982), An Experimental Analysis of Ultimatum Bargaining, *Journal of Economic Behavior and Organization* 3, 367–388.

Heal, G.M., Millner, A. (2014), Agreeing to Disagree on Climate Policy, *Proceedings of the National Academy of Sciences* 111, 3695–3698.

Hoffman, E., McCabe, K., Shachat, K., Smith, V. (1994), Preferences, Property Rights, and Anonymity in Bargaining Games, *Games and Economic Behavior* 7, 346–380.

Jarvis Thomson, J. (1985), *The Trolley Problem, Yale Law Journal* 94, 1395–1415.

Kahneman, D., Knetsch, J.L., Thaler, R.H. (1986), Fairness as a Constraint on Profit Seeking: Entitlements in the Market, *American Economic Review* 76, 728–41.

Kahneman, D., Wakker, P.P., Sarin, R. (1997), Back to Bentham? Explorations of Experienced Utility, *Quarterly Journal of Economics* 112, 375–405.

Kant, I. (1785), *Groundwork of the Metaphysic of Morals*, H.J. Paton (trans.), Harper and Row, New York (1964).

Lange, A., Löschel, A., Vogt, C., Ziegler, A. (2010), On the Self-Interested Use of Equity in International Climate Negotiations, *European Economic Review* 54, 359–375.

Levitt, S.D., List, J.A. (2007), What Do Laboratory Experiments Measuring Social Preferences Reveal About the Real World? *Journal of Economic Perspectives* 21, 153–174.

Nordhaus, W.D. (2008), *A Question of Balance*, New Haven, CT: Yale University Press.

Nordhaus, W.D. (2019), Climate Change: The Ultimate Challenge for Economics, *American Economic Review* 109, 1991–2014.

Nozick, R. (1974), *Anarchy, State and Utopia*, New York: Basic Books.

Perman, R., Ma, Y., Common, M., Maddison, D., McGilvray, J. (2011), *Natural Resource and Environmental Economics*, Fourth Edition, Pearson Education Limited.

Rawls, J. (1971), *A Theory of Justice*, Cambridge, MA: Harvard University Press.

Singer, P. (1981), *The Expanding Circle: Ethics and Sociobiology*, Oxford, UK: Clarendon Press.

Singer, P. (1993), *Practical Ethics*, Second Edition, Cambridge, UK: Cambridge University Press.

Sinnott-Armstrong, W. (2019), Consequentialism. In: Edward N. Zalta (ed.), *The Stanford Encyclopedia of Philosophy* (Summer 2019 Edition), https://plato.stanford.edu/archives/sum2019/entries/consequentialism/.

Smith A. (1759). *The Theory of Moral Sentiments*, London: Andrew Millar (1967).

Solnick, S., Hemenway, D. (1998), Is More Always Better? A Survey on Positional Concerns, *Journal of Economic Behavior and Organization* 37, 373–383.

Solnick, S., Hemenway, D. (2005), Are Positional Concerns Stronger in Some Domains than in Others? *American Economic Review* 95, 147–151.

Stern, N. (2007), *The Economics of Climate Change: The Stern Review*, Cambridge, UK: Cambridge University Press.

Tomasello, M. (2016), *A Natural History of Human Morality*, Cambridge, MA: Harvard University Press.

Waytz, A., Iyer, R., Young, L., Haidt, J., Graham, J. (2019), Ideological Differences in the Expanse of the Moral Circle, *Nature Communications* 10, 4389.

6 The Cooperation Dilemma and Deontological Behavior

Introduction

The preceding chapter has discussed consequentialism and deontology mainly from a normative perspective: what do consequentialist and deontological moral philosophies imply with respect to the ethical principles individuals' and policy makers' *should* obey in morally relevant situations, and what does individuals' behavior reveal about their ethical or moral standards? The morally relevant issues considered in the preceding chapter were mainly those of distribution.

In contrast to the normative perspective, this chapter will be concerned with consequentialism and deontology as positive (descriptive) theories – theories that make predictions about how people actually behave. The type of issue to be considered will not be distribution, but cooperation, in particular the cooperative provision of public goods. Similar to distribution, cooperation has moral relevance, as one agent's choices and behaviors affect the wellbeing of others.

Some of the most important issues that affect people's wellbeing worldwide have to do with public goods: equality, employment, financial and monetary stability (Chapter 3), clean air and water, the climate, and biodiversity (Chapter 4). Those are public goods, since (a) one agent benefiting from them does not interfere with other agents' benefit (non-rivalry), and (b) a provider of the good cannot exclude any potential beneficiary from the benefit (non-excludability).

In spite of their common general characteristics (non-rivalry and non-excludability), the conditions for the provision of those public goods vary. While some of them are local, regional, or national public goods, others are transnational or global in nature. For example, many kinds of air and water pollution arise within the boundaries of a country and can be addressed by national legislation. Others, for example, the climate, biodiversity, and financial stability, are global public goods, which no single nation can provide. It is here, where voluntary cooperation (of nations and individuals) – and the underlying consequentialist and deontological motives – come into play.

DOI: 10.4324/9781003206163-8

The standard economic model of choices and behaviors is based on a consequentialist paradigm, and this applies, in particular, to the provision of public goods. The consequentialist paradigm assumes that individuals choose among alternative actions solely based on how actions' expected outcomes (consequences) will affect individuals' interests – and possibly those of others. Intrinsic properties of actions are assumed to have no influence on what actions are chosen.

This chapter deals with the voluntary provision of public goods from a consequentialist and a deontological perspective. In a consequentialist framework, voluntary public goods provision poses a social dilemma: a situation in which actions taken independently by agents result in an outcome that is inferior to some other feasible outcome that could have occurred if agents had coordinated their actions. The focus will be on climate change mitigation by means of reducing greenhouse gases that affect the world climate. A major purpose of the chapter is to highlight the limitations of the conventional consequentialist model and the role of deontological motives when it comes to voluntary public goods provision.

Social Dilemmas

Economic choices often involve social dilemmas. As noted earlier, a social dilemma is a situation in which actions taken independently by agents who rationally pursue their self-interest result in an outcome that is inferior to some other feasible outcome that could have occurred if agents had acted together, rather than independently. Social dilemmas, in other words, are situations in which *individually rational* behavior leads to outcomes that fail to be *collectively rational*.

Social dilemmas occur frequently in our lives. Overusing antibiotics for minor illnesses, for example, may help the sick person who takes them recover more quickly but creates antibiotic-resistant bacteria that have a much more harmful effect on many others. A further example, to be thoroughly discussed later in this chapter, is the overuse of the global atmosphere, which brings about climate change. As these examples demonstrate, social dilemmas typically arise if a person's actions involve an externality: it affects another person's wellbeing without adequate compensation. The channel through which people affect others' wellbeing is often the impairment of a public good.

While many of the global challenges ahead involve social dilemmas, not all social interactions lead to them, even if individuals act in pursuit of their own interests. Accordingly, much of economics has focused on situations in which individually rational behavior leads to collectively rational outcomes – as if through the working of an *Invisible Hand* (Adam Smith). As a foil for the discussion of social dilemmas, we will therefore start by discussing an "invisible hand game" (CORE Team 2017, Unit 4).

The Invisible Hand Game

Like social dilemmas, the "invisible hand" is most easily illustrated in terms of just two people interacting. Consider the case of two farmers, each owning a piece of land (CORE Team 2017, Unit 4); in honor of two great economists, call them Adam Smith and David Ricardo.

The situation is described by the following assumptions: (a) Smith and Ricardo have to independently decide whether to grow wheat or corn; (b) Smith's land is better suited for growing wheat, while Ricardo's is better suited for corn; (c) if they bring less wheat to the market, the price will be higher, and the same goes for corn.

Table 6.1 describes Smith's and Ricardo's interaction – conventionally referred to as a *game* – in terms of their choices and payoffs. Each cell describes the outcome of one of four possible configurations of choices. For example, the upper-left cell shows the payoffs to Smith and Ricardo if both produce corn, whereas the upper-right cell shows the payoffs if Smith produces corn and Ricardo produces wheat.

In each cell, the number at the bottom-left corner is Smith's payoff, whereas the number at the top-right corner is Ricardo's payoff. For example, if both grow corn, Smith earns $10,000 per year, whereas Ricardo earns $30,000, reflecting the different suitability of their land for growing corn.

A natural (and indeed the standard) way of analyzing such situations is to assume that each player seeks to find the best (payoff-maximizing) response to the other player's hypothetical choices (Nash 1951) – a mode of behavior called Nash optimization. Suppose Smith considers the hypothetical case in which Ricardo has chosen to grow corn. Smith would grow wheat (in this case, he would get a payoff of $40,000, but he would get a payoff of only $10,000 if he grew corn instead). As can be seen, choosing wheat is also Smith's best response if Ricardo chooses wheat. So wheat is Smith's *dominant strategy*: it will give him the highest payoff, whatever Ricardo does. Similar to Smith, Ricardo also has a dominant strategy, which is growing corn.

Because both farmers have a dominant strategy, there is a simple prediction about what each will do: play their dominant strategy. Smith will grow wheat,

Table 6.1 The Invisible Hand Game

Smith's payoff	*Ricardo's payoff*	*Ricardo*: *Corn*	*Ricardo*: *Wheat*
Smith	*Corn*	$30,000 (Ricardo) $10,000 (Smith)	$20,000 (Ricardo) $20,000 (Smith)
Smith	*Wheat*	$40,000 (Ricardo) $40,000 (Smith)	$10,000 (Ricardo) $30,000 (Smith)

and Ricardo will grow corn. This pair of strategies is a *dominant strategy Nash equilibrium* of the game. Referring to it as an *equilibrium* captures the circumstance that it is a self-perpetuating configuration of choices that neither player would want to change unilaterally after seeing what the other player chose.

In the Nash equilibrium, Smith and Ricardo have specialized in producing the good for which their land is better suited. Simply pursuing their self-interest – choosing the strategy for which they got the highest payoff – resulted in an outcome that was:

- The best of the four possible outcomes for each player.
- The strategy that yielded the largest total payoffs for the two farmers combined.

In this example, the Nash equilibrium coincides with the outcome that each would have chosen if they had a way of coordinating their decisions so as to attain the collectively optimal outcome. Although they independently pursued their self-interest, they were guided "as if by an invisible hand" (Smith 1776) to an outcome that was in both of their best interests. In this sense, the Nash equilibrium is efficient; there is no other configuration of choices in which anybody is better off.

The Cooperation Dilemma

Let us add a couple of assumptions to the preceding example to arrive at a situation in which independent pursuit of self-interest leads to an equilibrium that could well be improved upon if the farmers coordinated their decisions, rather than acting independently. Those assumptions involve the *method* of producing wheat and corn, respectively.

Assume that the game depicted in Table 6.1 refers to "conventional" farming, which involves the use of pesticides. Alternatively, the farmers could engage in "organic" farming, which involves abstaining from using pesticides. Pesticide use leads to contamination of water in a common reservoir, from which both farmers draw.

The situation is described by the following assumptions: (a) Smith and Ricardo have to independently decide whether to engage in conventional or organic farming. (b) Organic farming *per se* leads to lower yields (negative direct effect). (c) By avoiding water contamination, organic farming leads to a higher yield (positive indirect effect). (d) *Unilaterally* switching to organic farming has a negative total effect on the respective farmer's yield (the negative direct exceeds the positive indirect effect), whereas *jointly* switching to organic farming has a positive total effect on both farmers' yield (the negative direct effect is smaller than the sum of positive indirect effects).

This situation is bound to lead to a cooperation dilemma under certain circumstances. An example is shown in Table 6.2. The structure of the table is similar to Table 6.1, except that the choice is between "conventional" and "organic".

Table 6.2 The Cooperation Dilemma

	Ricardo's payoff	*Ricardo*	
Smith's payoff		*Conventional*	*Organic*
Smith	*Conventional*	$40,000 $40,000	$30,000 $60,000
	Organic	$60,000 $30,000	$50,000 $50,000

The payoffs in the upper-left cell of Table 6.2 correspond to those in the lower-left cell of Table 6.1: Smith and Ricardo specialize in wheat and corn, respectively, both of them producing their crop "conventionally". If Smith unilaterally switches to organic farming (bottom-left cell), the negative direct effect on the yield exceeds the positive effect from better water quality, such that his payoff falls from $40,000 to $30,000. Ricardo, by continuing to produce conventionally, benefits from the better water quality without incurring a negative direct effect, such that his payoff rises to $60,000. The same reasoning holds if Ricardo unilaterally switches to organic farming (upper-right cell): his payoff drops, whereas Smith's rises. Overall, unilaterally switching to organic farming does not pay. Only if both *jointly* switch to organic farming is the improvement of water quality large enough to exceed the respective negative direct effects on yield, such that both farmers' payoff rises (bottom-right cell).

This example illustrates the existence of gains from cooperation. Cooperatively choosing "organic" rather than "conventional" makes both farmers better off.

That gains from cooperation are feasible is good news. The bad news is that – as readers can easily check – both farmers choosing "conventional" (that is, to use pesticides) is the dominant strategy Nash equilibrium of this game: if the farmers independently pursue their self-interest, it is better for each farmer to choose "conventional" than to choose "organic", no matter whether the other farmer chooses "conventional" or "organic". In contrast to the choice of which crop to grow (Table 6.1), independently choosing the method of farming leads to an equilibrium that fails to be efficient. The reason is that the reliance on a common water reservoir whose quality depends on the method of farming implies a *strategic interdependence* of the farmers' choices, which is absent in the choice of crops.

Worse than that: even if the farmers strike an agreement not to use pesticides, there is an incentive to defect. By (secretly) using pesticides, Smith can raise his payoff, provided Ricardo sticks to the agreement, and vice versa. Any such agreement is thus inherently unstable – if the farmers act in their own self-interest.

This highly stylized example is a first illustration of a cooperation dilemma. It arises because both farmers rely on a common production input, water quality, which they impair by using pesticides. The water quality here is a public good, from which both farmers benefit in a non-rivalrous and non-excludable fashion.[1]

The remainder of this chapter will discuss real-world global public goods – in particular the world climate – and the theory and evidence of behavior pertaining to their use.

Global Public Goods

Before discussing public goods in detail, it should be noted that the provision of a public good often involves the avoidance or mitigation of a public "bad". This is, in particular, the case with respect to environmental public goods: the "provision" of clean air or water – a public good – is actually the avoidance of pollution – a public bad. Models of environmental public goods can therefore take two forms. One is to focus on (production and consumption) activities that yield a private benefit to those who undertake them, but are associated with negative spillovers (through emissions) that create a public damage or public "bad". The other is to focus on the mitigation of the public bad (through limiting emissions), which is associated with private costs to those who engage in mitigation. Both ways of conceptualizing the issue are equivalent. In what follows, the second perspective will be adopted throughout and the term "provision of a public good" will be used, keeping in mind that it may refer to the mitigation of a public bad.

The example of pesticide pollution illustrates the nature of the cooperation dilemma – the cooperative provision or preservation of a public good – but the issue is relatively simple to address. Since groundwater pollution is a local or regional issue, it can be addressed by regional, national, or supranational (e.g., European Union) legislation that regulates and monitors the use of pesticides and similar pollutants.

The situation is different in the case of transnational or global public goods – environmental or other – for which no governmental institutions exist. Here, the issue is one of international voluntary cooperation. As will be discussed further later in the chapter, the cooperation dilemmas that arise in these circumstances are aggravated by the fact that large numbers of agents are involved in the respective issues.

This section discusses the nature of global public goods in general, whereas the next section will focus on climate change mitigation more specifically.

Properties of Global Public Goods

Public goods can be differentiated into several classes, depending on four properties: the degree of benefit non-rivalry, the degree of benefit non-excludability, the range of benefit spillovers, and the specific way in which the level of a public good depends on individual contributions to it (Buchholz and Sandler 2021).

The degrees of non-rivalry and non-excludability differentiate pure public goods from impure public goods. While *pure public goods* are characterized by complete non-rivalry and non-excludability (Samuelson 1954), public goods may possess one of these properties, but not the other. For example, deploying peace-keeping forces offers non-rivalrous and excludable benefits, whereas open-seas fisheries and other global commons contain rivalrous and non-excludable benefits. It is the non-excludability that has been early identified as giving rise to the "Tragedy of the Commons" (Hardin 1968), that is, their overuse.

The range of benefit spillovers differentiates global public goods and transnational public goods from national, regional, or local ones. An example of a pure global public good is the stratospheric ozone layer: (a) it benefits people worldwide (through protection from ultraviolet radiation); (b) the benefit that one individual derives from it does not reduce any other individual's benefit; and (c) no individual can be excluded from benefiting from it. Other examples of pure global public goods are curbing global warming and the preservation of biodiversity. By contrast, given the range of benefit spillovers, clean air is a sub-global – typically regional or local – public good.

The difference between global and transboundary public goods on one hand and national and subnational public goods on the other is important, because the latter can be provided by national governments through national legislation, without any need for transnational cooperation, whereas provision of the former requires precisely this: international cooperation. Because global public goods possess the property of non-excludability, international cooperation tends to be undermined by the threat of free-riding behavior: due to non-excludability, contributions by one agent benefit all other agents, which reduces the incentives for the latter to contribute themselves.

Aggregator Technology

The fourth property of global public goods concerns the technology of aggregation, which indicates how countries' contributions determine the overall level of the public good. Important types of aggregation are summation, weighted sum, and weakest link (Buchholz and Sandler 2021). A global public good with summation technology is the limiting of greenhouse gas emissions: greenhouse gases uniformly mix in the atmosphere, and each ton of gas emitted has the same effect on the global climate, irrespective of the place from which emissions originate. What matters for curbing climate change, thus, is the global sum of emissions. By contrast, curbing ambient air pollution is a public good with a weighted-sum technology: since the effects of emissions decay with distance, air pollution in a given place responds to emissions of the relevant pollutants, depending on emissions' place of origin. In general, the level of air pollution in a given place responds more strongly to emissions in proximate than in more distant places; it thus depends on the sum of emissions weighted by proximity to the places where emissions originate (possibly adjusted for wind direction). Finally, safety from financial crises or a disease outbreak are public goods with a weakest-link technology: the level of safety is only as good as the smallest effort.

Together with the degree of excludability, the type of aggregation technology is an important determinant of how severe the cooperation dilemma of public goods provision is. In the weighted-sum case, the level of a public good in a given place typically depends more strongly on contributions by agents close to that place than on more distant agents. There is thus a close correspondence between beneficiaries and contributors – closer than in the case of unweighted summation. Put differently, with weighted-sum aggregation, contributions by other agents are an imperfect substitute for contributions by the beneficiaries themselves, whereas with summation aggregation they are perfect substitutes. In the weakest-link case, contributions by others are no substitute at all for one's own contributions: one's own contributions are indispensable to the provision of the public good in question. It is obvious that the less one's own contributions can be substituted by others' contributions, the greater is the incentive to contribute rather than free ride on others' contributions.

If we focus on countries (that is, their governments) as the relevant agents in global public good problems, it can be said that each country plays a twin role as a potential contributor to and beneficiary from the public good in question. If the public good is one with summation aggregation, each country's contribution is a perfect substitute for any other country's contribution.

International Climate Policy as a Cooperation Dilemma

Climate change mitigation is a global public good, to which this description applies. The preservation of biodiversity is another, and the two are related to each other, as species loss is one of the consequences of climate change. In addition, climate change and biodiversity loss have at least one common cause: deforestation. As described in Chapter 1, climate change and biodiversity loss are considered to be among the most important challenges to public policy in the 21st century.

In contrast to conventional air pollutants, the most important greenhouse gases involved in human-made climate change – carbon dioxide, methane, and nitrous oxides – are difficult to capture using end-of-pipe technologies on a large scale. Fighting climate change thus implies limiting the economic activities that produce greenhouse gases, notably the extraction, transport, and use of fossil fuels (coal, oil, and gas); deforestation; wet rice production; and livestock. Given the ubiquity of these activities, virtually every country adds to the accumulation of greenhouse gases.

This section will provide a discussion of climate change mitigation as a pure global public good. As will be seen, mitigating climate change is a big challenge, not only because the impacts of climate change are large but also because the structural properties of the issue (benefit non-excludability and perfect substitutability of contributions) give rise to a cooperation dilemma unprecedented in human history.[2]

For the sake of accessibility, the model used to illustrate the issue will be highly stylized. In addition, part of the discussion will involve the counterfactual assumption that all countries are identical. Importantly, however, the following findings apply to more general models of international climate policy, and indeed to global public goods in general:

- *Mutual crowding out*: Due to free-riding incentives, each country rationally responds to other countries unilaterally reducing their greenhouse gas emissions by increasing their emissions. Individual countries' actions to curb climate change thus crowd out each other.
- *Cooperation gap*: Crowding out implies a cooperation gap – a discrepancy between mitigation levels that are rational from each country's individual perspective and those that are rational from a global perspective – a gap which increases in the number of countries involved.

These quintessential features make the curbing of climate change a supremely challenging global public good to supply.[3]

Consequentialist Climate Policy Analysis: A Stylized Model

Given the large predicted impacts of climate change, cutting back emissions of greenhouse gases is expected to yield large benefits worldwide, which far exceed the associated costs (Stern 2007). In spite of the positive cost-benefit balance on the global level, however, the problem is that the benefits of any measures to reduce greenhouse gas emissions spread across all nations of the world, whereas the costs accrue to the individual nations that undertake them. This gives rise to a cooperation dilemma, which can be illustrated as follows.

Assume there is a set of identical countries. Denote by $cutback_1$, $cutback_2$, and so on, the proportional cutback of emissions of greenhouse gases (measured in carbon dioxide equivalents) undertaken in countries 1, 2, and so on, relative to the emission levels in a business-as-usual (*BAU*) baseline scenario. The variables $cutback_1$, $cutback_2$, and so on, can take values between 0, which means that emissions remain at *BAU* levels, and 1, which means complete decarbonization (*DECARB*) of the respective economies. The climate change mitigation problem is described by the following assumptions on the benefits and costs of cutting back emissions, where benefits are monetized avoided damages from climate change.

1. Each nation benefits from the *sum* of cutbacks undertaken by all nations collectively, but at diminishing rates (diminishing marginal benefit): the higher the level of aggregate (global) cutback is, the smaller the

additional physical benefit (avoided greenhouse warming) is from any further increase in cutback. The benefit to any arbitrary nation, indexed "*i*", is specified as: $Benefit_i = B \cdot \sqrt{cutback_1 + cutback_2 + \cdots}$. In this formulation, the square root captures the property of diminishing marginal benefit, and *B* is a positive parameter that translates the physical effect of global emission reductions into a nation's monetary benefit.
2. Each nation has costs from cutting back its emissions. Costs rise at increasing rates (increasing marginal costs): the higher the level of a nation's cutback is, the greater the additional cost is from any further increase in cutback. To capture increasing marginal costs, the cost to any arbitrary nation "*i*" is specified as a quadratic function: $Cost_i = C \cdot cutback_i^2$, where *C* is a positive parameter that translates a nation's emission reduction into the associated monetary cost.
3. Each nation's payoff is the difference between its monetized benefit and its cost: $Payoff_i = Benefit_i - Cost_i$. Benefits, costs, and payoffs are in percent of the countries' GDP.

With these assumptions, the discussion will proceed as follows. We first consider a case in which nations independently have to make a choice between the binary options *BAU* (i.e., $cutback_i = 0$) and *DECARB* (i.e. $cutback_i = 1$). We then discuss which intermediate choices, between *BAU* and *DECARB*, are payoff-maximizing from the point of view of each nation acting independently, and which choices are optimal if they cooperate so as to maximize the sum of payoffs.

Binary Choice: BAU versus DECARB

We start by considering the choice between *BAU* and *DECARB* if only two countries, called *One* and *Two*, are involved. Four cases can arise, for which the payoffs are as follows.

- Both choose *BAU*. There are neither costs nor benefits: Payoff for *One* = Payoff for *Two* $= B \cdot 0 - C \cdot 0 = 0$.
- Both choose *DECARB*. They incur their respective costs and benefit from their joint effort: Payoff for *One* = Payoff for *Two* $= B \cdot \sqrt{1+1} - C \cdot 1$.
- *One* chooses *DECARB*, *Two* chooses *BAU*. *One* incurs its costs and benefits from its effort: Payoff for *One* $= B \cdot \sqrt{1} - C \cdot 1$. *Two* incurs no cost and benefits from *One*'s effort: Payoff for *Two* $= B \cdot \sqrt{1}$.
- *Two* chooses *DECARB*, *One* chooses *BAU*. *Two* incurs its costs and benefits from its effort: Payoff for *Two* $= B \cdot \sqrt{1} - C \cdot 1$. *One* incurs no cost and benefits from *Two*'s effort: Payoff for *One* $= B \cdot \sqrt{1}$.

Whether a cooperation dilemma arises or not depends on the benefit and cost parameters. Table 6.3 is a payoff matrix for the case $B = 5$ and $C = 6$. Following similar reasoning as in the pesticide example shown in Table 6.2, it is a dominant

Table 6.3 The Climate Change Cooperation Dilemma ($B = 5$, $C = 6$)

Payoff for One		*Payoff for Two*: *Two* *BAU*	*DECARB*
One	*BAU*	Two: $5 \cdot 0 - 6 \cdot 0 = 0$; One: $5 \cdot 0 - 6 \cdot 0 = 0$	Two: $5 \cdot \sqrt{1} - 6 \cdot 1 = -1$; One: $5 \cdot \sqrt{1} = 5$
	DECARB	Two: $5 \cdot \sqrt{1} = 5$; One: $5 \cdot \sqrt{1} - 6 \cdot 1 = -1$	Two: $5 \cdot \sqrt{1+1} - 6 \cdot 1 = 1$; One: $5 \cdot \sqrt{1+1} - 6 \cdot 1 = 1$

strategy for both countries to choose *BAU*: Whatever the other country chooses, choosing *BAU* yields a higher payoff than choosing *DECARB*. We thus have a dominant strategy equilibrium with payoff = 0 for both countries. If they cooperated, both of them choosing *DECARB*, both would get payoff = 1. But there is no incentive to do so. Rather, both have an incentive to try and free-ride on the other's effort, but this is a self-defeating strategy. The only stable outcome is the equilibrium in which both choose *BAU*.

More Countries: Climate Clubs

If there are more than just two countries, the incentive to free ride on other countries' decarbonization is greater, the greater the number of other countries is that choose *DECARB*. This can be seen by focusing on one arbitrarily chosen country, called *Home*. As illustrated in Table 6.4, *Home*'s payoff depends on the configuration of the parameters *B* and *C* and on the number of other countries (*Others*) that choose *DECARB*. If none of the other countries chooses *DECARB* (all stay at *BAU*), *Home*'s choice of *BAU* yields $Payoff = 0$, whereas *Home*'s choice of *DECARB* yields $Payoff = B \cdot \sqrt{1} - C \cdot 1 = B - C$. *Home* will thus choose *DECARB* if *B* is greater than *C*.

If one of the other countries chooses *DECARB*, *Home*'s choice of *BAU* yields $Payoff = B \cdot \sqrt{1} = B$, whereas *Home*'s choice of *DECARB* yields

Table 6.4 Home Country's Choice between *BAU* and *DECARB*

	Number of other countries choosing DECARB					
	0	*1*	*2*	*3*	*4*	*10*
BAU	0	*B*	1.41 *B*	1.73 *B*	2 *B*	3.16 *B*
DECARB	*B* – *C*	1.41 *B* – *C*	1.73 *B* – *C*	2 *B* – *C*	2.24 *B* – *C*	3.32 *B* – *C*
DECARB chosen if	*B* > *C*	*B* > 2.44 *C*	*B* > 3.13 *C*	*B* > 3.70 *C*	*B* > 4.17 *C*	*B* > 6.25 *C*

Note: Entries show the payoff to *Home* country.

Payoff $= B \cdot \sqrt{1+1} - C \cdot 1 = 1.41 \cdot B - C$. For *DECARB* to be chosen (rather than *BAU*), $1.41 \cdot B - C$ must be greater than *B*, that is: $0.41 \cdot B > C$ or $B > 2.44 \cdot C$.

As the number of other countries that choose *DECARB* grows, the requirements on the cost-benefit configuration for *Home* to choose *DECARB* become increasingly strict. If ten of the other countries choose *DECARB*, the requirement is $0.16 \cdot B > C$ or $B > 6.25 \cdot C$.

The logic behind this result is that – due to the property of diminishing marginal benefit – the *additional* benefit of one more country choosing *DECARB* is smaller the larger the number of other countries is that choose *DECARB*. For any given configuration of the parameters *B* and *C*, there is thus a maximum number of countries for which jointly choosing *DECARB* pays – a maximum size for which a hypothetical climate coalition, or "climate club", is stable.[4] If the size of the coalition exceeds that number, it pays for each country not to be a member, as the benefit to itself is smaller than the cost.

The bottom line from this discussion is that the larger the number of other countries is that choose *DECARB*, the less likely it is that the benefit from joining them covers the costs. Rather, it is individually rational to free ride on others' decarbonization efforts.

Optimal Response and Carbon Leakage

A similar point can be made if we focus not on the binary choice between *BAU* and *DECARB*, but on countries independently choosing their individually rational *degree* of decarbonization. The task is to choose that value of the variable *cutback* that maximizes a country's payoff, depending on the other countries' *cutback* choices. The condition for a cutback level to maximize a country's payoff is that the marginal benefit from *cutback* equals the marginal cost. The logic is that if the marginal benefit exceeds the marginal cost, the payoff (benefit minus cost) can be increased by increasing the cutback level, whereas if the marginal benefit is less than the marginal cost, the payoff can be increased by reducing the cutback level.

Denoting by $cutback_{Home}$ the cutback level of the home country and by $cutback_{Others}$ the aggregate cutback of all other countries, *Home*'s benefit is $B \cdot \sqrt{cutback_{Home} + cutback_{Others}}$ and *Home*'s marginal benefit is $B / \sqrt{cutback_{Home} + cutback_{Others}}$ (the partial derivative with respect to $cutback_{Home}$). Since the marginal cost equals $2 \cdot C \cdot cutback_{Home}$, the condition for a payoff maximum thus reads as follows: $\frac{B}{\sqrt{cutback_{Home} + cutback_{Others}}} = 2 \cdot C \cdot cutback_{Home}$.

Two important conclusions can be drawn from this condition. First, the condition implies a relationship between *Home*'s payoff-maximizing choice of its cutback level and the cutback levels of *Others*. This relationship specifies *Home*'s optimal response to any choice made by *Others*. As shown in the Appendix, the relationship is negative: *Home*'s payoff-maximizing response to *Others* increasing their cutback level is to reduce its cutback level. The same, of course, holds vice versa: *Others*' payoff-maximizing response to *Home* increasing its cutback level is to reduce their cutback levels. There is thus a mutual crowding out of cutback levels. This phenomenon is known as *carbon leakage*: if one country unilaterally reduces its carbon emissions, carbon "leaks" to other countries, leading to higher emissions there. The rate of carbon leakage is greater than zero and less than 100 percent. Carbon leakage, in this range, is predicted not just by the highly stylized model considered here but also by all models that involve diminishing marginal benefit and increasing marginal costs of mitigation.

In the real world, carbon leakage need not necessarily reflect an explicit response of one country's government to another country's mitigation decision. Rather, it results from the circumstance that one country unilaterally limiting its emissions triggers a relocation of emission-intensive production activities to other countries. Part of those countries' additional, carbon-intensive output will be exported to the country that has limited its emissions, leading to the import of *embodied carbon*. Reflecting such circumstances, real-world country-specific leakage rates are estimated to be between 10 and 45 percent (Misch and Wingender 2021). Since carbon leakage undermines the effectiveness of national climate change mitigation action, tariffs on embodied carbon have been proposed (Böhringer et al. 2021).

Equilibrium Cutback Levels and the Cooperation Gap

A second conclusion to be drawn from the condition for payoff-maximizing emission cutback (marginal benefit = marginal cost) concerns the equilibrium levels of cutback, and their dependence on the number of countries involved.

An equilibrium here is the set of cutback levels that solves the set of conditions for each country's payoff-maximizing cutback: $\frac{B}{\sqrt{cutback_1 + cutback_2 + \cdots}} = 2 \cdot C \cdot cutback_i$ for all countries i. Denoting the number of countries by N, there are N such conditions for N unknowns. As we continue to assume that agents (countries) are identical (an assumption to be dropped in the next section), their equilibrium cutback levels are the same. Importantly, the payoff-maximizing cutback levels are lower the larger the number of countries is (see Appendix): mutual crowding out of emission cutback is stronger the more countries are involved. This is an analog to the circumstance, discussed earlier, that it is rational from each country's point of view to free ride on other countries' decarbonization efforts, and more so, the more other countries there are.

The results from countries maximizing their individual payoffs by independently (non-cooperatively) choosing their cutback levels can be compared with a scenario in which countries (cooperatively) strive to maximize the sum of their payoffs, that is, the sum of benefits minus costs. Such an endeavor would take account of the fact that each country's cutback of emissions benefits not only the country itself, but – due to the public good characteristics of emission cutback – all countries. Accordingly, the conditions for maximizing the sum of payoffs is that the *sum of marginal benefits*, across all beneficiaries, of each country's emission cutback be equal to its marginal cost (Samuelson rule). With many beneficiaries, the sum of marginal benefits is likely to be much greater than the marginal benefit to the respective country alone. It is intuitive that this implies larger cutback levels than those that arise in the case of non-cooperative payoff maximization. Moreover, as is also intuitive, the cutback levels in the cooperation scenario are larger if there are more beneficiaries (countries).

The cooperation dilemma thus manifests itself as a *cooperation gap*: a gap between cutback levels that are individually optimal (from each country's national perspective) and those that are collectively optimal (from a global perspective). With benefit and cost functions as specified earlier (square root and quadratic, respectively), the gap amounts to 37 percent of the globally optimal level in the case of 2 countries, 79 percent in the case of 10 countries, and 95 percent in the case of 100 countries (see Appendix). In other words, if the world were composed of 10 countries, each contributing 10 percent to global emissions, each country's cutback rate would amount to slightly more than 20 percent of what is globally optimal.

Voluntary Public Goods Provision and Deontological Behavior

Consequentialist analysis of voluntary public goods provision predicts very low levels of contributions to public goods. This section discusses some evidence on the level of contributions that occur in the real world, in particular with respect to climate change mitigation, and describes how integration of deontological motives into the model of public goods provision can help explain the evidence.

Voluntary Contributions to Climate Change Mitigation

Considering nation-states, the Paris Agreement on climate change, concluded in 2015, marked the international community's abandonment of cooperative climate policy (involving the quest for binding "targets and timetables") in favor of voluntary "nationally determined contributions" (NDCs). Determining NDCs comes down to each country voluntarily and independently choosing its level of emission cutback. In spite of voluntariness, the vast majority of nations submitted significant NDCs. The NDCs submitted by the 8 largest emitters of greenhouse gases (except the United States, India, and the Russian Federation) amount to between 9 percent (China) and

31 percent (Canada) below business-as-usual (*BAU*) levels in 2030. The United States, after rejoining the Paris Agreement in April 2021, submitted an NDC that amounts to 50–52 percent below 2005 levels in 2030, which corresponds to 40 percent below *BAU* projections (see PBL Climate Pledge NDC tool at https://themasites.pbl.nl/o/climate-ndc-policies-tool/). Only India and Russia submitted NDCs that are actually above *BAU* projections. While the aggregate NDCs fall short of what would be required to limit global warming to 1.5–2°C, as stipulated in the Paris Agreement, they certainly exceed most countries' individually rational levels in the sense of the standard model of voluntary climate change mitigation.

Not only countries but individuals voluntarily engage in costly efforts to mitigate climate change, for example by buying energy-efficient household appliances. While energy-efficient household appliances are more expensive than less efficient ones, and those extra costs typically are not compensated by expected pay-back in terms of lower energy bills (Andor et al. 2020), considerable fractions of people opt for energy efficient appliances. In a representative survey of 23 European countries (European Social Survey, Round 8), 28.4 percent of the respondents say it is "extremely likely" (the highest category on an 11-point scale) that they would buy the most energy efficient one if they were to buy a large electrical appliance for their home, and this percentage is largely invariant with respect to the position in the income distribution. Conversely, only 1.7 percent of the respondents say it is "not at all likely", and even in the lowest income decile only 3.7 percent say so.

Additional insights on voluntary contributions to public goods come from public goods games. These are choice experiments in which subjects secretly choose how much of a private monetary endowment they put into a public pot. The sum of contributions to this pot is multiplied by a factor (greater than one and less than the number of players), and this "public good" is evenly distributed among the subjects. Each subject also keeps that part of the endowment they do not contribute. Each subject's payoff is the sum of the public good and that part of the endowment not contributed. With this construction (and the multiplication factor being less than the number of players), it is a dominant strategy for each player to contribute nothing, whereas the total payoff of the group is maximized if everybody contributes their total endowment – the cooperation dilemma. Refuting the prediction of all subjects choosing zero contributions (the dominant strategy equilibrium), only few do so, and average contributions are typically positive, amounting to about 50 percent of the endowment (Levitt and List 2007).

If, in contrast to the experimental design just described, the public good is not distributed among the subjects but used as a donation for mitigating climate change (of which subjects are informed before making their choice), contributions are lower. In particular, the proportion of subjects who contribute nothing (strict free riders) is three times larger, amounting to close to 40 percent (Goeschl et al. 2020). Nevertheless, the prediction of zero contributions throughout is refuted in this setting too.

The evidence on sizeable voluntary contributions to climate change mitigation at both country and household levels is hardly consistent with purely consequentialist calculus – only outcomes matter – and suggests that some non-consequentialist motives may be at play, that is, actions are taken because they are valued *per se*.

Extending the Consequentialist Model: Deontological Behavior

In the preceding section – by focusing on climate change mitigation – contributors to a public good were taken to be countries, that is, national governments that make decisions on the regulation and limitation of greenhouse gas emissions. The discussion relied on the simplifying assumption that potential contributors to a public good are identical.

Models of climate change mitigation by national governments conceive of greenhouse gas emissions as a by-product of the generation of national income (GDP). Accordingly, income depends on the level of emissions, and cutting back on emissions (relative to a business-as-usual scenario) implies costs in terms of reduced national income.

Models of climate change mitigation by national governments thus follow a macroeconomic approach in which income is endogenous. By contrast, many models of voluntary public good provision refer to individuals as the providers, and they follow a microeconomic approach. In these models, it is assumed that individuals have a fixed (exogenous) level of income, which they can allocate to the consumption of a private good and a contribution to a public good, such as charity. Importantly, individuals are assumed not to be identical, but to differ with respect to their levels of income.

Conclusions from such models corroborate those discussed in the preceding section, but are more comprehensive in that they involve assertions as to the effect of income on the contributions to a public good. Using such a framework, the following proposition can be derived: as the size of the population (the number of potential contributors) increases to infinity (a) the proportion of the population contributing to the public good decreases to zero; (b) only the very richest members of the population will contribute; and (c) average contributions decrease to zero (Andreoni 1988). Importantly, these predictions arise even if individuals act out of pure altruism (as in the case of charitable giving) rather than out of self-interest in the availability of a public good.

It is clear that assertion (c) is consistent with the models discussed in the preceding section, but assertions (a) and (b) are much more far-reaching. Their logic relies on the crowding-out mechanism discussed earlier and complements it with the effect of income on the contribution to the public good: (a) richer individuals contribute more to the public good than do poorer individuals; (b) poorer individuals respond to larger contributions by richer individuals by contributing less (crowding out); (c) in large populations the crowding-out effect can be so large that only the rich contribute at all.

Even though populations in the real world are not literally infinitely large, predictions (a)–(c) can nevertheless be validated in terms of observations from the real world. Simulations based on the US income distribution showed that the predicted proportion of non-contributors (free riders) amounts to 40 percent for $N = 2$ and increases to 89 percent for $N = 20$, and to 97 percent for $N = 200$. These predictions stand in stark contrast to evidence on charitable giving: 85 percent of US households make donations to charities, with average giving amounting to $200 in 1971, ranging from $70 for the lowest income quartile to $350 for the highest quartile (Andreoni 1988). Similarly, as mentioned previously, only 1.7 percent of European citizens say it is "not at all likely" that they will buy the most energy efficient but expensive electrical appliances, and even in the lowest income decile only 3.7 percent say so. This strongly contradicts the notion that in large economies only the richest individuals will contribute, whereas the majority will take a free-rider position.

The lack of predictive power of the standard model has spurred the development of an extended model that combines consequentialist and deontological elements (Andreoni 1990). In this formulation, it is not only the level of the public good – being the sum of individual contributions – that yields a benefit (utility) but also any individual contribution yields additional utility to the contributor. The crucial difference between the utility stemming from the public good and that stemming from the individual contribution is that the former is related to the contributions' *consequences* in terms of the public good, whereas the latter – dubbed a "warm glow" – is related to the contributions *per se*. The utility function (payoff function) thus captures deontological motives in addition to the consequentialist ones of the standard model.

From a different perspective, the extended model captures the fact that an individual's own contribution has properties of a private good, in particular excludability, that are independent of its properties as part of the public good. Unlike the benefits arising from the public good, the "warm glow" cannot be gained through others' contributions. Hence, there is no free-rider problem associated with this part of the utility function, and the predictions discussed earlier no longer apply. In particular, with deontological utility, everybody will contribute a positive amount even in large populations – as observed with respect to many public goods, including climate change mitigation.

While the deontologically augmented model explains non-zero contributions in large populations, its consequentialist part still implies that others' contributions crowd out own contributions, but crowding out will not be complete. The deontological motive, if present, ensures that some positive contribution will be made.

Conclusion

The voluntary provision of public goods is hampered by a generic cooperation dilemma: benefit non-excludability implies the possibility for every beneficiary to free ride on others' contributions to the public good. Agents independently maximizing their payoffs will thus contribute less than if they coordinated their actions. As a result, independent payoff maximization fails to be collectively rational, meaning that not only the sum of payoffs but also each agent's individual payoff is lower than it would be if agents acted cooperatively. There is thus a cooperation gap: a discrepancy between what is individually rational and what is collectively rational. Put differently, the "invisible hand" that aligns individual rationality with collective rationality under certain circumstances fails if there are non-excludable benefit spillovers. The cooperation gap gets larger as the number of potential contributors increases.

Chances to cope with the cooperation dilemma differ according to the range of benefit spillovers. If a public good's benefits are restricted to the boundaries of nation-states, the respective governments can implement regulations that resolve the dilemma. If benefits are of a transboundary and, in particular, global nature, no regulatory authority exists to devise and enforce such regulation. The issue then is one of voluntary cooperation of nations and/or individuals. Voluntary cooperation, however, is impeded by mutual crowding out: for every agent it is payoff-increasing to reduce their contribution if others' contributions rise. This implies that agreements that aim to improve over the individually rational outcome are unstable.

The mitigation of climate change is (along with biodiversity preservation) the most important public good problem of our time, and it is an issue to which this analysis applies. Reflecting the difficulties discussed earlier, a quarter century of climate diplomacy failed to establish binding "targets and timetables" for nations' limitation of greenhouse gas emissions, and the Paris Agreement of 2015 reverted to leaving it to each nation to define their voluntary "nationally determined contributions" (NDCs).

While, in view of the reasoning presented earlier, it should be expected that voluntary contributions are very low, many countries have submitted NDCs that go beyond what the aforementioned analysis predicts (though they fall short of the Paris Agreement's aim of limiting global warming to 1.5–2°C.) In addition, contrary to predictions, many people engage in actions to try and limit climate change as well as in other activities that constitute contributions to public goods. Overall, there is thus a discrepancy between the predictions of standard public goods theory and what we observe in the real world.

An approach to aligning theory with observations is to transcend the exclusively consequentialist framework on which the standard theory relies and to account for deontological utility that may arise from the respective actions themselves, in addition to the utility from actions' tangible outcomes. The deontologically extended model implies that an agent's own contribution has properties of a private good, in particular excludability, which yields a benefit that cannot be gained through others' contributions. To the extent that people enjoy such deontological utility – dubbed a "warm glow" – everybody will contribute a positive amount, even in large populations – as observed with respect to many public goods, including climate change mitigation.

The idea of a warm glow is consistent with evidence, discussed in Chapter 4, that engaging in pro-social and pro-environmental behavior is associated with higher levels of subjective wellbeing. The substantive psychological sources of the warm glow have recently started to be integrated into economic analysis, as will be discussed in the next chapter.

Notes

1 The cooperation dilemma is frequently dubbed the prisoner's dilemma. It arises in a hypothetical situation in which two prisoners are accused of having committed a crime together. They are interrogated individually and cannot communicate with each other. If both deny the crime, both will receive a light sentence, as they can only be proven to have committed a less-severe crime. If both confess, both receive a high penalty, but not the maximum penalty because of their confession. However, if only one of the two prisoners confesses, she goes unpunished, while the other, as a convicted but unconfessed perpetrator, receives the maximum sentence. The choice facing the prisoners is between denying and confessing. The choices are *strategic* in that the outcome for one agent depends not only on her choice, but on that of the other (CORE Team 2017, Unit 4).

2 While most countries will be losers from climate change (and, hence, beneficiaries of climate change mitigation) there may be some gainers, like countries in the high latitudes that may get warmer, longer, and wetter growing seasons. This is, however, a contested proposition. If true, it will obviously aggravate rather than facilitate cooperation (Buchholz and Sandler 2021) and will be neglected for the sake of clarity.

3 See Buchholz and Sandler (2021) for a comprehensive discussion of global public goods.

4 "Climate clubs" were suggested by Nordhaus (2015) as an institutional avenue for addressing climate change. The term is inconsistent with standard terminology since a club good is a good characterized by (partly) non-rivalrous but excludable benefits, a characteristic whose absence is precisely the reason why international climate policy is so difficult (Buchholz and Sandler 2021). The issue of stability (and free riding) would not arise if climate change mitigation were a club good: excludability prevents that benefits spill over to nonmembers, which provides an incentive to join. Since the term "climate club" has entered the public debate, it will be used here, as a synonym for climate coalition, keeping the appropriate caveat in mind.

Bibliography

Andor, M., Gerster, A., Sommer, S. (2020), Consumer Inattention, Heuristic Thinking and the Role of Energy Labels, *Energy Journal* 41, 83–122.

Andreoni, J. (1988), Privately Provided Public Goods in a Large Economy: The Limits of Altruism, *Journal of Public Economics* 35, 57–73.

Andreoni, J. (1990), Impure Altruism and Donations to Public Goods: A Theory of Warm-Glow Giving, *Economic Journal* 100, 464–477.

Böhringer, C., Schneider, J., Asane-Otoo, E. (2021), Trade in Carbon and Carbon Tariffs, *Environmental and Resource Economics* 78, 669–708.

Buchholz, W., Sandler, T. (2021), Global Public Goods: A Survey, *Journal of Economic Literature* 59, 488–545.

CORE Team (2017), *The Economy*, Oxford: Oxford University Press (e-book available at https://Core-Econ.Org/the-Economy/?Lang=En).

Goeschl, T., Kettner, S.E., Lohse, J., Schwieren, C. (2020), How Much Can We Learn About Voluntary Climate Action from Behavior in Public Good Games? *Ecological Economics* 171, 106591.

Hardin, G. (1968), The Tragedy of the Commons, *Science* 162, 1243–1248.

Levitt, S.D., List, J.A. (2007), What Do Laboratory Experiments Measuring Social Preferences Reveal About the Real World? *Journal of Economic Perspectives* 21, 153–174.

Misch, F., Wingender, P. (2021), Revisiting Carbon Leakage, IMF Working Paper WP/21/207.

Nash, J. (1951), Non-cooperative Games, *Annals of Mathematics* 54, 286–295.

Nordhaus, W.D. (2015), Climate Clubs: Overcoming Free-Riding in International Climate Policy, *American Economic Review* 105, 1339–1370.

Samuelson, P.A. (1954), The Pure Theory of Public Expenditure, *Review of Economics and Statistics* 36, 387–389.

Smith, A. (1776), *An Inquiry into the Nature and Causes of the Wealth of Nations*, London: Strahan and Caddel.

Stern, N. (2007), *The Economics of Climate Change: The Stern Review*, Cambridge: Cambridge University Press.

Appendix

This appendix shows how carbon leakage and emission cutbacks under independent (non-cooperative) and joint (cooperative) payoff maximization are computed.

Optimal Response and Carbon Leakage

The condition for payoff maximization (marginal benefit = marginal cost) stated in the main text

$$\frac{B}{\sqrt{cutback_{Home} + cutback_{Others}}} = 2 \cdot C \cdot cutback_{Home} \tag{6.1}$$

can be rewritten as:

$$\frac{B}{2C} = cutback_{Home} \cdot \sqrt{cutback_{Home} + cutback_{Others}}. \tag{6.2}$$

The left-hand side of equation (6.2) does not vary with respect to $cutback_{Home}$ and $cutback_{Others}$, whereas the expression on the right-hand side is increasing in both. Hence, if $cutback_{Others}$ rises, $cutback_{Home}$ must fall to keep the expression on the left-hand side constant.

Equilibrium Cutback Levels and the Cooperation Gap

Since countries are assumed to be identical, all countries end up with the same payoff-maximizing cutback rate. The expression $cutback_{Home} + cutback_{Others}$ in equation (6.1) can thus be written as $N \cdot cutback_{Home}$ (aggregate cutback is the *N*-fold of each country's cutback). Using this relationship, equation (6.1) can be solved to yield:

$$cutback_{Home}^{Non-cooperative} = \frac{\left(\frac{B}{2C}\right)^{2/3}}{N^{1/3}}$$

The right-hand side decreases as *N* increases.

By similar reasoning, the condition for a cooperative optimum (sum of marginal benefits = marginal cost) can be written as:

$$\frac{N \cdot B}{\sqrt{N \cdot cutback_{Home}}} = 2C \cdot cutback_{Home}$$

This can be solved to yield:

$$cutback_{Home}^{Cooperative} = N^{1/3}\left(\frac{B}{2C}\right)^{2/3}$$

which increases as *N* increases.

By comparing the non-cooperative and the cooperative cutback levels, it follows that the ratio of non-cooperative to cooperative cutback is $1/N^{2/3}$, which decreases as *N* increases. Accordingly, the cooperation gap $1-1/N^{2/3}$ gets larger as *N* increases.

7 Morality in Modern Economics

Introduction

As discussed in the preceding chapter, conventional analysis of voluntary public goods provision – in particular climate change mitigation – follows a consequentialist (outcome-focused) approach and predicts virtually zero contributions in large populations. Yet, voluntary contributions to climate change mitigation can be observed that go beyond what consequentialist theory predicts.

To explain observations of significant contributions to public goods, recent expansions of the standard economic model have considered moral determinants of the respective behaviors. Some departures from the standard model revise the assumption of self-regarding preferences by assuming other-regarding motivations, whereas other approaches retain the assumption of selfishness and propose that people do not engage in Nash optimization – as explained in the preceding chapter – but pursue a different mode of behavior – so-called Kantian optimization.

While assuming other-regarding preferences and Kantian optimization both stay within a consequentialist framework, other approaches pursue the idea that socially desired behaviors may be taken because people place a value on those behaviors *per se*, independent of outcomes. Building on the notion of "warm glow" giving (Chapter 6), recent research has been concerned with identifying more precisely the nature of warm-glow-like feelings and established compliance with social and moral norms as a pertinent factor, which complements consequentialist considerations with deontological (action-focused) ones.

This chapter starts with a conceptual discussion of the relevant departures from the standard model and then proceeds by presenting evidence of the role of social and moral norms for pro-environmental behavior. A focus will be on the specific set of moral values that has been identified by psychological Moral Foundations Theory. It will be shown that moral identity – the pattern of endorsement of the moral foundations – shapes not only pro-environmental behaviors but also cognitions relevant to those, notably cognitions concerning climate change. Since the outcome-focused element

DOI: 10.4324/9781003206163-9

of decision making relies on such cognitions, moral values not only have a direct, deontological effect on behaviors but also an indirect effect through the consequentialist mode of decision making.

Approaches to Morality

Many economists, dating back to Adam Smith (1759), have emphasized that factors beyond wealth – moral concerns – enter into the utility function, but the standard economic model crafted in the 19th and 20th centuries has ignored the moral dimension of economic behavior. It is only recently that moral concerns have started to be reinserted into theoretical and empirical economic analysis, possibly triggered by the increasing importance of phenomena that standard analysis fails to capture adequately (Chapter 6).

Approaches to taking moral concerns into account can be conceptualized as departures from and expansions of the standard model into several directions. To categorize these departures, it is useful to sketch some relevant features of the standard model.

Background: The Standard Model

The standard behavioral model of economics is based on three assumptions. First, agents have outcome-focused (consequentialist) preferences: they do not place any value on actions *per se*, but only on actions' outcomes (consequences). Second, agents have self-regarding preferences: they do not place any value on the outcomes of their actions for other agents, and so do not take account of the (positive or negative) effects that their actions inflict on others. Third, they engage in Nash optimization: they independently choose those actions that constitute the best response to any set of feasible choices of others. The overall outcome of such behavior is a *Nash equilibrium*, that is, a configuration of actions that no agent can improve upon – in terms of one's self-regarding preferences – by unilaterally choosing a different action.

As we learned in the preceding chapter, the Nash equilibrium is *efficient* under certain circumstances: (a) it yields the best possible outcome (highest payoff) for each agent, and (b) it yields the largest total payoff for all agents combined. Put differently, individually, rational behavior leads to a result that is collectively rational, as it could not be improved upon by acting cooperatively (collectively) rather than independently. The efficient outcome, thus, is attained by independent action as if there were an "invisible hand" (Smith 1776).

A major condition for a Nash equilibrium to be efficient is the absence of strategic interaction: one agent's actions have no effect on other agents' payoffs. If, by contrast, strategic social interaction exists, a social dilemma arises:

independent preference optimization results in an outcome that fails to yield the highest payoff for each agent and, hence, the highest sum of payoffs.

An important case of a social dilemma is the cooperation dilemma that arises if agents' payoffs depend on the level of a public good to which the agents make voluntary contributions. Using the case of climate change mitigation as a lead example, the preceding chapter has shown that independent voluntary provision of a public good leads to undersupply: in the Nash equilibrium, the levels of voluntary mitigation actions as well as the resulting payoffs are lower than they could be if agents coordinated their actions. The reason for undersupply is free-riding behavior that arises because the benefits from mitigation action are non-excludible.

In sum, the standard model of economic behavior predicts inefficiently low contributions to public goods due to free riding. More than that, individual contributions decrease as the number of agents increases.

Departures from the Standard Model

As worrying as these predictions are from a normative point of view, they fail to be descriptively valid. While voluntary contributions to public goods fall short of efficient levels, they are typically greater than predicted by the standard model (Chapter 6). This lack of predictive power is rooted in the model's assumptions, stated earlier (outcome-focused, self-regarding preferences, and Nash-optimizing behavior), and recent revisions of the standard model have departed from those assumptions. These departures take account of moral aspects of human behavior in situations that involve cooperation dilemmas – in line with the assertion of one leading scholar in the study of moral behavior that ". . . moral life is really about cooperation and alliance . . ." (Haidt 2012, Chapter 4, note 10).

The approaches to morality that have been pursued in recent accounts of strategic social interaction are displayed in Table 7.1. The benchmark (standard) model is that of consequentialist behavior, involving Nash optimization with respect to self-regarding preferences. The discussion that follows will focus on voluntary climate change mitigation as the paradigmatic example of a cooperation dilemma.

Table 7.1 Approaches to Morality in Social Interactions

	Consequentialist behavior (outcome-focused)		*Deontological behavior (action-focused)*	
Self-regarding preferences	Nash optimization	Kantian optimization	Social norm	Moral norm
Other-regarding preferences	Nash optimization with altruism			

Altruism

Accounting for other-regarding preferences is probably the most prominent departure from the standard economic model of behavior. Assuming other-regarding preferences means that individuals are taken to place a value not just on outcomes for themselves but also on outcomes for others. That value may be negative, as in the case of envy, which gives rise to the comparison effects on people's wellbeing discussed in Chapter 3. By contrast, accounting for morality in terms of other-regarding preferences means that individuals place a positive value on (positive) outcomes for others, that is, they display altruism (selflessness).

Tables 7.2 and 7.3 illustrate how altruistic preferences can resolve the cooperation dilemma of climate change mitigation. Both tables are based on the illustrative specification of the payoff from cutting back on greenhouse gases relative to business-as-usual (*BAU*) introduced in Chapter 6: $Payoff_i = B \cdot \sqrt{cutback_1 + cutback_2 + \cdots} - C \cdot cutback_i^2$. Focusing on the binary choice between *BAU* (*cutback* = 0) and *DECARB* (*cutback* = 1) in the case of two countries (*One* and *Two*) with parameters $B = 5$ and $C = 6$, Table 7.2 reproduces the cooperation dilemma (prisoner's dilemma) shown in Table 6.3: choosing *BAU* is the dominant strategy for both countries, and (*BAU*, *BAU*) is the dominant-strategy Nash equilibrium (Chapter 6). It is inefficient, since both countries would be better off if both chose *DECARB*.

Altruistic preferences can be captured by assuming that each country places a value on the benefit from the public good not just to itself but also to the other country. While the (material) benefit for each country itself remains to be measured by the parameter $B = 5$, the combined self-regarding and other-regarding benefit can be captured by a parameter $B' > B$. The altruism-adjusted payoffs (rounded to integers) are shown in Table 7.3 for $B' = 20$. Based on altruism-adjusted payoffs, (*DECARB*, *DECARB*) is now the dominant strategy Nash equilibrium: *DECARB* is the best choice for each country no matter if the other country chooses *BAU* or *DECARB*. While the material payoffs remain as in Table 7.2,

Table 7.2 The Climate Change Cooperation Dilemma Revisited ($B = 5$, $C = 6$)

Payoff for One	*Payoff for Two*	*Two*	
		BAU	*DECARB*
One	*BAU*	0	-1
		0	5
	DECARB	5	1
		-1	1

Notes: $Payoff_i = B \cdot \sqrt{cutback_1 + cutback_2} - C \cdot cutback_i^2$. *BAU* means *cutback* = 0; *DECARB* means *cutback* = 1.

Table 7.3 The Climate Change Game with Altruistic Preferences ($B' = 20$, $C = 6$); Altruism-Adjusted Payoffs

Adjusted payoff for Two / *Adjusted payoff for One*		*Two*: *BAU*	*Two*: *DECARB*
One	*BAU*	One: 0, Two: 0	One: 20, Two: 14
	DECARB	One: 14, Two: 20	One: 22, Two: 22

Notes: $AdjustedPayoff_i = B' \cdot \sqrt{cutback_1 + cutback_2} - C \cdot cutback_i$. *BAU* means *cutback* = 0; *DECARB* means *cutback* = 1.

the moral payoff from altruism turns the choices that are efficient according to Table 7.2 (*DECARB*, *DECARB*), but fail to be chosen with self-regarding preferences, into equilibrium choices.

It may be noted that in this example the moral payoff from altruism required to turn the efficient solution into an equilibrium is large (B' = 20 versus B = 5). A smaller degree of altruism (B' = 10) would turn the cooperation dilemma (Table 7.2) into a so-called chicken game (Table 7.4). In this case, there exists no dominant strategy Nash equilibrium, but two equilibria. It is the best choice for *One* to choose *DECARB* if *Two* chooses *BAU*, while it is best for *One* to choose *BAU* if *Two* chooses *DECARB*. The logic is that in the former case, the benefit from choosing *DECARB* is greater than the cost, whereas in the latter case, the *additional* benefit from choosing *DECARB* is less than the cost. The same reasoning applies to the choices of *Two*. Solutions where the countries choose differently are thus Nash equilibria, and there is no alternative set of choices in which both

Table 7.4 Chicken Game with Altruistic Preferences ($B' = 10$, $C = 6$); Altruism-Adjusted Payoffs

Adjusted payoff for Two / *Adjusted payoff for One*		*Two*: *BAU*	*Two*: *DECARB*
One	*BAU*	One: 0, Two: 0	One: 10, Two: 4
	DECARB	One: 4, Two: 10	One: 8, Two: 8

Notes: $AdjustedPayoff_i = B' \cdot \sqrt{cutback_1 + cutback_2} - C \cdot cutback_i$. *BAU* means *cutback* = 0; *DECARB* means *cutback* = 1.

are better off. Yet, the *sum* of (adjusted) payoffs arising under (*DECARB*, *DECARB*) is greater than in either of the two equilibria, so that there are potential gains from cooperation.

The binary-choice, two-country case is indicative of high degrees of altruism to be required for an efficient outcome to arise from independent Nash optimization. As the number of countries rises, so does the required degree of altruism. Treating *cutback* as a continuous variable, it was seen in Chapter 6 that the conditions for independent Nash optimization require equality of marginal costs and marginal benefit from each country's cutback, whereas efficient cutback levels require that the respective marginal costs be equal to the *sum* (across beneficiaries) of marginal benefits (Samuelson rule). For individual optimization to lead to an efficient outcome, each country would thus have to be so altruistic as to account for the entire benefit of its action for all countries. Moreover, if contributors are not identical, but differ (in terms of wealth), zero contributions are predicted to arise for most potential contributors, even with highly altruistic preferences (Andreoni 1988).

Kantian Optimization

Accounting for altruism while retaining the assumption of Nash optimization is one approach to capturing moral behavior. Another is to retain the assumption of self-regarding preferences, but to consider a different kind of optimization: Kantian optimization (Table 7.1).

The idea of Kantian optimization is inspired by Immanuel Kant's *categorical imperative*, which says: "Act only in accordance with that maxim through which you can at the same time will that it become a universal law" (Kant 1785). The categorical imperative has recently been taken to suggest that agents choose that action that, *if taken by everybody*, would maximize those agents' preferences, where the latter are taken to be purely self-interested and outcome-focused (Roemer 2015, 2019). The theory of Kantian optimization thus explicitly rules out that people care for others' wellbeing (altruism) and that actions are valued *per se* (deontology).

From a normative point of view, Kantian optimization has attractive properties. Consider the cooperation dilemma depicted in Table 7.2. By knocking out the off-diagonal cells where one agent chooses *BAU* and the other chooses *DECARB*, the choice is restricted to those options where both act in the same way. It is then the best choice for each agent to choose *DECARB*. The solution (*DECARB*, *DECARB*) is an equilibrium – there is no incentive to deviate (under the premise of uniform action) – and the equilibrium (Kantian equilibrium) is efficient – it cannot be improved upon.

Similarly, consider the chicken game (Table 7.4), assuming now that the payoffs shown are material payoffs rather than altruism-adjusted payoffs. Again, the off-diagonal cells are ruled out, and (*DECARB*, *DECARB*) emerges as an efficient Kantian equilibrium characterized by a maximum of the sum of payoffs.

While Kantian optimization leads to efficient outcomes in many situations that constitute social dilemmas (for example, cooperation dilemma and chicken game) under Nash optimization (Roemer 2019), the question is how psychologically plausible it is: why should people act upon the premise that everybody else act in the same way as they do? Two possible explanations can be distinguished (Elster 2017). One possibility is that people act upon an *illusion of control*, an irrational (possibly subconscious) belief that their choices have an influence on other people's choices. The other is that people follow a decision rule of *matching*, according to which they adjust their behavior to the prevailing behavior of others, and assume others to behave similarly.

While some evidence consistent with the control illusion has been found in cooperation experiments (Morris et al. 1998), survey research found people to mention matching as a reason for acting cooperatively. In a survey that asked people about their recycling behavior, 12 percent of those who recycled said they do it because "People in my neighborhood do", whereas 28 percent of non-recyclers said, "People in my neighborhood don't" (Roemer 2019).

Whether "doing what others do" implies the belief that "others do what I do", as is implicit in Kantian optimization, is not clear. Yet, independent of Kantian optimization theory, matching, or following, behavior is an essential element of another explanation of cooperation: conformity to a social norm.

Social and Moral Norms

Whereas altruism and Kantian optimization are approaches to morality that stay within the domain of consequentialist (outcome-focused) decision making, other approaches have focused on deontological (action-focused) factors, that is, people place a value on certain actions *per se*, independent of outcomes.

Consequentialist and deontological concerns may be at work at the same time and, as noted in Chapter 5, may imply conflicting prescriptions as to which actions to take. The so-called trolley problem of whether to kill one person to save a larger number is a case in point (Jarvis Thomson 1985). It is ruled out by deontology, but seems to be demanded by (Utilitarian) consequentialism. In spite of such moral dilemmas, deontological and consequentialist concerns have come to be viewed as complements. Specifically, deontological morality is instrumental to achieving "good" outcomes in many situations. As maintained by a functionalist view of human morality (Tomasello 2016), precisely those norms have evolved in (human) natural history that – by facilitating and enhancing cooperation – are beneficial to the survival of those groups whose members comply with them.[1] Such an evolutionary advantage from acting morally will arise as a statistical tendency, irrespective of single instances where consequences may be bad. In addition, acting morally, according to norms "approved by evolution", may be a useful way of dealing with uncertainties regarding the consequences of actions in particular situations.

Accordingly, while several deontological factors may influence an individual's behavior in general and the individual's contribution to a public good in particular (such as status-seeking or a desire for recognition and distinction) a major factor studied in recent behavioral economics is compliance with norms, that is, some rules of conduct.

Norms relevant to environmental behavior can be differentiated into social norms and moral norms (Nyborg 2018). Social norms are generally understood to be shared rules of conduct that are partly sustained by social approval and disapproval (Elster 1989). Proceeding from this general definition of a social norm, several distinctions have been proposed (Farrow et al. 2017). The most prominent and widely used distinction is that between descriptive and injunctive norms. Whereas descriptive norms refer to what most relevant people do, injunctive norms describe what most relevant people approve of doing. Depending on who those "relevant people" are, a further distinction can be made between within-group social norms and broader societal norms. A reason why people conform to what most others do (descriptive norm) may be that they take the prevalence of the respective behaviors to indicate that those behaviors are supported by a shared belief that they are approved of (injunctive norm).

In contrast to social norms, moral norms refer to inner feelings of what is right or wrong. They are enforced by an individual through emotions such as guilt and a bad conscience (Nyborg 2018). Through similar mechanisms, social norms – what most people do or approve of doing – may guide behaviors even if the behaviors are not observable by others, in which case they are referred to as quasi-moral norms (Elster 2017).

The remainder of this chapter discusses recent evidence on how social norms and a specific set of moral norms – so-called moral foundations – shape pro-environmental behavior.

Social Norms and Pro-Environmental Behavior

The influence of social norms on pro-environmental behavior has been extensively studied over the past two decades, and has recently been expanded to account for so-called social tipping points.

Social Norm Interventions

By 2017, 42 studies of social norms and pro-environmental behavior had been identified, of which 11 referred to energy use; 11 referred to recycling; and 20 referred to green consumption, littering, water conservation, towel reuse, and pesticide use (Farrow et al. 2017). These studies covered both (reported) behaviors and behavior intentions, and they referred to both descriptive norms (individuals' beliefs about what most people actually do) and injunctive norms (individuals' beliefs about what most people approve or disapprove of doing). The studies typically involved social norm interventions, that is, subjects were informed about the relevant behaviors of most others or others' approval/disapproval of such behaviors.

Informing people about what others approve/disapprove of was found to significantly positively affect the behaviors studied in 10 out of 19 cases. The proportion of significant results was highest in the case of energy use. This included energy use in the workplace and in public places (e.g., switching off lights when not used) and can thus be considered to be highly observable. Supplying information about what most people actually do (e.g., reuse towels in hotels) was also often found to enhance the corresponding behaviors, possibly because the information about what people do is taken as a signal of which behaviors are socially approved of and which are not (Farrow et al. 2017).

In a number of cases, however, boomerang effects were found, particularly with respect to domestic energy use. When informed about average energy consumption in their neighborhoods, some people who learned that they outperformed the norm increased rather than decreased their consumption (Allcott and Rogers 2014; Schultz et al. 2007). Evidently, this is consistent with the consequentialist notion that one's own and others' contributions are strategic substitutes: when individuals learn that the goal of climate change mitigation is closer to being achieved than they believed (as others consumed less energy than expected), it is rational to free ride and reduce one's own mitigation effort.

Another mechanism that may imply a boomerang effect of informing people about the prevalence of a behavior is social distinction: people may engage in a desirable behavior to seek distinction (Bénabou and Tirole 2006), and this works only when the overall level (prevalence) of the behavior is low. When they learn that the overall level is higher than expected, the behavior becomes less attractive as a vehicle for attaining distinction and may thus be reduced.

The distinction mechanism suggests that the relationship between one's own behavior and the average level of a desired behavior may be nonlinear, possibly being negative at low levels (where distinction plays a role) and turning positive at higher levels (where conformity becomes the dominant concern). Perhaps more fundamentally, such a U-shaped relationship between one's own behavior and others' behavior may also arise from the interplay of consequentialist and conformity considerations, where the latter take grip only when the behavior is sufficiently widespread in the population.

Social Tipping Points and Voluntary Climate Change Mitigation

A U-shaped relationship between an individual's desired behavior and the behavior's overall (average) level is consistent with the idea of social tipping points (Nyborg et al. 2016). Recent history has seen large-scale changes of norms and behaviors, for instance with respect to fertility behavior or the cessation of smoking in public places. However, for such changes to be self-reinforcing, it is necessary that *social tipping points* are passed; that is, for social conformity to induce behavior changes, a sufficiently large number of people must already have changed their behavior so that a "new" social norm emerges.

Though fertility and smoking behaviors do not necessarily refer to public goods, the notion of threshold values or tipping points may be even more relevant when public goods are involved. In such cases, "new" norms of behavior (e.g., environmental sustainability) do not only compete with "old" ones (e.g., "keeping up with the Joneses") but also – as discussed earlier – with incentives to free ride on others' contributions to the public good.

Evidence of social tipping points with respect to climate change mitigation is provided by a study involving about 30,000 individuals from 23 European countries (Welsch 2022a). The study used survey data on the purchase of energy-efficient home appliances as a means to contribute to climate change mitigation. Controlling for a large set of potential confounders (people's sense of responsibility for climate change, sense of effectiveness of taking individual action, income, and a battery of sociodemographic correlates), the study found that, up to a threshold level of others perceived to engage in mitigation, individuals' willingness to engage in mitigation themselves is lower the more other individuals are perceived to engage in such behavior, whereas the relationship is positive when the threshold (tipping point) is passed. The U-shaped relationship between one's own and others' perceived behavior was found to exist in all subgroups of the population (by age, gender, level of education, and ideological position) and in 15 out of the 23 countries.

Since the percentage of others perceived to engage in mitigation was found to be lower than the estimated threshold (30 to 56 percent) in a number of (but not all) countries, it was concluded that policies that induce *marginal* increases in the number of people who behave in a climate-friendly way may backfire by enhancing free-rider behavior. For the social norm to take grip, policy-induced *non-marginal* increases may be warranted in such cases to shift the system past the tipping point. For those countries where the percentage of others perceived to engage in mitigation was found to be higher than the threshold, the social norm mechanism is self-reinforcing, prompting ever greater numbers of people to follow the norm.

Moral Norms and Pro-Environmental Behavior

Moral norms may be issue-specific, for example, duties pertaining specifically to certain behaviors, or general, involving fundamental moral values. Recent research has studied the influence of both types of moral norms on pro-environmental behavior.

Issue-Specific Pro-Environmental Norms

Moral norms considered in studies of pro-environmental behavior are typically issue-specific, rather than referring to *general* moral values. For instance, a discrete-choice study of waste sorting used a latent variable that involves endorsement of the statements "Sorting waste at home is my moral/ethical duty" and "Sorting waste is something everybody should do", and found this latent variable to be significantly positively associated with choosing more thorough waste-sorting activities (Czajkowski et al. 2017). Similarly, a study of carbon offsetting used items designed to measure individuals' sense of duty toward climate change mitigation and found the willingness to pay for carbon offsets to mainly depend on the moral duty indicator (Blasch and Ohndorf 2015). Outside the environment context, it was found that appeals to moral duty were effective in stimulating several behaviors for mitigation of the Covid-19 pandemic, whereas pointing out the behaviors' favorable social consequences was effective only with respect to relatively low-cost behaviors (Bos et al. 2020).

While engaging in various kinds of pro-environmental and pro-social behaviors has been found to depend on some issue/behavior-specific sense of duty ("It is my duty to . . ."), it has long been unclear whether the respective duties and behaviors rely on some general and fundamental moral values or principles. Understanding such general/ultimate (rather than specific/proximate) moral motivations is important because, as will be discussed in the next section, individuals' general moral profiles are characteristics of their identities, and as such hardly malleable after adolescence. The heterogeneity of moral profiles may therefore imply persistent heterogeneity of the relevant behaviors.

Moral Foundations Theory

A stringent general and empirically applicable theory of moral values has recently been proposed by moral psychologists: Moral Foundations Theory (MFT). MFT defines generic foundations of moral behavior by measuring how people make moral decisions, rather than prescribing *a priori* what is moral and what is not. MFT is directly relevant to the issue of voluntary public goods provision, as it is based on a functionalist view of human morality (discussed earlier), according to which moral systems have emerged in biological-cultural evolution in order to facilitate the cooperative creation of common goods by curbing free-rider behavior (e.g., Graham et al. 2011; Haidt 2012; Tomasello 2016).

MFT was developed by relating the elementary challenges of community life described by evolutionary anthropology to virtues found in one way or another in all cultures of the world (Haidt and Joseph 2007). The basic values are Care, Fairness, Liberty, Loyalty, Authority, and Purity/Sanctity (Graham et al. 2011; Haidt 2012). The associated challenges in community life are the protection of vulnerable children (Care), the sharing of gains from cooperation (Fairness), the containment of despotic tendencies (Liberty), the stabilization of coalitions in competition with other coalitions (Loyalty), the support of efficient status hierarchies (Authority), and protection against impure substances (Purity/Sanctity). The set of moral concerns is thus more encompassing than the concern for Fairness, which economic accounts of ethics focus on (Chapter 5).

In behavioral psychology, the basic moral values are conceived of as moral norms that are activated by certain triggers. These triggers are sometimes more general or abstract than the original challenges just described. Likewise, the contemporary manifestations of the principles themselves are sometimes more general or abstract than the original ones. So the principle of Care presents itself as humanity, and the principle of Purity/Sanctity as inviolability of some values, traditions, and customs.

Table 7.5 describes the moral foundations in terms of the underlying adaptive challenges, the triggers that activate the respective mental modules, and some virtue words that characterize the moral foundations. The triggers listed give an indication of which principles could be relevant for pro-environmental and climate-friendly behavior. The virtue words serve to illustrate the meaning of the principles in terms of content. For example, the virtues of moderation or piety associated with the principle of Purity/Sanctity suggest that this principle implies an appreciation for traditions, manners, and customs.

An orientation toward the basic moral principles can be found in all cultures, societies, and socioeconomic groups, but to different extents. In particular, a distinction is important here between individual-focused (universalist) principles – Care, Fairness, and Liberty – which apply to all people regardless of belonging to their own group, and group-focused (parochial) principles – Loyalty, Authority, and Purity/Sanctity. While the individual-focused, universalist principles have a high priority in "Western" culture, "Eastern" cultures tend to be characterized by stronger endorsement of group-focused, parochial values (Haidt 2012).

The difference between universalist and parochial morality is of potential importance for climate-friendly behavior because climate protection is a *global* public good, that is, climate-friendly behavior has a reach that extends

Table 7.5 Moral Foundations Theory

	Care	*Fairness*	*Liberty*	*Loyalty*	*Authority*	*Purity/Sanctity*
Adaptive challenges	Caring for vulnerable children	Reaping benefits from cooperation	Constraining domination and bullying	Forming cohesive coalitions	Forging beneficial status hierarchies	Avoiding contaminants
Original triggers	Suffering, distress, neediness	Cheating, cooperation, deception	Bullies, tyrants	Threat or challenge to group	Signs of dominance and submission	Waste products, diseased people
Relevant virtues	Caring, kindness	Fairness, justice,	Sovereignty	Loyalty, patriotism, self-sacrifice	Obedience, deference	Temperance, moderation, chastity, piety, cleanliness

Source: Adapted from Haidt (2012), p. 146 and pp. 200–211.

beyond one's own group (e.g., region or nation), rendering parochial morality potentially less relevant or powerful. Having a greater reach than parochial morality, universalist morality may explain why people's moral circle comprises nonhuman beings (Chapter 5).

Moral Foundations and Voluntary Climate Change Mitigation

The relationship between an environment-specific moral norm (sense of duty toward the environment), endorsement of the moral foundations, and a set of climate-friendly behaviors was studied using representative survey data from the European Social Survey (ESS) for about 25,000 individuals from 16 West European countries (Welsch 2020). The moral foundations were approximated by items from the human values inventory of the ESS. The study found that the likelihood to buy energy-efficient appliances and to reduce energy use through behavior changes as well as the support of climate-related regulations (taxes, subsidies, and ban on energy-inefficient appliances) were significantly positively related to endorsement of the moral foundations, most strongly so to endorsement of Care, Fairness, and Loyalty (concern for the wellbeing of people close). In addition, the relationships were partially mediated by a measure of individuals' sense of duty toward environmental protection (proxied by a measure of environmental concern), that is, the behavior variables were positively related to the sense-of-duty indicator, which, in turn, was positively related to the moral foundations. The relationship between sense of duty toward the environment and the moral foundations was particularly strong with respect to the Loyalty foundation, that is, concern for the wellbeing of "people close" (Loyalty) strongly shaped individuals' environmental concern.

In addition to the *indirect* relationships between behaviors and moral foundations – through the sense of duty toward the environment – a significantly positive *direct* relationship was found with respect to the universalist values of Care and Fairness. By contrast, a significantly *negative* direct behavior-morality relationship was found with respect to the parochial values of Loyalty, Authority, and Sanctity. The relationships between the climate-friendly behaviors and the parochial foundations, in particular Loyalty, thus switched sign (from positive to negative) once the sense of duty toward environmental protection was controlled for: people with the same level of environmental concern engage less in climate-friendly behaviors, the more they endorse the parochial moral values.

In interpreting these findings, it is argued in the study that the indicator of duty toward the environment does not differentiate between the global public good of climate change mitigation and more local or regional environmental issues. Once this general environmental concern is controlled for, the focus is on the relationship between protection of the global environmental good and the moral foundations. In this perspective, the results suggest a strong influence of universalist morality on contributions to the global environmental good, whereas endorsement of parochial morality – while potentially beneficial to local/regional public goods – tends to be detrimental to the global public good.

A positive relationship between universalist moral values and climate-friendly behaviors was also found in samples from the United States (Dickinson et al. 2016) and Finland (Vainio and Mäkiniemi 2016), but these studies did not consider the mediating role of a sense of duty toward environmental protection. The first of these papers used a random sample of 1,000 US adults and found that valuations of Care and Fairness were strong, positive predictors of willingness to take personal actions on climate change, whereas Purity/Sanctity had a non-significant tendency in the positive direction. Loyalty and Authority were not supported as important predictor variables. The second paper used a sample of 272 Finnish students and found that universalist moral foundations were associated with increased climate-friendly choices with respect to transport, energy use at home, and food, whereas parochial foundations were associated with decreased climate-friendly choices.

A further study investigated the role for climate change mitigation of the moral foundations jointly with social norms and social preferences (including altruism) in a representative sample of 8,000 US adults (Falk et al. 2021). In that study, the moral foundations indicator was *relative* universalism, specified as Care and Fairness minus Loyalty and Authority. In a choice experiment, it was found that donations targeted to climate change mitigation were significantly positively related to relative universalism as well as to individuals' perceived social norms with respect to climate change mitigation, and social preferences such as patience and altruism.

In sum, the studies discussed consistently found a positive association between universalist moral values and climate-friendly behaviors, whereas the association tended to be negative in the case of parochial moral foundations. This is important in two ways. First, individuals' moral profile in terms of universalism-parochialism is a stable feature of their identity that is hardly malleable after early adulthood. Second, as will be seen, individuals' moral identity influences not only their climate-relevant behaviors but also their beliefs about climate change. Since those beliefs likely affect their behaviors, there is a second, indirect channel through which moral identity and climate-relevant behaviors may be related. The next section discusses these issues more thoroughly.

Identity, Cognitions, and Climate Change Mitigation

While group-specific social norms and moral norms become effective through different mechanisms, there is an important similarity between them: group-specific social norms (not society-wide social norms) and moral norms can be characteristics of an individual's identity or self-image – one's social identity in the former case and one's personal identity in the latter. If a social or moral norm is essential to an individual's identity, it can affect not only the individual's behavior but also the individual's beliefs and cognitions. As found by cognitive psychologists, individuals typically hold those behavior-relevant beliefs that are consistent with what the relevant behavioral norms demand (Kahan 2017). To illustrate, an individual for whom climate change mitigation is inconsistent with her (consumption-focused) social or personal identity is expected to downplay the severity of climate change, the extent to which it is human-made, and the effectiveness of mitigation activities, and to exaggerate the costs of mitigation. An individual who views herself as an environmentalist or climate activist, conversely, is expected to hold the opposite beliefs. This way, climate change mitigation and other environmental behaviors may depend on norms not only directly but also indirectly through the relevant beliefs and cognitions.

Moral Identity

The norms an individual adheres to are important characteristics of her identity. While her group identity – her feeling about what social group she belongs to – is linked to the group's social norms, her personal identity – her self-image – relies *inter alia* on her moral norms. To the extent that moral norms are shared by a group and differentiate it from other groups, those shared moral norms constitute within-group social norms that characterize an individual's group identity.

The individual-specific endorsement pattern of the moral foundations constitutes the moral dimension of an individual's identity, her moral identity, which is a stable and characteristic feature of an individual's self (Strominger and Nichols 2014). Depending on the emphasis an individual places on Care, Fairness, and Liberty on one hand and Loyalty, Authority, and Sanctity on the other, the individual's moral identity is more individual-focused or more group-focused (Haidt 2012).

Moral identity is acquired during adolescence and early adulthood and is stable thereafter. The development of moral identity involves three steps (McAdams and Pals 2006). The first step refers to a genetic predisposition that manifests itself in the personality trait of "openness to experience": a tendency to cherishing novelty, variety, and diversity, while simultaneously being less sensitive to signs of threat. People with this trait are predisposed (but not predestined) to become individual-focused, whereas people with the opposite settings are predisposed to become group-focused. These basic dispositional traits undergo so-called characteristic adaptations during adolescence in response to the specific environments and challenges individuals happen to face. For instance, an individual scoring high on "openness to experience" may respond to strict rules in school by developing a general sense of dissatisfaction with existing arrangements, which would not have happened to the same degree had the individual gone to a more individual-focused and less structured school (Haidt 2012).

Given dispositional traits and characteristic adaptations, the final step in the development of moral identity is the construction of "life narratives", that is, simplified and selective reconstructions of one's past, connected to an idealized vision of the future, and saturated with morality. Life narratives provide a bridge between an individual's developing adolescent self and the individual's adult moral identity as individual-focused – with a taste for Care, Fairness, and Liberty – or group-focused – with a taste for Loyalty, Authority, and Sanctity and a heightened sense for the interests of the group.

Identity-Protective Cognition and Climate Change

People's identity not only guides their decisions but may also shape their cognition of decision-relevant phenomena. One motive underlying identity's influence on cognitions is a desire to minimize cognitive dissonance, that is, a psychological discomfort arising from a misalignment between an individual's values and choices and the facts that characterize the choice situation. Cognitive dissonance can be resolved by changing one's identity-relevant values or, conversely, by interpreting the facts to match one's values. Given an individual's desire for a stable moral identity, interpreting reality in an identity-compatible way is a widespread strategy (Festinger 1957). With respect to group identity, an important motive for maintaining identity-consistent cognitions is the individual's desire to secure for herself the group's material and psychological support. With respect to voluntary public goods provision, the utility to the individual from group support is larger than the disutility from supplying too small contributions to the public good, a phenomenon referred to as "the tragedy of the science communication commons" (Kahan 2017). Individuals are therefore expected to align their decision-relevant cognitions to those of the group.

Identity-protective cognition involves individuals' differentially attending to (through selective exposure or avoidance) and/or processing (through motivated reasoning) information (e.g. Garrett et al. 2011; Kunda 1990, respectively) in a way that agrees with their (and their group's) worldview, norms, and values. Identity-protective information selection and directionally motivated reasoning have been found to lead to polarized views around science and policy issues (Druckman and McGrath 2019; Kahan 2013; Kraft et al. 2015). Polarized views on science are better explained by identity-protecting cognitive strategies than by the competing hypothesis of deficits in the public's capacity to comprehend scientific evidence (Kahan et al. (2017).

Many existing studies on identity-protective cognition refer to political partisanship as the relevant identity category. With respect to energy issues, one study investigated motivated processing of media information about biofuels in the United States and found that liberals (Democrats) and conservatives (Republicans) are affected differently by media use when forming opinions about the associated risks and benefits (Cacciatore et al. 2012). Similarly, polarization of support for fracking (horizontal oil and gas drilling using polluting chemicals) can be understood by how risk and benefit perceptions differ between liberals and conservatives, with liberals seeing greater risk and less benefit (Howell et al. 2019).

More important than those specific issues (biofuels and fracking), there is ample evidence that despite scientific consensus, liberal-progressive and conservative US citizens hold widely different views on climate change. Specifically, liberals tend to believe that human activity is a primary cause of climate change, whereas conservatives are much less likely to hold this belief (Brewer 2012; McCright and Dunlap 2011). Using an international sample, it was found that a positive relationship between a more right-leaning or conservative political orientation and "climate skepticism" exists not only in the United States but also in a pool of 24 other nations from all around the world, as well as in the majority of individual nations (Hornsey et al. 2018).

In addition to political orientation, a cultural polarization of perceived climate change risk between "hierarchical individualists" and "egalitarian communitarians" was found to exist in the United States (Kahan et al. 2012). Similarly, a positive association between hierarchical/individualist values and climate skepticism exists not only in the United States but also in a pool of 24 other nations (Hornsey et al. 2018). A meta-analysis that considered political orientation and cultural and human values jointly revealed that both, political affiliation and ideology, and cultural and human values, shape climate change beliefs, in particular the view that climate change is human-made (Hornsey et al. 2016). The same meta-study found that climate change beliefs, in turn, shape climate-friendly behaviors or behavior intentions.

Overall, this literature suggests that individuals' values shape their cognitions concerning the existence and origin of climate change and the risks associated with it. Since such cognitions are likely to influence their propensity to act in climate-friendly ways (as suggested by consequentialist reasoning), climate change cognitions may act as a mediator in the relationship between values and behaviors, that is, values affect cognitions and cognitions affect behaviors. This indirect relationship between values and actions potentially complements the usually considered direct relationship between them.

Moral Values, Identity-Protective Cognition, and Voluntary Climate Change Mitigation

While the bulk of the literature on identity-protective climate change cognitions focused on *ideological* identity (political affiliation or position on the left-right scale), one recent paper has studied the relationship between *moral* identity, climate change cognitions, and voluntary climate change mitigation (Welsch 2021). Specifically, the paper studied whether moral identity – as captured by the endorsement pattern of the moral foundations – may be related to climate-friendly behavior not only directly but, in addition, indirectly through a relationship between moral foundations and behavior-relevant cognitions, for example, a perception that climate change is (or is not) bad or that individual mitigation efforts are effective (or ineffective).

Using a large-scale representative data set (the European Social Survey) for a set of West European countries, the research found that endorsement of the individual-focused (universalist) moral foundations (Care, Fairness, Liberty) and endorsement of the group-focused (parochial) moral foundations (Loyalty, Authority, Sanctity) are both related to climate-friendly behavior through the direct channel, the former one and a half times stronger than the latter. In addition, individual-focused moral foundations were found to enhance the cognitions that climate change is bad and that individual action to mitigate it is effective. Since these cognitions, in turn, were found to enhance the behaviors studied (consistent with consequentialist calculus), there are indirect relationships between the universalist moral values and climate-friendly behavior. The indirect relationships amount to up to one-third of the direct relationships. Comparing different behaviors, moral identity is more important (through both channels) with respect to costly behavior than with respect to costless behavior. Comparing different moral foundations, the Care and Fairness foundations stand out by exhibiting the strongest (positive) relationship to the perception that climate change is bad and individual action is effective. Importantly, all of the relationships found hold while controlling for political position (left-right scale).

Identity, Climate Change Cognitions, and Educational Attainment

Given that climate change cognitions – and in particular "climate skepticism" – are shaped by identity protection strategies, an important question is, if and how biased cognitions may be corrected. An obvious source of more accurate knowledge about climate change is better education. Indeed, educational attainment has long been identified as a consistent predictor of environment-related perceptions and concerns (Dietz et al. 1998). Whether better education goes with less identity-related cognition bias is, however, not obvious. As shown recently, ideology-dependence of climate change cognitions is stronger rather than weaker in individuals with greater science literacy and numeracy, on the grounds that these abilities facilitate adjustment of beliefs to identity through selection and processing of information (Kahan et al. 2017).

Whether – similar to the dependence of climate change cognitions on *ideological* identity – their dependence on *moral* identity varies with cognitive ability was studied using data for 23 countries from the European Social Survey (Welsch 2022b). The study involved four climate change cognitions (the world climate is changing; climate change is caused by human activities; climate change has bad impacts; reducing personal-level energy use can reduce climate change), individuals' placement on the left-right scale, and individuals' endorsement of the moral foundations. The analysis revealed that all cognitions studied are significantly negatively related to a more right-leaning ideological position and significantly positively related to stronger endorsement of Fairness, whereas all but one of the cognitions are significantly negatively related to stronger endorsement of Authority and Sanctity. Similar to the literature on the role of science literacy, the research found that the ideology-dependence of the cognitions studied is significantly stronger in individuals with a tertiary education (that is, a bachelor's degree or higher). In addition to the ideology-cognition relationships, 9 of the 24 morality-cognition relationships were also significantly stronger in individuals with tertiary education. In particular, the cognitions that climate change is human-made and that climate change impacts are bad are more morality-dependent in individuals with better education than in less-educated people. In contrast to the latter cognitions, the belief that the climate is changing is less morality-dependent in better-educated than in less-well-educated people. The level of education *per se* is positively related to the cognitions that the climate is changing, that climate change is human-made, and that climate change impacts are bad.

The role of better education in shaping climate change cognitions is thus ambiguous, as better education *per se* improves climate knowledge but tends to amplify biases in the relevant cognitions that result from identity-protective information selection and processing. In particular, better-educated people with a more right-leaning ideological position and stronger endorsement of group-focused moral values have a greater propensity toward "climate skepticism" than their less-educated counterparts.

Conclusion

While conventional consequentialist analysis of voluntary public goods provision – and, in particular, climate change mitigation – predicts virtually zero contributions in large populations, voluntary contributions to climate change mitigation can be observed that go beyond what consequentialist theory predicts.

Compliance with social and moral norms offers an explanation for such observations, an explanation that relies on the deontological notion that some behaviors are valued *per se*, independent of their outcomes. With respect to social norms and associated behaviors, recent history has seen large-scale changes, for instance with respect to fertility behavior, indoor smoking, and the growing popularity of vegetarian and vegan diets. Some of the evidence discussed in this chapter suggests that social norms and changes thereof may affect climate-relevant behavior, in particular energy use, in a similar way. For this to happen, however, the prevalence of the respective social norms in society needs to pass a threshold level. As suggested by other evidence, however, group identities and polarized worldviews may impede this, as they imply a divide with respect to climate-related norms and cognitions. A major divide in this respect refers to political orientation toward the left (liberals) and the right (conservatives). Another refers to individuals' prevailing moral identity in terms of universalism and parochialism.

While political and moral identities are not the same, there is nevertheless a close association between them, in that conservatives display a stronger endorsement of parochial (group-focused) moral values, whereas liberals tend toward a more universalist morality. Irrespective of their relationship to political orientation, however, individuals' moral values can be expected to be of generic importance for climate change mitigation because, as discussed earlier, human morality is generally viewed as the answer of biological and cultural evolution to the challenges involved in the cooperative production of public goods.

The empirical findings discussed in this chapter are consistent with this view. The more people orient themselves toward the basic moral principles identified by modern moral psychology, the more likely they are to engage in pro-environmental behaviors and to support environmental policy measures. The appreciation of basic moral principles thus helps to mitigate the negative effects of individually rational behavior, that is, free riding: morality supports collective rationality where individual rationality fails.

In terms of specific moral values, the universalist values play a stronger role than the parochial, group-focused ones when it comes to climate change mitigation. While parochial values are important for environmental protection in general, they play a smaller – sometimes even negative – role with respect to the climate in particular. This is theoretically plausible: the preservation of a global common good is supported more by the appreciation of a universalist morality that refers to all people, than by a group-focused morality. The latter, especially the principle of loyalty to one's own group, is more relevant to local and regional environmental problems.

Universalist morality was put forth by various thinkers and religions around two and a half millennia ago and, in the wake of the European Enlightenment philosophy, was elevated to a political program (freedom, equality, humanity). Since then, universalist morality has spread and developed. At the same time – and accelerated in the wake of the Enlightenment – an unprecedented expansion of technological forces took place, which brought with it anthropogenic climate change and threats to biodiversity as undesirable by-products. Whether moral change, in the sense of a stronger emphasis on universalist morality, is sufficient to curb the adverse effects of technological change of the last two centuries or to steer it in the required direction is an open question.

Note

1 In contrast to the apparent antagonism between outcome-oriented and action-oriented behavior, evolutionary anthropology views some forms of action-oriented decision making as instrumental to eventually achieving favorable outcomes where a direct orientation of behaviors toward outcomes would fail. In this perspective, deontological moral behavior involves unconditionally choosing acts with apparently unfavorable outcomes to the individual if it serves a common purpose, and such behavior developed evolutionarily as a means of coping with the free-rider problem

in the cooperative creation of public goods (Haidt 2012, Tomasello 2016). As shown by Price (1970, 1972), a disposition to such behavior survives in (biological-cultural) evolution if the implied disadvantage of such a person within the group is less than the advantage the person gains from the fact that the group as a whole asserts itself better in competition with other groups (group selection).

Bibliography

Allcott, H., Rogers, T. (2014), The Short-run and Long-run Effects of Behavioral Interventions: Experimental Evidence from Energy Conservation, *American Economic Review* 104 (10), 3003–3037.

Andreoni, J. (1988), Privately Provided Public Goods in a Large Economy: The Limits of Altruism, *Journal of Public Economics* 35, 57–73.

Bénabou, R., Tirole, J. (2006), Incentives and Prosocial Behavior, *American Economic Review* 96, 1652–1678.

Blasch, J., Ohndorf, M. (2015), Altruism, Moral Norms and Social Approval: Joint Determinants of Individual Offset Behavior, *Ecological Economics* 116, 251–260.

Bos, B., Drupp, M.A., Meya, J.N., Quaas, M.F. (2020), Moral Suasion and the Private Provision of Public Goods: Evidence from the Covid-19 Pandemic, *Environmental and Resource Economics* 76, 1117–1138.

Brewer, P.R. (2012), Polarization in the USA: Climate Change, Party Politics and Public Opinion in the Obama Era, *European Political Science* 11, 7–17.

Cacciatore, M.A., Scheufele, D.A., Binder, A.R., Shaw, B.R. (2012), Public Attitudes Toward Biofuels: Effects of Knowledge, Political Partisanship, and media Use, *Politics and the Life Sciences* 31 (1–2), 36–51.

Czajkowski, M., Hanley, N., Nyborg, K. (2017), Social Norms, Morals and Self-Interest as Determinants of Pro-Environment Behaviour: The Case of Household Recycling, *Environmental and Resource Economics* 66, 647–670.

Dickinson, J.L., McLeod, P., Bloomfield, R., Allred, S. (2016), Which Moral Foundations Predict Willingness to Make Lifestyle Changes to Avert Climate Changes in the USA?, *PLoS ONE* 11(10): e0163852. doi:10.1371/journal.pone.0163852.

Dietz, T., Stern, P.C., Guagnano, G.A. (1998), Social Structural and Social Psychological Bases of Environmental Concern, *Environment and Behavior* 30(4), 450–471.

Druckman, J.N., McGrath, M.C. (2019), The Evidence for Motivated Reasoning in Climate Change Preference Formation, *Nature Climate Change* 9, 111–119.

Elster, J. (1989), Social Norms and Economic-Theory, *Journal of Economic Perspectives* 3, 99–117.

Elster, J. (2017), On Seeing and Being Seen, *Social Choice and Welfare* 49, 721–734.

Falk, A., Andre, P., Boneva, T., Chopra, F. (2021), Fighting Climate Change: The Role of Norms, Preferences, and Moral Values, CESifo Working Paper No. 9175.

Farrow, K., Grolleau, G., Ibanez, L. (2017), Social Norms and Pro-Environmental Behavior: A Review of the Evidence, *Ecological Economics* 140, 1–13.

Festinger, L. (1957), *A Theory of Cognitive Dissonance*, Stanford, CA: Stanford University Press.

Garrett, R.K., Carnahan, D., Lynch, E.K. (2011), A Turn Toward Avoidance? Selective Exposure to Online Political Information, 2004–2008, *Political. Behavior* 35 (1), 113–134.

Graham, J., Nosek, B.A., Haidt, J., Iyer, R., Koleva, S., Ditto, P.H. (2011), Mapping the Moral Domain, *Journal of Personality and Social Psychology* 101, 366–385.

Haidt, J. (2012), *The Righteous Mind: Why Good People Are Divided by Politics and Religion*, Harmondsworth: Penguin Books.

Haidt, J., Joseph, C. (2007), The Moral Mind: How 5 Sets of Innate Intuitions Guide the Development of Many Culture-Specific Virtues and Perhaps Even Modules. In: P. Carruthers, S. Laurence, S. Stich (eds.), *The Innate Mind* (pp. 367–391), New York: Oxford University Press.

Hornsey, M.J., Harris, E.A., Fielding, K.S. (2018), Relationships Among Conspiratorial Beliefs, Conservatism and Climate Scepticism Across Nations, *Nature Climate Change* 8, 614–620.

Hornsey, M.J., Harris, E.A., Bain, P.G., Fielding, K.S. (2016), Meta-Analyses of the Determinants and Outcomes of Belief in Climate Change, *Nature Climate Change* 6, 622–626.

Howell, E.L., Wirz, C.D., Brossard, D., Scheufele, D.A., Xenos, M.A. (2019), Seeing Through Risk-Colored Glasses: Risk and Benefit Perceptions, Knowledge, and the Politics of Fracking in the United States, *Energy Research and Social Science* 55, 168–178.

Jarvis Thomson, J. (1985), The Trolley Problem, *Yale Law Journal* 94, 1395–1415.

Kahan, D.M. (2013), Ideology, Motivated Reasoning, and Cognitive Reflection, *Judgment and Decision Making* 8 (4), 407–424.

Kahan, D.M. (2017), Misconceptions, Misinformation and the Logic of Identity-Protective Cognition, Yale Law & Economics Research Paper No. 575.

Kahan, D.M., Cantrell Dawson, E., Peters, E., Slovic, P. (2017), Motivated Numeracy and Enlightened Self-Government, *Behavioral Public Policy* 1, 54–86.

Kahan, D.M., Peters, E., Wittlin, M., Slovic, P., Larrimore Ouellette, L., Braman, D., Mandel, G. (2012), The Polarizing Impact of Science Literacy and Numeracy on Perceived Climate Change Risks, *Nature Climate Change* 2, 732–735.

Kant, I., (1785), *Groundwork of the Metaphysic of Morals*, H.J. Paton (trans.), New York: Harper and Row (1964).

Kraft, P.W., Lodge, M., Taber, C.S. (2015), Why People Don't Trust the Evidence: Motivated Reasoning and Scientific Beliefs, *Annals of the American Academy of Political and Social Sciences* 658, 121–133.

Kunda, Z. (1990), The Case for Motivated Reasoning, *Psychological Bulletin* 108 (3), 480–498.

McAdams, D.P., Pals, J.L. (2006), A New Big Five: Fundamental Principles for an Integrative Science of Personality, *American Psychologist* 61, 204–217.

McCright, A.M., Dunlap, R.P. (2011), Cool Dudes: The Denial of Climate Change Among Conservative White Males in the United States, *Global Environmental Change* 21, 1163–1172.

Morris, M., Sim, D., Girotto, V. (1998), Distinguishing Sources of Cooperation in the One-Round Prisoner's Dilemma, *Journal of Experimental Social Psychology* 34, 494–512.

Nyborg, K. (2018), Social Norms and the Environment, *Annual Review of Resource Economics* 10, 405–423.

Nyborg, K., Anderies, J.M., Dannenberg, A., Lindahl, T., Schill, C., Schlüter, M., Adger, W.N., Arrow, K.J., Barrett, S., Carpenter, S., Chapin, F.S. III, Crépin, A.-S., Daily, G., Ehrlich, P., Folke, C., Jager, W., Kautsky, N., Levin, S.A., Madsen, O.J., Polasky, S., Scheffer, M., Walker, B., Weber, E.U., Wilen, J., Xepapadeas, A., de Zeeuw, A. (2016), Social Norms as Solutions, *Science* 354 (6308), 42–43. doi:10.1126/science.aaf8317.

Price, G. (1970), Selection and Covariance, *Nature* 227, 520–521.

Price, G. (1972), Extension of Covariance Selection Mathematics, *Annals of Human Genetics* 35 (4), 485–490.

Roemer, J. (2015), Kantian Optimization: A Microfoundation for Cooperation, *Journal of Public Economics* 127, 45–57.

Roemer, J. (2019), *How We Cooperate: A Theory of Kantian Optimization*, New Haven, CT: Yale University Press.

Schultz, P.W., Nolan, J.M., Cialdini, R.B., Goldstein, N.J., Griskevicius, V. (2007), The Constructive, Destructive and Reconstructive Power of Social Norms, *Psychological Science* 18 (5), 429–434.

Smith, A. (1759), *The Theory of Moral Sentiments*, London: Andrew Millar (1967).

Smith, A. (1776), *The Wealth of Nations*, London: J.M. Dent & Sons (1910).

Strominger, N., Nichols, S. (2014), The Essential Moral Self, *Cognition* 131, 159–171.

Tomasello, M. (2016), *A Natural History of Human Morality*, Cambridge, MA: Harvard University Press.

Vainio, A., Mäkiniemi, J.P. (2016), How Are Moral Foundations Associated With Climate-Friendly Consumption? *Journal of Agricultural and Environmental Ethics* 29, 265–283.

Welsch, H. (2020), Moral Foundations and Voluntary Public Good Provision: The Case of Climate Change, *Ecological Economics* 175, 106696.

Welsch, H. (2021), How Climate-Friendly Behavior Relates to Moral Identity and Identity-Protective Cognition: Evidence from the European Social Surveys, *Ecological Economics* 185, 107026.

Welsch, H. (2022a), Do Social Norms Trump Rational Choice? Multi-Country Evidence of Social Tipping Points, *Ecological Economics* 20, 107509.

Welsch, H. (2022b), What Shapes Cognitions of Climate Change in Europe? Ideology, Morality and the Role of Educational Attainment, *Journal of Environmental Studies and Sciences* 12, 386–395.

8 Prospects and Future Directions

The past three decades have seen a twofold revolution in economics. One refers to how the outcomes of economic activities are being measured and evaluated. Since the 1990s, earlier discontent with the level and growth of GDP as measures of economic performance has been rising further, and subjective wellbeing (happiness) has become increasingly accepted as an alternative, more comprehensive indicator of individual and social welfare (Frijters and Krekel 2021; Stiglitz et al. 2009).

The availability of valid data on subjective wellbeing for a large majority of countries around the world is a fortunate circumstance, not least because the scope and scale of economic outcomes beyond GDP have been rapidly increasing. Many of these outcomes have the characteristics of public goods, which implies that no market prices are available to measure their contribution to welfare. Such measurement – and in particular how public goods trade off against private consumption goods – is of paramount importance for making adequate cost-benefit analysis of their provision and taking appropriate policy action.

Data on subjective wellbeing are valuable tools for making such measurements, and they have been increasingly used for this purpose, particularly with respect to environmental public goods (Chapter 4). In this way, happiness and nature, which were of major concern to the classical economists, have made a comeback in modern economic analysis.

While the increased focus on subjective wellbeing refers to the evaluation of outcomes of economic activities and behaviors, a second major change to economic analysis involves the drivers of such behaviors. The standard conceptualization of those drivers has been in terms of self-regarding, consequentialist (outcome-focused) preferences. While the notion that people have other-regarding (altruistic) preferences has been around for some time, it was not until the late 1980s that the "limits of altruism" (Andreoni 1988)) in explaining behavior with respect to public goods were recognized. To adequately explain voluntary contributions to public goods in large populations, it must be assumed that people have deontological (action-focused) preferences, that is, they place a value on actions *per se*, not just on actions'

DOI: 10.4324/9781003206163-10

consequences (Andreoni 1990). Important sources of deontological value are the psychological benefits from compliance with social and moral norms – notions practically absent in economic analysis three decades ago (Nyborg 2018). With the recognition of "moral sentiments" as drivers of economic behavior, another element of classical economic thinking made a comeback. In the light of evolutionary anthropology, psychological benefits from acting morally are precisely those sentiments that facilitate the voluntary provision of or contribution to public goods (Tomasello 2016).

Since important public goods refer to the natural environment, there is a close connection not only between wellbeing and nature but also between moral values and nature. Overall, wellbeing, nature, and moral values constitute a triad of essential elements of modern economic analysis.

Pressing Economic Problems: What Economists Say

As described in Chapter 1, economics students around the world have stated what they considered to be the pressing problems economics should address (Bowles and Carlin 2020). How are these problems to be assessed from the point of view of their impact on subjective wellbeing? To what extent have economists addressed these problems over the last three decades? And how important is it that economic analysis addresses these problems? Economists from Germany, Ireland, the Netherlands, the United Kingdom, the United States, and Spain, who are experts in subjective wellbeing, have provided their views on these questions.[1] Respondents were asked to allocate a total of 100 points to a set of nine issues, where the points allocated were to reflect respondents' assessment as to the relative importance of the various issues with respect to the questions stated earlier, abstracting from the fact that some issues may be related to each other. Results are displayed in Table 8.1.

Climate change is by far the most important factor affecting wellbeing (life satisfaction) to the middle of this century, followed by inequality, poverty, and unemployment, whereas business cycle volatility and inflation are the least important factors in terms of wellbeing. With respect to the intensity with which economists have addressed the various issues over the past three decades, unemployment and poverty rank first, whereas biodiversity and infectious diseases rank last. The most important issues that economists should address are unemployment, inequality, poverty, and climate change.

There is some consistency between what experts consider to be important for wellbeing and what they consider important to be addressed by economists, but the consistency is incomplete. In particular, the issues of business cycle volatility and inflation are considered to be more important topics for economic analysis than corresponds to their estimated impact on wellbeing. Part of this divergence seems to be related to the view that economic analysis has a greater *capacity* to help deal with issues such as the business cycle and inflation than with respect to biodiversity and infectious diseases, even

Table 8.1 What Economists Say on Pressing Economic Problems

	To what extent will the following problems affect people's life satisfaction up to the middle of the century?	*To what extent have economists addressed these problems over the last three decades?*	*How important is it that economic analysis addresses these problems?*	*What is the capacity of economic analysis to help deal with these problems?*
Biodiversity loss	8	4	9	6
Business cycle volatility	4	12	9	12
Climate change	24	12	13	9
Inequality (including relative poverty)	12	13	13	9
Infectious diseases	8	4	6	2
Inflation	4	9	9	10
Pollution (air, water, soil)	9	7	9	9
Poverty (absolute)	11	15	12	15
Unemployment	11	18	15	19
Other	9	6	5	9

Note: The entries in each column are the mean number of points (out of 100) allocated to the respective problems (rounded to integers).

if the latter are considered to be more relevant to wellbeing than the former. What is considered important to be studied thus seems to reflect ideas about the comparative advantage of economics as a discipline. In spite of this, the nature-related issues (biodiversity, climate, and pollution) account for close to one-third of stated research priorities – not much less than their estimated relevance for wellbeing (41 percent).

If we compare the various issues' estimated wellbeing relevance with the intensity with which they were addressed by economists over the last three decades, climate change, biodiversity, infectious diseases, and pollution appear to be relatively under-researched, whereas the business cycle, inflation, poverty, and unemployment appear to be relatively over-researched. A caveat to this conclusion, however, is that some of the issues are related to each other. For instance, one channel through which climate change and the loss of biodiversity may affect wellbeing – and jointly so – is through inflation and increased poverty due to reduced agricultural output in hot and dry regions. The economics of climate change and biodiversity will thus have to include poverty as one important aspect. In addition, it must be noted that the statements made involve *comparisons* of several important problems. Much of economic research, however, has not been concerned with *any* of those pressing economic issues; some economic research has rather focused on issues such as baseball and basketball (Oswald and Stern 2019).

In addition to the pre-specified pressing issues, some respondents mentioned sociological factors such as social cohesion and trust, and the quality of government as being highly relevant to wellbeing and worthy of investigation. The importance for wellbeing of social cohesion, or conversely fragmentation and polarization, has recently started to be studied (Binder et al. 2020; Welsch et al. 2021).

Respondents were also asked how important they think it is for adequate behavioral analysis of voluntary public goods provision (e.g., with respect to climate change and biodiversity preservation) to account for other-regarding preferences (altruism) and deontological values (e.g., "warm glow", social conformity, sense of duty). With respect to altruism, about two-thirds said it was "important", whereas the rest of the responses were approximately equally split between "somewhat important" and "very important". With respect to deontological values, responses were approximately equally split between the options "somewhat important", "important", and "very important".

Economics and the Challenges Ahead

Table 8.1 reveals a discrepancy between which issues are important to address and the importance economic research has attributed to some of them. Climate change is a case in point: While climate change ranks first as a factor for wellbeing, it was under-researched against this standard of reference. Bibliometric analysis corroborates the discrepancy: while the economics of climate change has been present in *specialist journals* focusing on environmental and resource economics, only 57 pertinent articles have ever appeared in a set of nine leading *general economics journals* (as of August 2019). This compares to a total number of approximately 77,000 articles ever published (Oswald and Stern 2019).

In the *Quarterly Journal of Economics*, which is the oldest professional journal of economics in the English language and the top-ranked one in 2019, the number of articles dealing with climate change was *zero* by that time (Oswald and Stern 2019). It is only recently that the number rose to *one* (Carleton et al. 2022), and that article is remarkable. The paper estimated that in a high emission scenario, the mean global increase in mortality risk due to increased temperatures is 84.8 deaths per 100,000 in 2100, where today's hot and poor locations have larger projected risks due to differences in both the need and capacity for adaptation. Accordingly, the mortality risk is 376.0 in poor and hot Pakistan and 10.1 in the rich and (on average) less hot United States. Using earnings foregone to estimate the value of expected life years lost, climate-related mortality is valued at roughly 3.2 percent of global GDP in 2100, which varies between 1.0 percent in the United States and 27.5 percent in Pakistan.

Increased mortality is arguably the most tragic threat posed by global warming, but the associated losses in income may incompletely capture the consequences of lives lost. An aspect not captured this way is the psychological cost to those who lose people close to them. An impression of such intangible costs can be gained from a study of the wellbeing costs of armed conflict, which estimated that compensating people for the wellbeing loss from one fatality would cost approximately US$100,000 (Welsch 2008).

The study on the mortality consequences of climate change is an impressive illustration of why the economics of climate change matters so much. As noted earlier, the engagement of economists in facing the issue has largely been restricted to specialist journals and is far from receiving the necessary attention within the profession more generally. Relatedly, since the year 2000 only 11 (out of 47,000) articles on species decline and biodiversity have been published in a set of 50 leading professional journals (Goodall and Oswald 2019). To tackle these problems, contributions from right across the subject are needed, including the economics of growth and technical change, public economics, industrial and regulatory economics, agricultural economics, international and development economics, as well as ethics and moral philosophy (Oswald and Stern 2019).

Economics and the Role of Feelings

The increasing importance in economic analysis of subjective wellbeing on the one hand and moral values on the other have a common denominator: a focus on human feelings. Human feelings are both an outcome of economic and social circumstances and behaviors, and a driver of behavior, and they may influence each other in a dynamic fashion. While economic and environmental circumstances affect people's levels of satisfaction (Chapters 3 and 4), dissatisfaction and related feelings of frustration, anger, and "falling behind" lead to human actions, with significant impacts on politics and social cohesion. For example, people's narrow feelings about their own financial situations, rather than their objective income levels, contributed to Brexit (Liberini et al. 2019). Similarly, unhappiness was a strong predictor of populist voting in elections in Europe and the United States. Specifically, generalized unhappiness with one's personal wellbeing – and not merely dissatisfaction with governments – was found to play a significant role in the rise of European populism (Nowakowski 2021), and low levels of subjective wellbeing were found to predict anti-incumbent voting in the 2012 election in the United States and Donald Trump's victory in the presidential election in 2016 (Ward et al. 2021).

Similar to feelings of (un)happiness, people's "moral sentiments" shape their political preferences and behaviors. In this respect, a study from Germany found that people's patterns of endorsement of the Moral Foundations (Chapter 7) predicts their level of satisfaction with democracy, both directly and indirectly. On one hand, an individual's moral values (not just one's objective circumstances) influence what the individual demands the government to do (e.g., in terms of redistribution), and the degree to which those demands are satisfied influence the individual's satisfaction with democracy (indirect channel). On the other hand, people have an intrinsic preference for their moral values to be respected by the government, independent of their specific demands for government action (direct channel). Empirical results reveal that a stronger taste for Care and Fairness predicts a stronger demand for redistribution at any given level of income. There is thus an ethical, not just a self-interested, preference for redistribution. A stronger demand for redistribution, in turn, predicts lower levels of satisfaction with democracy. In sum, a stronger taste for Care and Fairness negatively predicts satisfaction with democracy in an indirect fashion. On the other hand, a stronger taste for Authority was found to predict higher satisfaction with democracy via the direct channel (Welsch 2022). Whether similar relationships apply to other countries remains to be studied, but the findings for Germany are suggestive of a role of moral values for satisfaction with and, ultimately, stability of our institutional architectures.

In striking dissonance with the importance that feelings have as outcomes and drivers of economic, social, and political behavior, economists have traditionally been taught to eschew all data on feelings. That was a mistake – one that has started to be corrected over the past three decades. In order to tackle the challenges ahead, economists must take account of human happiness and moral values, and of people's feelings of human resentment, frustration, anger, and "falling behind" (Oswald 2022).

Note

1 Respondents were recruited from the contributors to the *Handbook on Wellbeing, Happiness and the Environment* (Maddison et al. 2020). The survey was undertaken in July 2022.

Bibliography

Andreoni, J. (1988), Privately Provided Public Goods in a Large Economy: The Limits of Altruism, *Journal of Public Economics* 35, 57–73.

Andreoni, J. (1990), Impure Altruism and Donations to Public Goods: A Theory of Warm-Glow Giving, *Economic Journal* 100, 464–477.

Binder, M., Blankenburg, A.K., Welsch, H. (2020), Pro-Environmental Norms, Green Lifestyles, and Subjective Well-Being: Panel Evidence from the UK, *Social Indicators Research* 152, 1029–1060.

Bowles, S., Carlin, W. (2020), What Students Learn in Economics 101: Time for a Change, *Journal of Economic Literature* 58, 176–214.

Carleton, T., Jina, A., Delgado, M., Greenstone, M., Houser, T., Hsiang, S., Hultgren, A., Kopp, R.E., McCusker, K.E., Nath, I., Rising, J., Rode, A., Seo, H.K., Viaene, A., Yuan, J., Zhang, A.T. (2022), Valuing the Global Mortality Consequences of Climate Change Accounting for Adaptation Costs and Benefits, *Quarterly Journal of Economics* 137, 2037–2105.

Frijters, P., Krekel, C. (2021), *A Handbook for Wellbeing Policy Making: History, Theory, Measurement, Implementation, and Examples*, Oxford: Oxford University Press.

Goodall, A.H., Oswald, A.J. (2019), Researchers obsessed with *FT* Journals list are failing to tackle today's problems, *Financial Times*, 8 May, 2019.

Liberini, F., Oswald, A.J., Proto, E., Redoano, M. (2019), Was Brexit Triggered by the Old and Unhappy? Or by Financial Feelings? *Journal of Economic Behavior and Organization* 161, 287–302.

Maddison, D., Rehdanz, K., Welsch, H. (eds.) (2020), *Handbook on Wellbeing, Happiness and the Environment*, Cheltenham: Edward Elgar.

Nowakowski, A. (2021), Do Unhappy Citizens Vote for Populism? *European Journal of Political Economy* 68, Article Number 101985.

Nyborg, K. (2018), Social Norms and the Environment, *Annual Review of Environmental and Resource Economics* 10, 405–423.

Oswald, A. (2022), Trouble: A Brief Essay in Pictures, Presentation at the Oxford Wellbeing Conference, July 2022.

Oswald, A., Stern, N. (2019) Why Does the Economics of Climate Change Matter so Much – and Why Has the Engagement of Economists Been so Weak?, *Royal Economic Society Newsletter* 187, 5–9.

Stiglitz, J.E., Sen, A., Fitoussi, J.-P. (2009), Report by the Commission on the Measurement of Economic Performance and Social Progress (CMEPSP). http://www.stiglitz-sen-fitoussi.fr/en/documents.htm.

Tomasello, M. (2016), *A Natural History of Human Morality*, Cambridge, MA: Harvard University Press.

Ward, G., De Neve, J.E., Ungar, L.H., Eichstaedt, J.C. (2021), (Un)Happiness and Voting in US Presidential Elections, *Journal of Personality and Social Psychology* 120, 370–383.

Welsch, H. (2008), The Social Costs of Civil Conflict: Evidence from Surveys of Happiness, *Kyklos* 61, 320–340.

Welsch, H. (2022), What Shapes Satisfaction With Democracy? Interests, Morals, and the German East-West Divide, *Social Indicators Research* 163, 197–217.

Welsch, H., Biermann, P., Kühling, J. (2021), Immigration Attitudes and Subjective Well-Being: A Matter of Identity? *Journal of Happiness Studies* 22, 1563–1581.

Index

Note: Page numbers in **bold** refer to tables. Page numbers followed by "n" refer to notes.